TUNISIA
From Protectorate to Republic

INDIANA UNIVERSITY INTERNATIONAL STUDIES

TUNISIA

From Protectorate to Republic

DWIGHT L. LING

INDIANA UNIVERSITY PRESS

BLOOMINGTON AND LONDON

To My Family

PREFACE

What factors combine to make a nation, especially when the area has been dominated by a European power for decades? This is one of the key questions of our time. How is a drowsy, traditionalist society rallied to the struggle for national self-determination? It takes a long time to overcome lethargy in the political, economic, and social structure of a country dominated by a colonial power that has stifled nationalist voices of reform. Nationalists must agree upon a program which will convince the people that they have been exploited and that life would improve under their own government. Successful nationalist uprisings reported from around the world add incentive.

This is the story of Tunisia, conquered and tied by a foreign power, and how Tunisians strained and pulled until the ties were broken. The unfolding of Tunisian national development helps to answer many questions about emerging nations. As a new era punctuated by a widespread revolt against colonialism begins in Africa, many new nations study Tunisian developments to obtain answers to their own dilemmas. Despite his criticism of Tunisia, President Ahmed Ben Bella of Algeria patterned his political party after the Neo-Destour Party (now the Socialist Destour Party) of Tunisia.

In presenting the Tunisian story it is necessary to describe the French protectorate that was overthrown. Tunisia was dominated by France for seventy-five years. Although French capital and presence undoubtedly brought the benefits of Western technology and culture, Tunisia lacked an identity of its own. Only a few educated Tunisians fully recognized the exploitive nature of French rule. Until the reforms of 1922 Tunisians had little opportunity to gain political experience, and then only in subordinate positions. Tunisia, though a protectorate, literally "belonged to the French." Europeans owned the best land, held the skilled positions, and gave little technical training to the Tunisians, while Muslim education did not encourage Western customs or technology. Lacking a well organized movement in the early twentieth century, Tunisian nationalism awaited a maturity which came with the organization of the Destour Party (Liberal Constitution Party) after World War I.

Both world wars created situations favorable to a reevaluation of Western European imperialism. President Woodrow Wilson's doctrine of national self-determination, as one of the principles of settlement in 1919, captured the imagination of nationalist leaders. The League of Nations mandate system recognized that eventually independence would be accorded to former Turkish and German colonies, an encouraging promise to nationalists throughout the Arab world. After the devastation of World War II, the political collapse of Europe strengthened nationalist demands from colonies around the globe, and the United Nations Organization offered a voice and prestige to new nations in the world community.

The independence year 1956 was a turning-point in Tunisian history. Although not the midpoint in a chronological sense, the year divides the long struggle for independence from the fascinating story of a newborn nation beset with contemporary problems. The division is one between Tunisia's past and its future. The process of nation-making involves the whole being of a society fighting for its existence. Tunisia is a good example of the sacrifices, planning, and bloodshed necessary in the steep and rugged climb to independence. Once colonial military and political domination is broken, another enemy, underdevelopment, must be conquered. The new fight consumes the energy of Tunisia: it must be waged on a battlefield of climate, people, natural resources, and a world economy often hostile to small economic units.

The author is indebted to many organizations and individuals. Without a scholarship from the Tunisian government

I would not have been able to study and travel in Tunisia. A travel grant from the Penrose Fund of the American. Philosophical Society also helped make the trip possible. The writing of the work was aided by a grant in non-Western studies from the Great Lakes Colleges Association, and DePauw University was kind enough to encourage me to pursue this study.

This book is a culmination of ten years' interest and research beginning with my Ph.D. dissertation on the French protectorate and ending with my recent study of contemporary Tunisia. While in Tunisia I talked with so many people that it would be impossible to give them individual recognition. Moreover, since a few requested that they not be named or quoted directly, a general recognition seems prudent. My diary lists twenty-seven interviews and many casual conversations with a great variety of people—from government officials, professors, students, to the person who sold my daily newspaper. To all I offer my gratitude, but I accept the responsibility for my own analyses and interpretations.

All of the translations from the French in this book have been made by the author. Transliterations conform with the way names are written in official Tunisian and French documents.

D. L. L.

Greencastle, Indiana
June, 1966

CONTENTS

TUNISIA
From Protectorate to Republic

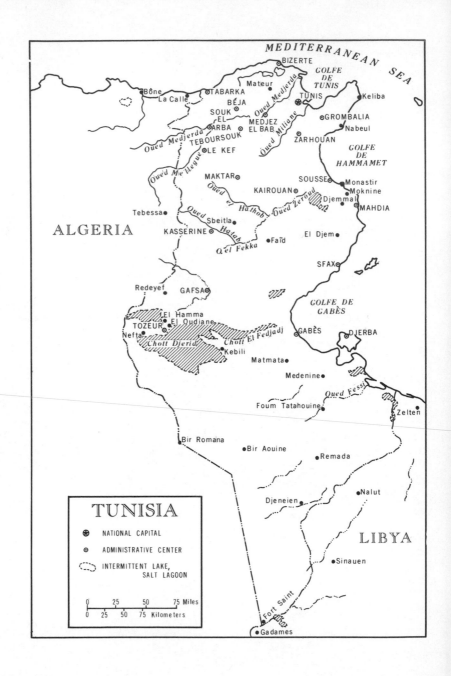

1

A Nation Conquered

Land, Climate, and People

Tunisia stands like a sentinel on the coast of North Africa with a mountainous arm, Cape Bon, pointed toward Sicily. This guardian of the African coast lies only ninety miles from Sicily and in effect divides the Mediterranean Sea into an eastern and a western basin—a fact not overlooked by all nations interested in dominating the Mediterranean area. For centuries the people living in Tunisia have defended their long coastline and interior from invaders. Ruins of Phoenician fortifications along with Spanish forts and the pillboxes of World War II still dot the coast. Danger generally came from the sea. Morocco, Algeria, and Tunisia form a natural region which the Arabs call the Maghreb, meaning western land. The area shares common flora and fauna in and around the Atlas mountain range, stretching some 1,400 miles in a northeasterly direction from Morocco to Tunisia, a range geographically related to the Sicilian mountains and the Apennines of Italy. The height of the chain descends from a high of 14,000 feet in Morocco to Tunisia, where two-thirds of the land is no higher than 1,500 feet. Tunisia is a land of blue and white.

White houses with blue shutters and doors predominate, reminding the observer of the surrounding blue sky and sea contrasted with the white sand.

Four geographical areas offering a variety of agricultural products can be distinguished.[1] The first region is bordered on the north by the sea and on the south by an imaginary line from La Calle, Algeria, to Cape Zbib just east of Bizerte. This division line follows the ridges of the small Atlas chain, from which the water drains by way of small rivers directly into the Mediterranean Sea. Forests, pastures, and grain land are found in the region, and fishing areas abound in its coastal waters. Wooded mountains in the western part of the region harbored the famed independent-minded Kroumir tribe, who long defied the central government.

The Medjerda and Miliane river basins form the second region, which is bounded on the north by the small Atlas chain and on the south by a line drawn from the Algerian town of Tebessa northeast to Cape Bon. The unnavigable Medjerda River created a broad grain-producing valley, forming the best route for the railway connecting Tunis with Algiers. Vineyards abound in the environs of Tunis, and sedentary farming life is prevalent. Terrain and life become more rugged as one moves westward in this region, and the city of Le Kef is the provincial seat of the government ruling the surrounding mountain tribes.

Great diversity is seen in the third region, which includes the eastern coastal area from Cape Bon in the north to the Libyan frontier in the south. It is bordered on the north and west by the larger Atlas mountain range, which forms a line running southwest from Cape Bon connecting with a small mountain range running north and south at a point west of the holy city of Kairouan. On the coast are the cities of Sousse, Monastir, Sfax, and Gabes. The interior of this region is characterized by low mountains and dry unproductive soil which supports nomads for only part of the year. However, Cape Bon is good for grain and citrus fruits, while the stony Sahel (meaning "coast"), stretching inland from Monastir south to the Sfax district, is an excellent area for olive culture. South of the Sahel is the arid area called the Arad, dotted infrequently with green oases.

The sparsely populated fourth area is the Tunisian Sahara, containing small villages around the date-producing oases of Gafsa, Touzeur, and Nefta. Here are found the Chott depressions, dried up lakes rumored to have been the home of the fleet of Atlantis. Geology explains, however, that the Chotts were never a Mediterranean gulf, but merely large inland bodies of water.[2] The crust of the Chott is hard enough in certain places to cross by caravan, but Arabs tell stories of camels straying from the path and sinking through the surface. The region merges imperceptibly with the shifting sands of the Algerian Sahara.

Contact with the sea on the north and east, along with low elevation of the mountains, has allowed the sea breeze to penetrate deeply and bring a more pleasant climate than that of Algeria. Still, howling winds and burning sun are trademarks of the country. Tunisia is often called a land with a cold climate and a hot sun because the contrast between shade and sunlight can be shocking. Northwesterly winds dominate the landscape during most of the year, and northern Tunisia can get as cold as southern Europe, forcing the most hardy souls to gather their cloaks tightly.[3] In midsummer the scorching, whirling sirocco wind off the desert reigns supreme, and Tunis can experience sweltering temperatures of 113° or more. The year falls into four unequal seasons. Summer lasts about six months from May through October. The autumn months of November and December signal the return of rain, which continues in the winter months of January until around the first of March. The green season includes the spring months of March and April. Some knowledge of the rainy season can be gained from the annual rainfall figures. In the high plateau which comprises almost one-half of northern Tunisia there is an average of 99 days of rain with an average yearly fall of

39 inches. The low plateau area of central Tunisia is wet on the average of 61 days with a fall of only 18 inches. The Sahel averages 16 inches, and the southern oases receive only 30 days of rain, amounting on the average to nine inches a year.[4]

In this environment Tunisians move noisily about their daily tasks, oblivious of their great racial diversity. An indigenous North African people called Berbers are said to have lived in the land for over three thousand years. They belonged to the Hamitic linguistic family, related to the general Semitic group.[5] On an invasion highroad Tunisia experienced the arrival of many peoples such as the Phoenicians, who moved westward along North Africa early in the first millennium B.C., creating the great commercial center of Carthage. The Romans conquered the area, establishing a province in 146 B.C., and left many traces of their culture, including the intriguing remains of Utica, the ancient administrative center for Africa. Christianity spread over the area in the first and second centuries A.D., but Vandals led by Gaiseric invaded and ruled Tunisia for about a hundred years until Belisarius, a general for Emperor Justinian, conquered it in A.D. 533 for Byzantine Christianity.

Like the earlier Phoenicians, the Arabs began to move westward over North Africa in the seventh century. A century after Arab expansion chroniclers tell us that Frenchmen under Charlemagne were in contact with Tunisia. Negro slaves had been brought to the area by Arab traders, who sometimes sold them to merchants from Marseille, Genoa, and Venice. Spain spread its influence over the coastal regions of North Africa during the crusade of Cardinal Ximenes (1507-1508). The Turks established themselves there in 1534, only to be subdued first by Charles V, the Holy Roman Emperor, and later by the Dey of Algeria. But Turkey fought back and set up regencies in Algeria and Tunisia in the seventeenth century. Obviously under these conditions racial unity was impossible, but the Muslim faith introduced by the Arabs and sustained by the Turks became the unifying force.

There are no census figures for Tunisia in the nineteenth

Sidi Bou Said

Modern housing in Monastir

Berbers on the island of Djerba

*Sailing boat
off Djerba*

Camel plowing in central Tunisia

Irrigation in the Medjerda River Valley

Village market in central Tunisia

Sheep market in Tunis

President Habib Bourguiba
(United Press International Photo)

century, so only an estimated population based on the capitation tax is available. This much seems certain: during the Roman domination Tunisia had a larger population than at any time since. Among windswept Roman ruins stone olive presses and grinding stones lie silently in arid soil that will no longer produce olives, grapes, or grain. Centuries of overworking and overgrazing the land have made large areas of North Africa less habitable than in ancient times. Political strife, disease, and the economic ineptitude of the government also helped reduce the population. The estimated population decline from 1828 to 1878 was from five million to one and a half million.[6] The American consul in Tunis, Gwin Harris Heap, sent a dispatch to Washington which explained:

> The population of the country has been so reduced of late years by famine, pestilences and emigration to Algeria and Tripoli that there is a great scarcity of hands for agriculture. The withdrawal of so large a number of men will be felt as a serious calamity, particularly as no encouragement is given to immigration.[7]

Of the one and a half million people in the late nineteenth century there were approximately 50,000 Europeans plus an equal number of Jews. The most numerous among the Europeans were Italians, Sicilians, French, and Maltese. Many of the Arabs and Berbers were nomads of the south, where tents outnumbered huts. Sedentary peasants lived in *gourbis*, or huts made of piled stone with mud-plastered walls and grass roofs. Sometimes *gourbis* were made entirely of sticks and grass, and one type used palm tree trunks for the walls.[8] Today 4,500,000 people inhabit Tunisia, and the European population has been reduced to around 25,000 people since independence.

Growing French Influence

The story of French influence covers many centuries, but from the very beginning the commercial value of the area was the main attraction. Marseille merchants in the late Middle Ages imported silks, perfumes, and products of the Sudan from Tunis, but Henry III further stimulated French commercial interest when he created a consulate at Tunis in 1577. All foreign merchants were protected by the French consulate until the seventeenth century, when Turkey conquered and established a regency, with the Bey of Tunis ruling as an autocrat under Turkish suzerainty.

By treaties of concession France steadily improved her position in the Regency during the seventeenth and eighteenth centuries despite Turkish suzerainty. The agreements solidified the commercial settlement at Cape Negro (founded in 1520 on the northern coast) and gave France the privilege of direct negotiations with Tunisians. A 1666 treaty gave the French company at the Cape the power "to maintain as many boats and launches or coral fishing boats as it will judge necessary."[9] Later France established the Company of Africa to strengthen and expand the Cape Negro concessions, but in 1741 a Tunisian fleet attacked the Cape, dispersed the employees, and destroyed the buildings; however, a few years later France gained permission to rebuild.[10] Napoleon's government signed a treaty of peace with the Turkish Regency in 1802 stating that France, "being the most distinguished and the most beneficial of all the nations established in Tunis . . . will be likewise the most favored."[11] Therefore, by the nineteenth century France enjoyed a relationship with the Bey unequaled by any other European power.

French relations with Tunisia took on new significance after France conquered Algeria in 1830. Now France and the Bey were neighbors without a clearly defined boundary to separate them. Almost immediately France improved commercial relations with Tunisia. In August, 1830, Hussein Bey[12] signed a treaty with France which abolished enslavement of Christians, attempted to protect foreign shipping, opened the Regency to commercial agents, and gave France the exclusive right of coral fishing up to Cape Negro.[13] A secret article ceded land to

France for a memorial honoring Louis IX, the leader of the thirteenth-century crusade against Tunisia.[14] In 1832, for an annual fee, France obtained the right to engage in coral fishing off the entire Tunisian coast.

Throughout the French activity Turkey and England stood ready to challenge France at every opportunity. After the Turks occupied Tripoli in 1835, they sought to increase their nominal suzerainty over Tunisia. Frequently the Sultan sent vessels to Tunisian waters, but France, wishing to maintain the status quo, dispatched her own squadrons to "protect" the Bey. A report from the Constantinople correspondent of the *Constitutional* to the effect that the Sultan planned an expedition against Tunisia alarmed the French. In January, 1836, the French ambassador explained to the Porte "that any enterprise tending to implant her domination in Tunis could expect to find us in its way and encounter on our part a real opposition."[15] Although the communiqué discouraged overt Turkish action, the Sultan still hoped that his weak suzerainty over the Bey could be strengthened. In 1843 he sent a firman to the Bey which offered him investiture for life. Under French pressure Tunisia rejected the offer with the claim that since the Bey owed his throne to the independent laws of the country, there was no need for a special investiture. Two years later the Sultan tried again and the English consul, Thomas Reade, advised the Bey to listen to the Porte. The French response was prompt and strong and promised "the maintenance of the family which governs this Regency, with hereditary title, of all the rights which it held for the predecessors and of all the relative conditions of independence which constituted his political existence and that of the Regency."[16] By this time the French consul optimistically reported, "we have now, in this part of Africa, nearly all the advantages of possession, without having the inconveniences."[17]

During Ahmed Bey's state visit to France in 1846 an incident occurred which illustrated that England and France held conflicting views concerning Turkish suzerainty over Tunisia. The visit in France was unmarred, but Ahmed Bey offended England by refusing to cross the Channel when he heard that the Ottoman ambassador was scheduled to introduce him to Queen Victoria. He preferred his twenty-one-gun salute at Toulon and his audience with Louis-Philippe minus the assistance of the Turkish ambassador.[18] It was evident that the Bey considered friendship with France his greatest protection against Turkey.

The problems facing the Tunisian government were not confined to international affairs, but included social and economic unrest at home. An event in Tunis excited the Jewish and European communities. A young Jew, Samuel Sfez, while intoxicated, knocked down a Muslim child in the crowded streets of Tunis. Attacked by the crowd, he responded by cursing the Muslim faith and the Bey's government.[19] The Sharaa religious tribunal sentenced him to death by having molten lead poured down his throat; his body was to be burned. His wife appealed to the consuls, but it was too late. "The head of the wretched man," reported the English consul, "was kicked about by the boys, while men were endeavouring to smash it with stones."[20] Léon Roches, the French consul, strongly protested the execution to the Bey:

> I know the Muslim law, illustrious Sovereign. Blasphemy is forbidden under pain of death and constantly my ear is offended by the blasphemies of the Muslims. The adulterous man or woman is to be stoned or drowned, and adultery is the permanent state of a third of your subjects. . . . Drunkenness is forbidden and it is impossible to take a step in the city without meeting a drunk Muslim. . . .[21]

Such incidents led the foreign consuls to urge Mohammed Bey to reform his government, whereupon the Fundamental Pact of 1857 was announced, which (1) guaranteed security to all inhabitants regardless of religion, nationality, or race (this was extended to their person, property, and reputation), (2) guaranteed equality of all before the law and in taxation, (3) guaranteed freedom of commerce for all without special privileges for anyone, and (4) allowed Jews to wear the Muslim red *chechia* (hat) if they wished, instead of black skullcaps. In Europe the pact was hailed as a great progressive step, and Napoleon III sent the cordon of the Legion of Honor to the Bey. However, in Tunisia there was grumbling about an agreement that made unbelievers equal with the followers of Allah, and many accused the Bey of selling his soul.

Upon the death of Mohammed Bey in 1859, Mohammed es Sadok Bey succeeded his brother and retained the prime minister, Mustapha Khaznadar, and his personal bureaucracy of mamelukes. Mamelukes were young men of Christian origin captured by the Turks and sold in Tunis. Raised as Muslims and adopted by Beys and dignitaries at the court, they now formed an elite governmental class which often ignored the plight of the average Tunisian. The Bey confused the situation by declaring himself sole ruler without outside dependence on any power and, at the same time, drawing closer to Turkey.[22] However, French influence became evident again the following year, when the Bey met Napoleon III in Algiers and gained his approval for reforms that would be announced as the Constitution of 1861. This document defined the power of the Bey and provided for hereditary succession; instituted an advisory assembly called the Supreme Council and composed of sixty members appointed by the Bey for five-year terms; recognized a judiciary independent of the legislative and executive powers; and affirmed the principles of the Fundamental Pact. The Supreme Council helped the monarch draft legislation and drew up a budget subject to his confirmation. Actually little reform had been accomplished because Mustapha Khaznadar and the Bey easily controlled the council and did as they pleased. General Khéréddine (Arabic: Khair Al-Din), who presided over the Supreme Council from 1861 until 1863, complained:

> Perceiving that the Bey, and especially his all-powerful Prime Minister, Mustapha Khaznadar, consented to these reforms merely to justify their own misdeeds as decisions emanating

from the Council, I first endeavored, by all the means in my power, to bring them back to the path of loyalty and integrity for the good of their country. My efforts proved fruitless and, as I was unwilling by taking part in public affairs to contribute to the hoax of my country of adoption, which was being dragged to ruin, in 1863 I resigned from office.[23]

Frustration over the "paper reforms" and over the general economic situation eventually led to the insurrection of 1864. A ruinous financial situation developed when Mustapha Khaznadar contracted foreign loans at a high interest rate which he attempted to repay by a direct *medjba* tax levied on the countryside but not on the cities. The country tribes refused to pay the tax and demanded the dismissal of Mustapha Khaznadar and the other mamelukes. The insurrectionists also asked for the abolition of the constitution. The Bey suspended the constitution and reduced the *medjba,* but the mamelukes led by Khaznadar seemed stronger than ever.

In the critical years from 1864 to 1867 revolt followed in the wake of high taxes, famine, typhus, and cholera. The Kroumir tribe attacked troops escorting the tax collectors, while three hundred Tunisian troops sent to restore order in the South were massacred. When the French consul Charles de Beauval asked the Bey to recall Mustapha Khaznadar, the prime minister retaliated by accusing the consul of ruining a Tunisian financial mission to Europe. Later while de Beauval was enjoying his Tunis garden, shots whistled around his head. It appeared that France would intervene and move into Tunisia from the Algerian province of Constantine, but instead she invited England and Italy to cooperate in a naval demonstration to help the Tunisian government quell the revolt. Turkey volunteered to help "save" the Bey, but France threatened to sink any Turkish vessel that disembarked a single man.[24] By bribery and intrigue Mustapha Khaznadar finally succeeded in disorganizing the revolt, and five hundred Tunisian officials were pulled through the streets of Tunis chained to one another by their necks.[25] The French fleet left La Goulette,

and the French consul, who never stopped denouncing Mustapha, was recalled. The internal plight caused many Tunisians
to cross the border into Tripoli. It was claimed that the
number of plows in use fell from one hundred thousand to
eight thousand in several years.[26] In addition, cholera and
typhus carried off many victims. These events plus bankruptcy
weighed heavy on Tunisia by 1868.

European creditors feared their entire investment in Tunisia
would be lost. The English consul Sir Richard Wood and the
Italian consul Luigi Pinna inaugurated a plan whereby the
creditors would agree to four debt conversions in which they
would receive, in exchange for their old claims with varying
interest rates, unified obligations at twelve per cent interest.
For some time French creditors resisted, but realizing they
were merely protecting depreciated claims that could not be
paid, they finally agreed to conversion. Since the greatest per-
centage of the debt was owed to them, the French creditors
felt entitled to the greatest voice in financial decisions. France
suggested a financial organization composed of two Tunisian
officials, two influential persons elected by the foreign creditors
of Tunis, two French creditors, and two French delegates. England and Italy flatly refused.[27] An international commission
was proposed instead, and France reluctantly agreed to equality
on one committee for a somewhat stronger position on the
Executive Committee. The International Financial Commission, established in 1869, was charged with the complete control of Tunisian finances. An Executive Committee was composed of the prime minister, a representative of the Bey, and
an inspector of finances, who was nominated by France and
appointed by the Bey.[28] This committee represented the rights
of the Bey, established the budget, and ruled over the expenses
of the state. A six-member Committee of Control, including
equal representation from France, England, and Italy, supervised the revenues designated by the state for the payment of
the European creditors.[29] After the creation of this commission
Tunisia no longer enjoyed financial autonomy.

With a total outstanding debt of 275,000,000 francs, the new commission confronted a momentous task. In 1870 the commission reduced the liability to 160,000,000 francs, bearing an annual interest of 19,500,000 francs. The reduction was accomplished by a careful examination of the claims in order to eliminate all but the most legitimate. Many creditors consented to the reduction of their claims when they were convinced there was a good chance to receive payment under the commission's program. However, a much more drastic program was necessary because the total revenue was only 13,500,000 francs, of which at least half was necessary for public services.

A more comprehensive plan was drawn up which remained the financial charter of Tunisia until 1884. The debt was reduced to 125,000,000 francs, and for its liquidation the commission issued 250,000 obligations of five hundred francs at five per cent semiannual interest. Added to this was eighteen million in coupons in arrears. Creditors holding obligations in arrears were issued coupons worth a certain amount without interest and reimbursable every six months by a drawing.[30] State revenue was divided two ways: first, designated revenues from import duties and taxes totaling 6,505,000 francs were to be used against the consolidated debt, and second, 6,500,000 francs were budgeted for operating the government. The International Financial Commission controlled the operational budget, and the Bey could not give any concessions or create new taxes without its consent. Adolphe-François de Botmiliau, the French consul, stressed the seriousness of the situation: "A last attempt is made in this moment to save this country by the financial commission. If it fails, we would have to be forcibly called upon to occupy Tunisia and this will be a troublesome extremity for us."[31]

One man, Mustapha Khaznadar, personified financial ruin for Tunisia. His career had been personally lucrative but nationally disastrous. His term as prime minister and finance minister, from 1837 to 1873, was a long and difficult period for Tunisia. Until 1837 Tunisia had no public debt, paid its public officials and army, and experienced enough expansion in agriculture to sustain the economy. However, the new ruler, Ahmed Bey, had expensive tastes encouraged by Mustapha Khaznadar. Without understanding government finance the Bey ordered the construction of industrial plants, expansion of the armed forces, and new palaces. Besides the palace of Le Bardo he had a summer residence at La Goulette and began constructing a huge palace called the Mohammedia, south of Tunis. Today the gaping ruins of this large complex shelter a Berber village. As one travels from Tunis to Zahgouan, the silhouette of Mohammedia attracts attention miles before one reaches its windswept hulk. Ahmed Bey planned to make this enormous palace the Versailles of Tunisia, but because of financial trouble the great walls of Mohammedia began to fall in ruin before they were completed.[32]

Mustapha Khaznadar used not only his official position but the fact that he was brother-in-law of the Bey to enhance his influence and increase his personal fortune. The only financial principles that Mustapha Khaznadar seemed to know were borrowing, issuing bonds, and going deeper into debt. Financial ruin threatened Tunisia as the annual revenue in 1871-1872 fell two million piasters below the sum of the previous year.[33] The French vice-president of the financial commission, Victor Villet, suggested a temporary moratorium on debt repayment, hoping for a better harvest the next year. The creditors opposed Villet, as did Mustapha Khaznadar, who suggested more borrowing. In January, 1872, the government could only pay one-half of its debt and Villet refused to authorize new loans.[34] All these problems culminated in the Bey's long overdue dismissal of Mustapha Khaznadar.

In a trying period the French consul scored an important success. By agitation through the financial commission and with the help of a young favorite of the Bey, Mustapha Ben Ismail, de Botmiliau finally convinced the Bey that Mustapha Khaznadar was incompetent. In 1873 the Bey replaced his erring finance minister with General Khéréddine.[35] The new minister showed a determination to compensate for the weaknesses of his ruler by establishing rigid financial policies and creating strict security throughout the Regency. It was claimed that "a young girl crowned with diamonds could travel alone, without fear, through the Regency from North to South."[36] Nevertheless, the minister's policy toward Turkey brought a sharp rebuke from France. Khéréddine planned to send four thousand men to help Turkey in the Russo-Turkish War. Recruitment was a hated word in Tunisia, and fortunately for the prime minister a peace treaty was signed before the Tunisian corps was completely established. A poor harvest in 1877 threatened the subscription of money that Khéréddine planned for the Sultan of Turkey, and he supplemented the money by reducing the pensions of the princes at the Bardo, a policy hardly likely to win friends at court. The loss of a great segment of Tunisian support, as well as French anger over his Turkish policy, led to the disgrace of Khéréddine in 1877. He sold his land, went to France, and later took refuge at Constantinople. Unlike his predecessor, Khéréddine had worked well with the financial commission; after his dismissal the financial situation once again deteriorated.[37]

Meanwhile, in December, 1874, Theodore Roustan arrived as the French consul-general and chargé d'affaires. This tenacious, energetic, and clever man had served in many diplomatic posts in the Middle East and was thoroughly conversant with the workings of Arab monarchies. He found French prestige in Tunisia waning, but by clever intrigue and diplomatic adroitness he reversed the trend. No project seemed beyond the ability of Roustan, who was instrumental in creating a climate leading to a French protectorate. Foreign consuls respected his skill and feared his Machiavellian tactics.

Mohammed Khaznadar, who succeeded Khéréddine, was distrusted by Roustan because he was friendly with the English consul. France wanted the Bey to name the young, pro-French Mustapha Ben Ismail as premier. The Bey had considered the young man his favorite, adopted him, and given his daughter to him in marriage. With the encouragement of Roustan, Mustapha Ben Ismail informed the Bey of the incumbent premier's "swindles" and in 1878 was rewarded for his vigilance with the office of the discredited Mohammed Khaznadar.[38] The triumphant new minister visited Algeria and then traveled to France for the Exposition of 1878.

Roustan soon found himself in a conflict with the financial commission. It was his theory that since the French in Tunisia were outnumbered by Italians and Maltese, French capital should be attracted to the country to make up for the deficiency. Victor Villet, the French inspector general of finances and vice-president of the Executive Committee of the financial commission, claimed that Roustan used deplorable intrigues to attract capital. The English and Italian consuls and the four non-French members of the Committee of Control supported Villet's complaint; even Mustapha Ben Ismail was disgusted with Roustan's methods. The dispute culminated in the de Sancy affair.

About thirteen years earlier Count Ferdinand de Sancy, a French citizen, had obtained from the Bey a stud farm near Tunis. The sovereign stipulated that de Sancy make certain improvements within an allotted period. For ten years the Bey protested that the property was going to ruin, and when he asked de Sancy for horses to send to the Sultan in 1877, he was refused. Consequently, the following year the Bey asked de Sancy to evacuate the property.[39] Springing to the defense of his countryman, Roustan demanded an inquiry, but three successive French vice-presidents of the financial commission turned him down and declared that the monarch was within his rights. The third, Eumène Queillé, who held office in 1878 and 1879, headed the Tunisian commission to expel de Sancy. Roustan sent soldiers from his consulate to prevent expulsion, and sharp words were exchanged between the two groups. The French foreign minister, William Henri Waddington, supported his consul and sent M. Depienne to replace Queillé. Roustan demanded an apology from the Bey and the dismissal of the officers who tried to expel de Sancy. If a satisfactory answer had not come within twenty-four hours, Roustan was directed to take down his flag and board a French ship anchored at La Goulette. The Bey yielded and his officers apologized and agreed to arbitration.[40] The resulting inquiry, for the most part, exonerated de Sancy.[41]

In the dispatch reporting the de Sancy affair, American consul W. G. W. Fish cited two other examples of French pressure on the Bey's government. One of the Bey's interpreters, Moses Santillana, who was appointed on Sir Richard Wood's recommendation, was dismissed. The French called him Wood's "spy at court." In the second incident, Elias Mussalli, who had been earlier removed from office under British insistence, was reinstated as interpreter and assistant director of foreign affairs.[42]

From this period on, the financial commission ceased to check the spread of French power in Tunisia. Sir Richard Wood was recalled from Tunis but, according to French claims, not until he had taught the new Italian consul, Signor Licurgo Maccio, how to combat mounting French influence. Consul Maccio had many worries because Italy had left the Congress of Berlin disappointed and fearful that France might have obtained a blank check in Tunisia. The fear proved to be well founded. England backed out of the Tunisian affair, and not only told France that she would not oppose France's influence in Tunisia, but gave in to pressure for the recall of Wood. Italy was alone in a critical period.

French Invasion

The major factors involved in the French invasion were the attitude of major European powers toward French intervention, the disruptive political and economic state of Tunisia which jeopardized French economic interests, and some particular events on the Tunisian-Algerian frontier leading to the immediate cause of the invasion and occupation.

Three European powers—Britain, Germany, and Italy—could have opposed French designs in Tunis. Britain and Germany proved to be no problem. France received British approval of its policies in Tunisia in the course of secret negotiations at the Congress of Berlin, where French Foreign Minister William Waddington conferred with his British counterpart, Lord Robert Salisbury.[43] Upon returning to Paris, Waddington reported that Lord Salisbury had advised, "Do at Tunis what you think proper; England will offer no opposition, and will respect your decision." Waddington reportedly replied:

> It is possible that the future may impose upon us, as regards Tunis, a more direct responsibility than now devolves on us. . . . We should not allow any foreign Power to establish itself there, and we should oppose by force any attempt of that kind.[44]

Although Lord Salisbury would not vouch for the authenticity of Waddington's statements as direct quotations, it became obvious when he explained the view of Her Majesty's Government that France need not fear British interference:

> They [Her Majesty's Government] have witnessed with lively satisfaction the success of the experiment conducted by France in Algiers, and the great work of civilization which it is accomplishing in that country. They have never been unaware that the presence of France on those shores, supported as it is by an imposing military force, must have the effect of giving to her, when she thinks fit to exercise it, the power of pressing with decisive force upon the Government of the neighbouring Province of Tunis. This is a result which they have long recognized as inevitable and have accepted without reluctance. England has no special interests in this region which could possibly lead her to view with apprehension or distrust the legitimate and expanding influence of France.[45]

Ending with a note of caution, Salisbury reminded France that it was not the only country in close proximity to Tunis and that he had no way of knowing the Italian views on the subject. Although Germany eventually adopted the British attitude,

German Chancellor Otto von Bismarck originally looked with contempt upon French designs in Tunisia. Late in 1873 the London *Times* reported French intrigues to persuade the Bey of Tunis to repudiate his ties with Turkey. When Britain supported Turkey, Bismarck complimented the British ambassador in Berlin and "burst forth about French diplomats being conspirators and enemies of order and Germany."[46] Nevertheless, in time, Bismarck began to see the advantage of occupying these "conspiring" diplomats in Tunisia rather than in Europe. Accordingly, during the Congress of Berlin he encouraged overt French action in Tunisia. In a confidential dispatch dated January 5, 1879, the French ambassador in Berlin reported an interesting conversation with Bismarck:

> Well! he said to me, I believe that the Tunisian pear is ripe and that it is time for you to pick it; the insolence of the Bey has been the sun of August on this African fruit which may spoil or be stolen by another if you leave it on the tree too long.[47]

Bismarck appeared to be relieved when France finally took Tunisia. The British ambassador in Berlin, Lord Odo Russell Ampthill, explained the chancellor's attitude:

> He is in great spirits since the French have gone into the Tunis trap, which he baited for them during the Congress, and chuckles over the security Germany will enjoy from a diminished Army in France with increased occupation in Africa.[48]

Italy, as Lord Salisbury had warned, did not share the apathy of the other powers with regard to French influence in Tunisia. If France pointed to the early interest of Marseille merchants in Tunis, Italy could counter with stories of Genoese and Venetian traders or, if necessary, call attention to the Roman conquest of North Africa. Italian influence in Tunisia had been established early in the nineteenth century when Italy opened the first European school in the Regency to educate its nationals. In 1860 Italy secured permission for its citizens to buy land in Tunisia and eight years later signed a treaty of friendship, commerce, and navigation with the Bey of Tunis.

The Italians appeared to be ready to conquer Tunisia in the 1860's and even claimed that Emperor Napoleon III had sanctioned the move, but English opposition delayed the plans. After the French defeat at the hands of Prussia in 1870, the Italian scheme was revived, only to meet renewed opposition from England abroad and from a strong pro-French group at home. Thus, when France officially questioned Italy in 1876 to determine how seriously it regarded the Tunisian problem, it was informed that Rome "did not dream in any way of a territorial aggrandizement at the expense of Tunisia and did not plan any annexation of this area."[49] Nevertheless, the situation became critical after the Congress of Berlin. In describing the Congress, Italian Prime Minister Francesco Crispi declared, "We were humiliated and treated as the last nation in Europe; we were mocked and scorned."[50] The humiliation undoubtedly stiffened later Italian policy.

After his secret conference with Salisbury, and aware of Italian opposition, Waddington sent a secret personal dispatch to Marquis de Nouilles, the French ambassador in Rome. He instructed the ambassador to explain that since France controlled Algeria, she had to maintain a close surveillance over the Regency because internal strife in Tunisia invariably led to trouble in Algeria. France clearly could not tolerate the establishment of another power in Tunisia. It was therefore necessary for Italy to understand that it could not entertain ideas of conquest in Tunisia without risking a conflict with France. The communiqué suggested that Italy turn its desires in another direction. Perhaps the port of Tobruk in North Africa or Avlona in Albania would be fertile areas for Italian expansion. Waddington concluded the lengthy dispatch with the caution:

> Finally, if Count Corti pressed you on the subject of the accord which exists between the English and us, and of the promise

that they made to allow us *carte blanche* in Tunis, you must not part from the generalities indicated above; because the English dispatch is secret, and I do not have the right to make any use of it in regard to the present.[51]

Seemingly unimpressed by these French warnings, Italy sent a new consul to Tunis, Licurgo Maccio, who had known the French consul, Theodore Roustan, when they both served in Syria. The rival consuls were soon embroiled in conflicts over economic concessions. When Maccio gained permission from the Bey to link Sicily and La Goulette by a submarine telegraphic cable, Roustan protested that this violated the French monopoly granted in the Telegraphic Convention of April 19, 1861. Although the convention had not granted France a monopoly, the Bey of Tunis retreated under French pressure and withdrew permission for the cable.[52]

The most serious conflict developed over the railroad from Tunis to La Goulette. Since its English owners had found this twenty miles of railway unprofitable, they had decided to sell. The French Bône-Guelma Company and the Italian Rubattino Company opened negotiations for the bankrupt road. As soon as the French bought the railway, the Rubattino Company pointed out that under British law such a sale had to be approved by the High Court of Justice of Great Britain. When the High Court delayed the sale, the Rubattino Company, assured by the Italian government's guarantee of over six hundred thousand francs annually, seized its opportunity and purchased the railroad for 4,125,000 francs—an amount several times what the railroad was worth.

The transaction caused Jules Ferry, who formed a new French cabinet in September, 1880, to complain, "It had been agreed between the two cabinets of Rome and Paris that the new action should be in place of and beyond all intervention of one or the other governments."[53] Roustan protested bitterly to the Bey, Mohammed es Sadok, demanding compensations for France. Specifically he wanted the Bey's permission to build a railroad around the southern shore of the Lake of Tunis to the port of Rhades. This would have competed directly with the newly acquired Italian line, which skirted the northern shore of the lake. A French naval squadron appeared off La Goulette, and the Bey was given a time limit in which to make a decision. Despite the presence of the naval vessels, the Bey refused the French demand; nevertheless, France received large concessions elsewhere. She was permitted to build a railroad from Tunis to Sousse, Sfax, Monastir, and Bizerte and was granted the right to make a harbor at Tunis by cutting a channel between the city and the sea. In addition the claims of French citizens to undeveloped mining property were confirmed: it was estimated that the concessions covered nearly one-fourth of the available agricultural surface of the Regency. However, these concessions did not satisfy the French, who maintained that the Rubattino purchase could lead to an Italian political advantage in Tunisia. Jules Ferry attributed the origin of the French expedition in Tunisia solely to this purchase.[54]

Thus, by 1881 France had secured the consent of England and Germany for its impending adventure in Tunisia, and had learned of Italy's active opposition. But substantial European support for the program was not enough, for France recognized that final control of Tunisia depended upon extending political and economic power over the Bey's government.

Tunisian financial and economic difficulties between 1879 and 1881 invited penetration. Having developed extensive interests in Tunisia, France felt that the inept policies of the Bey's government jeopardized them. In his report for 1878 the United States consul described this incompetence:

It is pitiable to see a country like this with a docile people, an excellent climate, rich soil and abundant resources reduced to the most abject poverty and misery by the misgovernment of a few men whose only thought is to find the means of gratifying their inordinate love of luxury and bad passions.[55]

Much of the mismanagement resulted from the confusion that attended the Bey's plea of bankruptcy in 1869 and the establishment of the International Financial Commission. For example, the Bey and the commission planned to devalue the coinage on the pretext that a large number of four-piaster silver pieces had been smuggled into the country. The reduction of the nominal value of ten- and five-piaster gold pieces and all silver pieces threw internal trade into confusion. Both the holders of large sums in silver, who faced a one-fifth reduction in the value of their deposits, and government employees and creditors, who were paid in depreciated coinage, suffered. The scandalous part of the affair was that before recommending the measure to the Bey, the members of the commission had gradually changed their silver for gold at a slight discount. The impunity with which it was done, although the guilty parties were known, led the American consul to charge that high government officials planned the financial swindle.[56]

More serious than the coinage problem was the inability of the financial commission to raise adequate revenue to meet payments on government bonds. Two conditions caused this situation: a drought in the winter of 1876-1877, killing cattle and sheep, resulted in a sharp reduction in revenue from the tax on livestock; and large-scale smuggling of exports deprived the government of a good portion of its customs revenue. Conditions were so serious that many lesser government employees were not even paid.

In 1880 the economic pattern of Tunisia was changing. The greatest factor in the change was the development of the railroad from the city of Tunis to the Algerian border, which greatly aided the French in establishing economic supremacy in the Regency. In 1871 the Tunisian government had granted the railway concession to an English company. However, when this company and its successor—another English company—failed to fulfill their contract obligations, a French company, Chemins de Fer de Bône-Guelma et Prolongements, took control. In 1876 this company established a Tunisian branch,

Ligne de Tunisie, to develop the concession. With headquarters in Paris the company, holding a capital stock of ninety million francs, enjoyed a governmental guarantee of six per cent on the money expended in construction. Later it secured a right of way to the frontier, ground for depots and shops, gravel and material, and the right to develop the lead mines near the projected railroad. Construction was begun in January, 1878, and completed in March, 1880.

From Tunis the railroad reached the fertile valley of the Medjerda River by a tunnel that pierced the high ridge of mountains separating the city from the valley; it then followed the winding river to the Algerian border. The American consul observed that the railroad placed the richest portion of the Regency in the hands of the French and that foreign capital, mostly French, was flowing into the country. The consul concluded, "European commerce, industry and enterprise are also quietly drifting hitherward, and the whole industrial, as well as political, aspect of the country is being silently, and almost imperceptibly revolutionized." Later he elaborated.

> When the link between Duvivier and Ghrardimaou is completed a French Army can be brought from Algeria to any part of Tunis in a few hours, which in cooperation with the French Navy—always in force within easy call of this coast—places the Regency of Tunis absolutely within the power of France whenever it may suit her purposes to use that power. I do not imagine that France intends to, violently, disturb the present order of things. She prefers accomplishing her purposes by using the Tunisian Government leaving the responsibility of governing the country with its present rulers. France is, however, fully prepared to hold the country, as against any other European power that might desire to grasp it. . . . This French railroad scheme has been from its inception to the present time a political rather than a financial enterprise.[57]

In addition to this valuable railway from Tunis to the Algerian border, France seized other opportunities to extend her economic power. A shipping company, liberally subsidized by

the French government, arranged to run steamers weekly between Marseille and Tunis and to establish service from Tunis
to Tripoli and Malta. France also enjoyed control of the telegraph system and established a Banque de Crédit, which
greatly facilitated the development of agriculture, commerce,
and industry by lowering the interest rates on loans. Moreover, a French company in 1880 bought the Enfida Domain,
which comprised about a thousand square miles in the fertile
olive-growing Sahel region between Tunis and Sousse. In
large measure France planned its occupation of Tunisia to
protect these economic interests.

France had difficulty timing the invasion. As early as the
summer of 1878, Foreign Minister Waddington informed
Consul Roustan in Tunis that he was contemplating negotiations with the Bey for a convention stipulating Tunisian recognition of a French protectorate. The project would involve
occupation of Le Kef, Bizerte, La Goulette, and one or two
points near Gabes; guarantee of the civil government of the
Bey during his lifetime; definition of the powers of the French
resident in relation to the Bey; and limitation of the Tunisian
army to a good police force. Roustan was ordered to regard
the communiqué as strictly confidential and to withhold action.
On September 1, 1878, however, Waddington wrote to his
consul, "It will probably be some time before we are able to
engage in the affair of the protectorate."[58] Four days later
the foreign minister canceled the project because too many
obstacles prevented successful negotiations: the Turkish Muslims were in a state of excitement, and France did not want
to furnish them with an excuse for fanaticism.

In 1879, under the Ministry of Charles de Freycinet, France
again began to consider moving into Tunisia. Acting under
Freycinet's orders and after preliminary talks with the Bey
in order to persuade him to sign a formal protectorate treaty,
Roustan suggested, "Authorize me to debark a company of
marines and the Bey will sign." Freycinet was about to comply
when he was forced to resign. He informed his successor, Jules

Ferry, "The fruit is ripe, you should gather it at the proper moment."[59]

Trouble on the Tunisian-Algerian frontier created the situation which finally led to French intervention. The border between Algeria and Tunisia had long been the object of pillaging Arab tribes, both Algerian and Tunisian. In the *Yellow Book,* explaining their case, the French mentioned 2,379 outrages between 1870 and 1881—all attributed to Tunisia. Although many of these claims were settled—the Tunisian government gave reparations in 1,867 cases—France became critical because the Bey had not pursued and arrested the culprits.[60] Actually, the Bey was unable to collect taxes from many of these obstinate mountain tribes, let alone arrest them or command them to stay at home. France knew this but constantly admonished the Bey for his inability to maintain order.

The pillaging of French vessels by Tunisian tribes was considered particularly odious because such acts involved attacks upon Frenchmen. In 1878 the packet-boat *L'Auvergne* ran aground near Tabarka, and the Kroumir tribe of western Tunisia looted the wreck under the very eyes of the Tunisian garrison in the neighboring fort.[61] Less than a year later a small ship, *Le Forbin,* was boarded by Tunisians and one sailor was seriously wounded. In April, 1881, the French brig *Le Santoni* was taken by the raiders.

The specific incident which brought about the invasion was the raid on March 30, 1881, in which several hundred members of the Tunisian Kroumir tribe swept into Algeria. The following day, after eleven hours of combat, French and Algerian troops repulsed the Kroumirs. The French suffered four dead and six wounded. The clash started negotiations between Roustan and the Bey in which Mohammed es Sadok finally offered the French an indemnity of three hundred thousand francs if they would allow his troops to occupy Kroumir territory in western Tunisia. But Roustan refused, insisting upon French punishment for the warring tribe.

The affair was taken to the French parliament by Premier

Jules Ferry on April 4. Three days later, by a vote of 474 to 2 with 50 abstentions, the Chamber voted a credit of 5,695,276 francs to finance the punishment of the Kroumirs. In the Senate the credit was approved unanimously. Ferry announced that France had two objectives: first, to punish the Kroumirs, and second to see that this sort of incident never occurred again.[62]

Meanwhile, Italy asked England what its attitude would be if France extended the mission beyond chastisement. Italy was disappointed to receive answers similar to this:

> While France claimed to exercise the influence over Tunis which is necessary for a powerful civilized country over a small and less civilized neighbour, she did not desire in any way to interfere with the rights of foreign residents or foreign traders in Tunis, and she had no intention to annex Tunis.[63]

Although English Foreign Minister Earl Granville and Prime Minister William Gladstone were not very sympathetic toward French designs in Tunisia, they both felt bound by the Salisbury-Waddington negotiations, which were published in the London *Times* on April 11, 1881. Gladstone realized also that no legal basis existed for contesting French power in Tunisia. In a debate on Anglo-Turkish relations the prime minister explained:

> We may lament the conduct of France in Tunis; but it is difficult to assert that France by her conduct in Tunis has been guilty of a breach of International Law. France has never for a very long time . . . admitted that Tunis belonged to the Turkish Empire, and, only a few years ago, France was joined by Italy in holding that view. We hold the contrary; but [as] it has only been a matter of opinion on one side and the other, it is impossible to assert as a proposition of European Law that Tunis belongs to the Turkish Empire.[64]

On April 9 British Consul Thomas Reade reported that a French cavalry detachment crossed into Tunisia from Algeria and encountered no opposition from the natives, one of whom they took prisoner. "Although thrown into a state of effervescence by the arrival of the aggressive force, the natives were with some difficulty restrained by their commanding Chief from engaging in the conflict to which they were provoked."[65] A few days later French vessels reached Bizerte, which surrendered without a shot. When French troops disembarked and moved southeast toward the city of Tunis instead of westward to Kroumir country, even the most naive observers realized the affair went beyond mere punishment. The anticipated terror, however, failed to materialize in Tunis. The American consul felt that the Bey's efforts to maintain order were responsible. Moreover, the consul, commending the behavior of the French soldiers, reported, "The rights of the people are, it is said, strictly respected, and whatever is taken for the use of the troops is paid for liberally."[66]

The illusion—apparently strong among Tunisian and Turkish leaders—that the great powers would aid Tunisia was dispelled in the early weeks of May. An appeal for help from Turkey on May 3, 1881, secured no support. Several days later the French ambassador in Constantinople informed the Sultan, "Since France is actually at war with a part of the population of Tunisia, any dispatch of military forces to Tunis, on the part of Turkey, will be regarded as an act of hostility."[67]

In the circular introducing the *Yellow Book,* Foreign Minister Barthélemy Saint-Hilaire announced that one policy governed French relations with Tunisia: namely, an absolute obligation to assure the security of Algeria. Nevertheless, later in the document he said that since Tunisia was jeopardizing French enterprises, "it was necessary to have recourse to other means than loyal discussion and persuasion, which have become absolutely useless." He denied Turkish sovereignty in Tunisia, declared that France had the support of Europe, and suggested the benefits France could bring to Tunisia, which "is a sacred obligation, that a superior civilization contracts to-

ward peoples less advanced."[68] When the circular reached
Rome, the *Libertà* editorialized:

> Events will show how far France intends to offend Italy and
> the high interests she has in Tunis. Anyway, it is well that we
> Italians should have a perfectly clear idea of what France has
> done against us, if for no other reason than to remember it.[69]

Italy did remember for some time. When France and Tunisia
signed the Treaty of Bardo, Cairoli's ministry fell; and the
dispute between Rome and Paris remained bitter until 1883.

Just sixteen days after the invasion began, French troops
camped within sight of the Bey's palace. Here on May 12,
1881, Mohammed es Sadok signed the famous Treaty of
Bardo,[70] which in essence established a French protectorate
without ever using the term. It was a brief ceremony: Roustan
and General Jules-Aimé Bréart had an audience with the Bey
in which the text of the treaty was read and the Bey was
given until nine o'clock that evening to reply. Several hours
before the deadline he signed. The Bey asked France not to
occupy the capital city so that he could maintain prestige with
his people and thereby lessen the possibility of riots. France
granted the request.

The treaty allowed France to occupy "the points which she
will judge necessary to assure the reestablishment of order and
security of the frontiers and the coast." The occupation would
cease when the local administration was in a state to guarantee
the maintenance of order. The French government promised
to protect the Bey against danger to his person or dynasty and
guaranteed the treaties existing between the European powers
and the Regency. Henceforth France would be represented at
Tunis by a resident-minister. Tunisia could not conclude any
international agreement without the consent of France. Article
Seven contained a financial arrangement whereby an organization could be established "to assure the service of the public
debt and to guarantee the rights of the creditors of Tunisia."

A war contribution would be levied on the tribes of the frontier and the coast. Finally, to protect Algeria against arms smuggling, the Tunisian government was obligated to prevent the introduction of arms and munitions from the island of Djerba, the port of Gabes, and all other ports of southern Tunisia.

While the treaty was generally welcomed in France, where public opinion appeared to favor a protectorate policy rather than annexation, Georges Clemenceau criticized it in the Chamber of Deputies for changing the European order. In referring to Italy he asserted that the treaty had cooled "precious friendships cemented on the field of battle."[71] Furthermore, he maintained that France had fallen for Germany's opportunistic policy of declarations of friendship. Deputy Anne-Armand Vicomte de Gontaut-Biron complained because the affair was carried out without a declaration of war, therefore without the consent of parliament. But a legislative commission reporting on the treaty declared it a sound document in international law, a treaty that assured the order and benefit of French civilization to Tunisia, protected Algeria, and opened "finally, under our auspices, a vast field of activity to the commerce of all nations."[72] The Treaty of Bardo passed the Chamber by a margin of 430 to 1; the Senate ratified it unanimously.

The English and particularly the Italian newspapers were critical of the treaty. A London *Times* editorial was highly skeptical of the method by which France accomplished her objective:

> The terms of the treaty seem to leave it in the discretion of the French to occupy Bizerte, though M. Barthélemy St. Hilaire is said to have disclaimed this intention to the Italian Ambassador. Disclaimers, however, by the French Minister for Foreign Affairs will, we fear, henceforth be viewed with some suspicion. . . . While foreign Governments were being soothed by declarations that the sole object of the French expedition was to punish

the Kroumirs, General Bréart, beyond reasonable doubt, had in his pocket a cut and dried treaty, prepared in Paris, to be forced upon the Bey at the point of the bayonet.[73]

The French blamed jealousy for the bad English press.

In Italy Garibaldi announced in the *Riforma* that he had lost his good opinion of the French Republic; he warned that Italy would not forget its old relationship with Nice and Corsica. In June a bloody riot broke out in Marseille between French and Italians, and similar outbreaks occurred at Rome, Turin, Naples, Genoa, and Palermo.[74] The following month the French ambassador in Rome reported continued threats against his life and a "manifestation" against the embassy by people carrying concealed weapons. France shrugged off these unfriendly incidents and turned to the task of deciding what to do with its newly acquired possession.

So many conditions encouraged the French invasion of Tunisia that the act appeared inevitable. The support of the major European powers and the attitude that the "superior" civilization of Europe must be "shared" with "unfortunates" gave the invasion an air of righteousness. The more realistic aspects of the situation also encouraged action: Algeria must be protected; Tunisia was a fertile area for economic penetration; the inept policies of the Tunisian government threatened French investments; and Italian nationals were challenging the supremacy of France in the Regency. For these reasons France acquired a territory that it would rule as a protectorate for seventy-four years.

2

Problems of the Young Protectorate

Organizing the Protectorate

The word "protectorate" did not appear in Franco-Tunisian negotiations until the Convention of La Marsa in 1883. Many problems required solution before France obtained satisfactory power in the Regency of Tunis. The laborious task fell to the capable Paul Cambon, who later became the famous French ambassador in England before the First World War, and his able assistants, Maurice Bompard and Baron d'Estournelles de Constant.

Paul Cambon began a long public career in September, 1870, when Jules Ferry, then prefect of the Seine, chose him as his secretary-general. In 1877 Cambon was named head of the department of the North, one of the most important prefectures in France, and while serving in this capacity he was appointed resident-minister in Tunisia on February 25, 1882.[1]

Maurice Bompard attracted Cambon's attention as the intelligent hard-working secretary-general of the prefecture of the North. Cambon persuaded him to enter the diplomatic service and accompany him to Tunis. Later, when the Tunisian administration was organized, Bompard held the important post of secretary-general of Tunisia. Baron d'Estournelles de Constant was not acquainted with Paul Cambon until he served with him in Tunisia; however, they soon became close friends and the baron was the administrative assistant to the resident-minister. Formerly d'Estournelles had been with the French embassy in London. His diplomatic experience as well as his personal contacts in the British Foreign Office proved valuable to the government of Tunisia.

Confusion shrouded the French policy in Tunisiâ when Cambon was appointed resident-minister. The Freycinet ministry was noncommittal concerning future plans. Cambon, who was above all an administrator, despised uncertainty and vowed to establish a definite policy before he sailed for Tunis. For a month and a half he interviewed various government officials to discover what the future policy for the Regency might be. Prime Minister Freycinet temporized, and the minister of war, General Billot, felt that the expedition to Tunisia had been a mistake but commented on Cambon's appointment, "He is a superior man, he will succeed . . . perhaps."[2] President Grévy comforted the new minister by telling him, "The task is difficult but nothing is beyond your intelligence and capacity."[3]

In the absence of a definite government program, Cambon advanced some ideas of his own. He wrote to his wife on March 1, 1882, stating that if France only wanted to exert diplomatic influence, it was hard to see why she planned to send forty thousand men and a former prefect. On the other hand, if France really wanted to extend control, it was necessary to establish a definite policy for Tunisia.[4] In his estimation two steps had to be taken before an effective protectorate could be realized: the Tunisian debt should be guaranteed and converted, and consular jurisdiction and capitulation rights must be abolished in favor of French justice.

Resident-Minister Cambon immediately inaugurated his

program to accomplish these objectives, but his initial efforts to bring about Tunisian debt redemption were frustrating. After much debate an extraparliamentary commission under the chairmanship of Prime Minister Freycinet was established to study the problem. The commission considered the following proposals: abandonment of the idea of annexation in favor of maintaining the Bey's government; subordination of military authority to that of the resident-minister; creation of a Tunisian army; establishment of French courts; and guarantee of the debt. These reforms were recommended by Paul Cambon, and gradually, during his four years in the Regency, all were instituted.

When the time came for Cambon to leave for Tunis, the commission had not yet decided the question of the Tunisian debt, a decision which Cambon considered fundamental. He reluctantly agreed to go under these circumstances but warned that if he could not adapt himself to the International Financial Commission he would say so in unmistakable terms.

Cambon departed for and arrived in Tunis amid great fanfare. At Toulon his train was met by an official delegation including his predecessor in Tunisia, Theodore Roustan. He had breakfast at the prefecture and that afternoon, April 1, 1882, in the company of Bompard and d'Estournelles, boarded the dispatch-boat *Hirondelle*. Saluted by the strains of "La Marseillaise," the ship glided between two flagships and pointed toward Tunisia. About twenty-four hours later the *Hirondelle* anchored off La Goulette, the port city of Tunis. The cannon of the Bey's timeworn forts fired salutes while shabby Tunisian soldiers presented arms. At the railroad station in Tunis French soldiers snapped to attention as Cambon walked between them to the Bey's carriage, where he was greeted by the Bey's interpreter, Elias Mussalli, and escorted to the residence.

The following morning he visited the Bey at the Bardo Palace. The Bey was restive because his horoscope had predicted his downfall, and upon hearing the cannon salutes for

Cambon, he thought the end was surely at hand. Informed that his rule would be protected, he and Cambon engaged in fifteen minutes of flowery compliments through Mussalli.

The French official's first reaction to conditions in Tunis was one of dejection. Ten days after his arrival Cambon wrote to his wife:

> The more I examine this Tunisian question the more I find it insoluble if the Government does not make great decisions. Misery, waste and ruin exist throughout. . . . This year the deficit will be fifteen millions. They will not be able to extricate themselves if the French government does not take the debt into its charge along with the financial administration and the suppression of capitulations.[5]

He threatened that unless there was early government action he would ask for another post. Bompard's estimation of the situation was just as discouraging:

> The public fortune had been given over to pillage, the offices of the state put up for sale, justice confined to venal hands, all the jurisdiction of the government weakened or broken, the country the prey of anarchy, the population squeezed by exactions or relieved of all authority. . . .[6]

The financial commission obliged Tunisia to pay European debts first, which left little money to carry on the administration. Foreign consuls, exercising old capitulation rights, had power to rule over their nationals and protégés. Commerce was sluggish, numbers of people were weakened by famine, others fled to Tripoli.[7] There were no vital statistics, births and deaths were not even registered, and the central government exercised only theoretical power in the provinces.

To a former French prefect the situation was intolerable, and Cambon set out to change it. In June of 1882 he returned to Paris to induce the government to sign a treaty with the Bey establishing a definite protectorate and guaranteeing the debt. He had launched an adventure that would seem like a nightmare before it was over. Freycinet was hopelessly embroiled in the Egyptian problem because England had invited France to undertake a joint expedition to Port Said for the protection of the Suez Canal. The situation was a strain on Freycinet, and Cambon added to the pressure by suggesting that France demand English renunciation of capitulation rights in Tunisia in return for French help in Egypt. After a debate in the Chamber, Cambon wrote to d'Estournelles, "You do not realize the physical and moral state that Freycinet is in since the session on Egypt. . . . His days are numbered."[8] Indeed the premier's political days were numbered, and his cabinet fell in August.

The visit was a frustrating one for Cambon. Nobody was willing to forget Egypt and talk about Tunisia, and even Cambon's repeated threats of resignation failed to break this preoccupation. Undaunted, Cambon returned to Tunisia and, with the help of Elias Mussalli, laid the groundwork for the Bey's signature of the proposed treaty. After the Bey had conferred upon Cambon the Order of the Bey and in return had received a saber, along with assurances that his sovereignty would be respected, he signed on July 8, 1882. Actually Cambon had no authority to negotiate the treaty. He planned to present the confused French government with a *fait accompli*.[9]

The Bey was cooperating handsomely, but Cambon still lacked the approval of his own government. Freycinet's toppled ministry was replaced on August 7 by that of Duclerc, who took the portfolio of foreign affairs, and Cambon renewed his efforts to gain approval of the treaty. Disturbed, he wrote to his wife that if the International Financial Commission was not suppressed, the only alternative would be to organize a purely military government in Tunisia.[10] His theory was that no efficient civil government could exist unless it had complete financial autonomy, and he plainly indicated he would fight for this independence.

The situation in Paris was uncertain, but at least the Bey had signed the treaty. While Cambon was finding some comfort in this, the Bey's death on October 27, 1882, reduced

Cambon's accomplishments to zero. Ignoring this reversal, he used the death of the Bey as an excuse for alterations in Tunisia. Cambon organized an investiture ceremony for the new ruler, Ali Bey, in the name of the French president. This unprecedented ceremonial, in which Cambon presented the foreign consuls to the new sovereign, strained the self-control of the Italian consul.

In March, 1883, the tenacious Cambon was back in Paris bargaining with the second Ferry ministry in behalf of his faltering convention. When at last the idea was supported by the government, he returned to Tunisia and concluded the Convention of La Marsa with Ali Bey on June 8, 1883.[11] The Convention was the essential first step toward an actual protectorate. Article One read: "His Highness the Bey of Tunis promises to proceed with the administrative, judicial and financial reforms that the French government will judge necessary." For its part the French government guaranteed a loan to the Bey of 125 million francs for the conversion or reimbursement of the consolidated debt and of the floating debt up to a maximum of 17,500,000 francs. In the future the Bey could not contract any loans without the authorization of France (Article Two). The Bey could deduct from the revenue of the Regency (1) a sum necessary to service the loan guaranteed by France, and (2) the sum of 1,200,000 francs for his civil government. The remainder was to be used for the expenses of the protectorate (Article Three). Article Four simply confirmed the Treaty of Bardo, and the last article provided for the submission of the treaty to France and the remittance of the ratification as soon as possible.

The expected brief delay became an eleven-month vigil. Although the Convention had not been ratified, Cambon put Article One into operation in the summer of 1883. The following spring he hurried to Paris and spoke to the Chamber in behalf of ratification. Here, before the Chamber, Paul Cambon displayed his administrative cleverness and political ability. He abhorred the needless oratory that characterized parliamentary debate and decided to base his arguments instead on fact. First he reviewed the financial situation of Tunisia. When France occupied Tunisia there was no budget, simply a list of expenses and receipts. The list of receipts was seldom accurate because the government was often faced with insurrections that prevented tax collection. Consequently, Cambon told the deputies, his first task was to establish a budget. The budget for 1884 allowed an excess of receipts over expenditures amounting to 183,000 francs.[12] Some important economies were introduced. By abolishing the ministry of marine and cutting the expenditures for the office of foreign affairs, whose functions were now performed by the resident-minister, enough money was saved to permit the creation of a forestry service and a service of public works and still show a favorable balance.

Cambon skillfully undermined the reputation of the International Financial Commission by telling the French deputies that the commission did not allow the state enough revenue to carry on public services. Furthermore, it was not interested in internal improvements, but only in paying off the Bey's creditors. From a political point of view this organization hurt France, because "it is composed mainly of foreigners; it contains nine members, of which only three are French."[13] This, he felt, was an inadmissible situation in a country which France had occupied for three years. Moreover, the commission had ruined the municipalities by conceding their revenues to the creditors of the Regency. As a result, Cambon added, "If you would visit Tunis, at this time, you would be very unpleasantly surprised by the state of dilapidation of the public streets, the absence of sewers, of public lighting, and we have been there three years."[14]

He observed that if France guaranteed the Tunisian debt, the *raison d'être* of the financial commission would be removed. Moreover, if the debt were guaranteed, France could convert it and realize an economy of about two million francs by servicing the debt under a new interest rate, leaving a substantial amount for the operation of the government. Cambon assured the Chamber that if the debt were converted and France controlled the finances, there was no doubt that "Tunisia could exist by herself."[15] He claimed,

> this guarantee is not only necessary to operate the conversion, it also allows us to put into operation indispensable economic reforms in Tunisia; it is necessary finally, in order to allow us to exercise an effective political action in the country under our protectorate.[16]

The Chamber approved the Convention of La Marsa. Jules Ferry, then prime minister, defended the measure before the Senate in what Cambon reported as a very short and satisfactory discussion, and the Convention was formally ratified on April 10, 1884.

Simultaneous with the resident-minister's efforts to win acceptance for his convention was his vigorous work for the abolition of capitulation rights. Under these rights foreign powers through consular courts maintained jurisdiction over their nationals and protégés. This privilege had existed for centuries; French capitulation rights were established in Tunisia as early as the sixteenth century. The Treaty of Bardo guaranteed the existing treaties between Tunisia and foreign powers, thereby recognizing these privileges.

Since the original and ostensible reason for capitulation was to protect foreigners from Muslim law, the French reasoned that with the establishment of their courts the need for consular jurisdiction would disappear. Under the confusing and annoying system of consular jurisdiction the new administration could not arrest anyone under foreign jurisdiction except in the presence of his consul's guard. If the consul refused to furnish janissaries, the pursuit of his protégé had to be abandoned. Sometimes Negroes, Arabs, or native Jews, who did not speak any European language, would associate themselves with a European nationality to escape native law, taxes, and military duty.[17] More annoying still was the fact that consular jurisdiction paralyzed the sources of revenue for public improvements. Municipal authority was challenged by the consuls, and ordinary municipal laws were inapplicable without consular consent. If the municipality wanted to tax carriages, those who owned carriages were exempted by their consuls, and the people who did not have a consul usually traveled on foot.[18] If a toll bridge was built, the natives alone paid. One consul used his right of protection to maintain a house of ill fame.[19]

Numerous incidents resulted from this complexity of jurisdiction. To add to the confused pattern the French minister of war, General Billot, decided that incidents involving French soldiers would be referred to the council of war. A short time later, Meschino, a Sicilian barber who fancied himself a comic, stole a saber from a *zouave* and took it to his consul. The next morning gendarmes knocked at his door and placed him under arrest. The Italian consul protested the barber's arrest, asserting that he alone had the right to judge the case. The council of war, unmoved by the humor of the situation, sentenced Meschino to a year in prison. The prankster wrote a letter of apology to the French general; nevertheless, it looked like a year in a smelly Tunis jail for Meschino. Cambon defended the right of the council of war to judge such cases. However, the affair did not end there; Italy made it a political issue. The Italian chargé d'affaires asked Minister of Foreign Affairs Duclerc to pardon Meschino. Duclerc had been misinformed and, believing that the Sicilian had attacked a French soldier, refused to intervene.[20] Telegrams from the French chargé d'affaires in Rome finally convinced Duclerc of the seriousness with which the Italian government regarded the affair, and the minister telegraphed a pardon for Meschino.[21]

Later, at La Goulette, a drunken Italian picked a quarrel with a French sentry. A passing patrol tried to corner him but he escaped and took refuge with his consul. The consul clandestinely sent the offender to Sicily in order to escape French military justice.[22]

Such incidents indicated that no efficient law enforcement would exist until the central government had a stronger position. Cambon advocated replacing consular jurisdiction with a system of French courts. Only a weak government, he claimed, would tolerate this hopeless confusion.

The first step toward abandonment of capitulations was taken when a commission of the Chamber of Deputies recommended the establishment of a French civil tribunal and six justices of the peace in Tunisia. The law of March 27, 1883, created a tribunal of the first instance at Tunis, and justices of the peace at Tunis, La Goulette, Bizerte, Sousse, Sfax, and Le Kef to preside over magistrate courts. The law further provided:

> These tribunals shall form part of the jurisdiction of the Court of Algiers. They shall take cognizance of all civil and commercial questions between French and French protected subjects.
>
> They shall take cognizance likewise of all proceedings instituted against the French and French protected subjects for infractions of the law, misdemeanours, or crimes.
>
> Their authority may be extended over all other persons by Edicts or Decrees of His Highness the Bey, issued with the assent of the French Government.[23]

The last clause was important because the Bey issued such a decree on May 5, 1883, announcing that "the nationals of the friendly powers of which the consular tribunals are suspended become amenable in the French tribunals under the same conditions as the French themselves."[24]

The basis for the renunciation of consular jurisdiction was now established, and only consent of the major powers was needed. French officials felt English renunciation would persuade the other powers to follow suit. Therefore, Cambon was greatly disturbed when he learned that Consul Thomas Reade, the British representative in Tunis, and the English journalist A. M. Broadley were conducting a press campaign against abrogation. On November 24, 1883, Cambon wrote to

Ferry requesting permission to send d'Estournelles de Constant to England for conferences with his friends in the foreign office. The resident-minister felt sure that d'Estournelles and Ambassador Waddington could persuade the English government to renounce consular jurisdiction.

In England, d'Estournelles was faced with the request that in return for abolition of capitulations France should arbitrate a large number of English claims in Tunisia. Cambon wrote that if the number of cases could not be limited, he would prefer keeping capitulations, which would also mean keeping the financial commission since it was the only safe guard against foreign consuls.[25]

Having heard from Rome that if England suppressed capitulations Italy would follow, and placing great confidence in d'Estournelles, Cambon felt that abrogation could be announced by January 1, 1884. Late in December, d'Estournelles wired, "Rejoice and embrace Depienne. Reade and Broadley erased. Will leave London Tuesday."[26] Cambon was elated. England informed her vice-consul in Tunis that her consular jurisdiction would be abolished from the first of January.

During a New Year's Day conference between Cambon and Bompard, the Italian consul, M. Mancini, arrived with the news that Italy agreed to end capitulations. The arrangement was signed on January 25, 1884, providing for the suspension of consular jurisdiction, a suspension which would last as long as the French protectorate existed. All other immunities which had been accorded Italians would remain in existence. With the exception of the United States[27] all major powers joined England and Italy in their renunciation.

Philosophy of a Protectorate

In theory a protectorate established control for the mother country without destroying the dignity of the protected nation or stirring up uncontrolled hatred. Therefore, the relationship between the protector and the protected was a delicate one whereby each possessed partial sovereign rights. The protected state did not vanish from the international community, and its subjects retained their nationality. Nor was its property merged with that of the protector, but two sovereignties existed side by side within the limits of the protectorate treaties. This contact not only introduced new political and economic ideas into the protected state but allowed a cultural penetration as well. In his *Essai sur les protectorats* Franz Despagnet wrote, "The protectorate therefore appears as a sort of moral conquest preceded and justified by the material conquest."[28]

D'Estournelles de Constant outlined the general principles of this government.

> The government of the protectorate allows the administration of the country that we occupy to remain, strengthens and controls it; it conserves, as much as possible, that which cannot be replaced at little cost and it only replaces slowly. An old, halting administration progresses still better than an administration created from the old; a body accustomed to its infirmities

TUNISIAN GOVERNMENT 1881-1892

TUNISIAN	MIXED	FRENCH
	Central	
	Government	
Bey		Resident-Minister 1881
Ouzara (central		Resident-General 1885
administration)		Secretary-General 1883
Prime Minister		Minister of War 1881
Minister of the		*Director of Public
Pen		Works 1882
		Forest Service 1884
		Topography Service
		1885
		*Director of Finances
		1882
		Directorate of Monopolies 1890

TUNISIAN GOVERNMENT 1881-1892
(continued)

TUNISIAN	MIXED	FRENCH

*Central
Government*

		FRENCH
	Mixed Army Companies 1883	*Director of Public Instruction 1883
		*Director of Postal and Telegraph Office 1888
		*Director of Agriculture and Colonization 1890
		**Consultative Conference 1892
		Chambers of Commerce
		Chambers of Agriculture
		Third College

*Provincial
Administration*

Local Officials		Civil Controllers 1884
Caid		
Khalifa		
Sheikh		

*Municipal
Administration*

Municipal Councils
1884
Municipal Commissions

*These services included Tunisian personnel, but the main officials were French.

**Mixed to a slight degree in the 1907 reform, but more fully by the Reform of 1922.

submits to a severe regime, furnishes more useful work than that of a newly-born. Therefore we have not introduced an army of officials behind our troops; we have contented ourselves with an administration which knows how to collect the taxes.[29]

The protectorate form of government was also less expensive than annexation, which appealed to the French guardians of the purse. Algeria had been a mismanaged headache for France since 1830, and there was a strong desire to avoid duplicating this sort of annexation.

Paul Cambon and his aides realized that French power must be instituted delicately because of the strong Tunisian opposition to change and the excitability of the European populace. D'Estournelles de Constant observed that discipline and regularity were unknown in Tunisia, that one might just as well try to discipline the birds. For example, when the coach lines were rerouted in Tunis, the Maltese coachmen became so excited that a Capuchin, their spiritual leader, had to be called to calm them. Even the placing of water meters in homes brought vehement protests, and the following laws almost caused riots:

1. To throw excrement, sloppy water, dirt, rubbish, etc., before the houses is prohibited.
2. Horses shall not gallop down narrow streets.
3. Carriages and coaches must be registered and taxed.
4. Streets are to be named and the houses numbered.[30]

Moving slowly, and particularly sensitive to Muslim customs, the French officials began a program of reform. The American vice-consul was convinced that keeping the Bey in power prevented native fanaticism from becoming unmanageable.[31]

French Control

At all levels of government France moved into the key positions while carefully maintaining a semblance of Tunisian rule. Before French occupation the central administration of Tunisia was the *Ouzara,* which comprised three sections: the ministry of state, which regulated internal affairs; another section with jurisdiction over criminal and civil justice; and a third section, which controlled foreign affairs.[32] The Bey wielded absolute power, enjoying the ultimate authority in the executive, legislative, and judicial realms, provided he respected the precepts of religious law. He was assisted by the following: the prime minister, who handled the departments of foreign affairs and interior; the minister of the pen, who aided the prime minister; and the ministers of war, marine, and finance, until the latter's functions were absorbed first by the International Financial Commission and later by France.

Since France was dedicated to the principle of using the existing government, the pattern of administrative reform was one of introducing French control as gradually and imperceptibly as possible. Eventually each main Tunisian official was given his French supervisor. After 1881 the Bey's guardian was the resident-minister (in 1885 he received the title resident-general). By the Bey's decree of June 9, 1881, the resident-minister became the foreign minister of Tunisia.[33] Guardedly, but surely, power was transferred from the Bey to the resident-minister.

In the estimation of Cambon one of the greatest advancements was instituted by President Grévy's proclamation of November 10, 1884. Article One of this decree gave the resident-minister the power to approve, in the name of the French government, the promulgation and execution in the Regency of all the decrees rendered by the Bey. Furthermore, the minister could give these acts of the Bey the force of French law.[34] Paul Cambon considered this of great importance because the French magistrates in Tunis were resisting his program and offending the Tunisians by their disrespect for Muslim customs and Qur'anic law. Armed with this new law, Cambon could compel the French to obey the Bey's decrees. No longer could French judges endanger the future of the French protectorate.[35]

The Tunisian prime minister and his assistant, the minister

of the pen, also had their French adviser. He was the secretary-general of the Tunisian government, charged with the general surveillance of the administration. He guarded the archives of the state, examined official correspondence between different public services, remitted this correspondence to the prime minister, and officially promulgated laws, decrees, and regulations. Since nothing could be executed until it was published in the *Journal Officiel Tunisien,* which was controlled by the secretary-general, no official act escaped his scrutiny. Maurice Bompard, whom Paul Cambon described as one living on unbridled work, held this key position. During the resident-minister's frequent absences, Bompard had full charge of the government.

The process of French infiltration continued as the commander of the French occupation forces became minister of war in the Tunisian government. The Ministry of Marine was abolished for financial reasons, and control of finances passed to France. After the disappearance of the financial commission the former French president of the commission, M. Depienne, was named Director General of Finances. M. Grant, who had served the Bey as the French engineer of mines, was appointed Director of Public Works by Paul Cambon.

Although seriously curtailed, the sovereignty of the Bey was not defunct. He still had his prime minister and minister of the pen, and he retained the administrative and judicial services of the *Ouzara* even though this organization no longer controlled foreign affairs. Only on rare occasions were acts of the French Chamber of Deputies or Ministry of Foreign Affairs issued in Tunisia by decree, most notably in the organization of French justice or for international acts and treaties. Although supervised by French officials, legislation at least was made in Tunis, not Paris. In this way it differed from colonial legislation or Algerian legislation. Bompard claimed this very arrangement was "the secret of the success of the Tunisian protectorate."[36]

The principal administrative officials, namely the prime minister, resident-general, and the directors of the public services, legislated by *arrêtés* or orders. The prime minister issued orders dealing with the internal administration of Tunisia, while matters relative uniquely to the French colony were handled by the resident-general.

It was relatively easy for France to maintain native influence in the central administration at Tunis and at the same time install French advisers, but the real problem was to apply the central power to the provinces. Indeed, it can hardly be contended that before the protectorate the Bey really ruled outside of Tunis and its environs. Tunisia was a conglomeration of intermingling sedentary and nomadic tribes. At the head of each tribe was a *caid,* or chief, who theoretically was responsible to the central government, but who actually enjoyed a great deal of local autonomy.[37] The *caid,* appointed by the Bey, had administrative, judicial, and financial power. He was charged with collecting taxes, maintaining order, and administering the laws of the central government. In minor cases he held judicial power and could inflict penalties up to fifteen days in prison. *Caids* did not have a fixed salary but were paid by an increased charge of five per cent on certain taxes they collected. They had to pay their own personnel, the chief of which was the *khalifa,* the main administrative assistant. The *khalifas* were appointed by the *caid* until 1889, when the Bey appointed them, although they were still paid by the *caid.*

Supposedly each tribe had one *caid;* however, some Beys over-exercised their patronage, and one tribe, the Zlass, had five. Because of these irregularities there were more than eighty *caids* in 1881. Moreover, the tribes were divided into factions ruled by sheikhs, who represented local power and were elected by the nobles or "best men" of each faction until the decree of 1889 gave the Bey power to appoint the sheikhs.

The native officials had ample opportunity to enrich themselves through graft and corruption. Stories of corruption, factionalism, and tribal warfare were rife when the French occupied Tunisia. Much of this disorder was attributed to the native police or *oudjak,* who were paid by those arrested. Persons who were arrested either had to pay ten piasters to those who took them to prison or run the risk of never getting out again.[38] Used by the national police as well as the *caid's* horsemen, this system was a continual harassment to the population.

Finally a commission of inquiry traveled throughout Tunisia hearing evidence leading to a plan for getting rid of incompetent *caids* and reducing the number of *caidats,* the districts they governed. By combining tribes of common origin, they hoped to reduce the number without offending the noble class. The number of *caidats* was reduced from eighty in 1881 to fifty-one in 1892, and later to thirty-six.[39]

The next problem was to effect central government surveillance over the *caids.* French President Grévy's decree in 1884 established a system of French civil controllers for this purpose.[40] Controllers were named by the President of the Republic upon the recommendation of the minister of foreign affairs, and all assistant controllers were named by the resident-general. In 1887 general instructions were issued to the controllers by Cambon's successor, Justin Massicault, to observe the native administration and report to the resident-general anything that was of importance to the welfare of the country. They were required to visit, as often as possible, all parts of their territory and send detailed reports to the resident-general three times a year. The civil controller was also charged with local police duties and was cautioned to watch for smuggled arms and powder.[41]

Certainly one of the most important functions of the controller was to supervise the collection of the *achour* tax on wheat and barley lands and the compilation of the *medjba* (capitation tax) rolls. Since these taxes were the ones on which the *caid* levied his five per cent charge, amazing discrepancies appeared in the collection. Some people testified that their *caids* required them to pay the capitation tax three or four times a year. For this reason the controller was asked to watch when the *caids* drew up the roll for the *medjba.*[42] A receipt had to be given to the taxpayer, and soon the Arabs understood the importance of this small piece of paper and would request it if by chance the officials proved forgetful.[43] Ultimately, in 1924, the *caids* were paid a fixed salary.

By 1887 civil controls had been established at Le Kef, La Goulette, Sfax, Sousse, Tozeur, Nabuel, Djerba, Tunis, Kairouan, Mateur, Souk el Arba, Beja, and Bizerte. On the theory that he knew the local needs better than anyone, the controller of an area was consulted on all proposed public works, especially those dealing with the vital problem of water supply.

While the French were formulating the central and provincial administrations, they were also concerned with municipal administration. Only Tunis had a municipal organization, and even this system was ineffective under the old financial commission, which arbitrarily conceded municipal revenues to the creditors of the Bey. After French occupation the central government appointed municipal councilors and saw that city revenues were not drained from the municipalities. The largest municipalities were created at La Goulette, Le Kef, Sfax, Sousse, and Bizerte. The city councils contained French, Tunisians, and even foreigners, all of whom were appointed by the central government.[44] The whole organization was integrated with the provincial administration. In a city which was the administrative center for a *caidat* the *caid* served as president of the city council, and a French vice-president represented the Europeans. The civil controllers were the intermediaries between the councils and the resident-general.

A deliberative organization known as the Consultative Conference completed the administration of Tunisia. The roots of this body were found in the Chambers of Commerce and the Chambers of Agriculture representing the French colonists. At the request of Resident-General Massicault, in 1891 these chambers met in an assembly to act as a deliberative council for the government. However, there were about three thousand Frenchmen who were not represented because they belonged to neither the Chambers of Commerce nor the Chambers of Agriculture.[45] In 1896 the situation was remedied by allowing all unrepresented Frenchmen to elect a third college. The Consultative Conference, which contained no Tunisians, met biannually to discuss all sorts of problems in the presence of the directors of the public services. Later this organization debated the budget, and after World War I became the nucleus around which the Grand Council, containing both French and Tunisian sections, was built.[46]

The real administrative nature of the protectorate assured French domination of a central government that reached into the provinces at all levels. Tunisian sovereignty was nominal.

Judicial System

In Europe religious and civil law struggled for supremacy, and after an exhaustive conflict lived concurrently. In the Middle East the civil and religious domains remained wedded. One specialist described the organic nature of Muslim law:

> The classical theory of Muhammadan law, as developed by the Muhammadan jurisprudents, traces the whole of the legal system to four principles or sources: the Koran, the *sunna* of the Prophet, that is, his model behaviour, the consensus of the orthodox community, and the method of analogy.[47]

He explained the method of analogy as reasoning "guided by the parallel of an existing institution or decision."[48]

Tunisians failed to see the need for the codification of the laws; therefore, a European could gain only a general knowledge of them. To complicate the situation further, four orthodox rites of law were recognized by Muslims, two of which were found in Tunisia—the malekite and hanefite. The majority of Tunisians were ruled under the malekite; since the hanefite had been brought to the Regency by the Turks and was becoming increasingly less common. Although Tunis had some hanefite judges in the supreme tribunal, all the provincial magistrates were of the malekite rite. In a few instances these codes were antagonistic and, indeed, sometimes directly opposite in their pronouncements. The plaintiff could choose the rite under which he wanted to be tried, but having chosen one, he had no recourse to the other in the same case.[49]

The religious or canon law of Islam called *sharaa* covered Qur'anic and religious issues comprising personal law—for example, those dealing with marriage, divorce, guardianship, inheritance, and property rights. These laws severely controlled the Muslim's life. Some traditional Muslim punishments were the loss of a hand for theft; eighty lashes for slander or wine-drinking; death for apostasy; stoning for fornication and adultery if the person was married, but a hundred lashes for the unmarried offender.[50] In Tunisia, in former times, a woman guilty of adultery met a horrible fate. She was sewn in a leather sack and thrown into the smelly lake of Tunis. Sometimes she had to share the sack with several half-starved cats.[51]

Each principal city had its *sharaa* court, but the one in Tunis was the supreme tribunal, which alone contained judges of both rites. Defendants could appeal their cases to this court. The tribes had no courts, only *cadis,* or magistrates, who judged cases under personal law. The jurisdiction rights were limited only by custom and usage since provincial tribunals could declare themselves competent in many cases. The defendant could ask a *mufti,* or jurisconsult, of the *sharaa* court of Tunis to write a *mrazla,* or consultation, on the case; if the verdict of the *cadis* differed from the *mufti's,* the defendant had the privilege of appealing to the *sharaa* tribunal of Tunis. The Bey could intervene in decisions of this court in two instances: (1) in the relatively rare case of a tie vote of the *muftis,* (2) if the court passed the death sentence.

Baron d'Estournelles de Constant was honored by an invitation to view the *sharaa* court of Tunis in action:

> At two opposite extremities of a very long hall, which a person can enter only if he takes off his shoes as for prayer,

seated facing one another on divans, at the right the *maleki* tribunal, at the left the *hanefi;* between the two, arriving by a central door which opens on a vast patio of marble colonnades where the crowd gathers, the litigants of the two rites and their lawyers enter and take their places; a bailiff directs them, they prostrate themselves, then remain on their knees before their respective judges. In this posture, the *hanefis* turn their backs to the *malekis,* and talk simultaneously of two affairs which have no relationship to each other—the litigants developing the arguments of accusation and of defense. Very rapidly, for each rite, a *cadi* questions, directs the debates, renders the sentence, consulting quite often the glances of the other members of the tribunal, a *bach-mufti,* and the *muftis.*[52]

One other religious court existed—the rabbinical tribunal for Jews, located in Tunis. Rabbis presided over this court and ruled the Tunisian Jews under Hebraic instead of Muslim law.

The law of the Qur'an was unalterable, but as Tunisian society became more complex many situations requiring judgment were outside the scope of religious law. For example, no industrial or commercial code existed in Tunisia. A secular court called the *ouzara* court was established to fill the gaps in the old legislation and handled civil, commercial, and penal affairs.[53] The *ouzara* law was divided into civil, criminal, and correctional sections with essentially the same procedure in each. For a long time, like the *sharaa* tribunals, the *ouzara* courts held public audiences, but there the resemblance ended. The members of the *ouzara* court did not pronounce judgment; they gathered the facts from the litigants and compiled a report which was handed to the chief of the section. The report, containing the suggested action, was submitted to the Bey, who ruled by decree on the basis of the tribunal's advice.[54] Finally, by decree in 1921 the Bey relinquished the power of judgment to the *ouzara* courts.

In the provinces the *caids* administered secular justice, but under a reform of the protectorate they could not inflict fines, imprisonment for more than fifteen days, or arrest for debt. All decisions of the *caids* could be appealed to the *ouzara* court in Tunis. Slowly specific jurisdiction emerged from these courts, and some of the decisions were codified.[55]

Arab justice recognized the right of asylum; that is, if an accused person escaped and found sanctuary, he could not be tried and sentenced in absentia. Many places offered him sanctuary: certain mosques, cemeteries, schools, chapels, and even quarters of a city or village. As long as the fugitive was able to live there he could not be apprehended. Relatives and friends were allowed to bring him food and visit when they wished. Baron d'Estournelles de Constant relates a fascinating account of an Arab enjoying sanctuary:

> For two years, in Tunis . . . I have seen nearly every day, at the same place, an Arab seated behind the window or before the door of a mosque. Not far from him, in a small plot of ground, grazed a cow which he surveyed from the corner of his eye while murmuring his prayers. I encountered him so regularly, I already considered him as an old acquaintance, when by chance I learned that he had been there for fourteen years! A former notary, he had wanted to appropriate to himself, in 1870, the property and the clientele of one of his colleagues, so he killed him. Discovered, he took refuge in the first asylum that he found. He was still there when I left Tunisia.[56]

The sequel to the story was that after having enjoyed the haven for sixteen years, the Arab made a fatal mistake. One morning the cow broke the rope and the old man ran after her, only to be apprehended and hung from a rope himself.[57] The protectorate government closed as many of the asylums as they could without alienating the Arabs. A decree in 1884 provided that if a guilty person took refuge in a certain quarter, the sheikh of the area should inform the *caid*, who would have the culprit chained and dragged to the *ouzara* court.

After the establishment of French tribunals consular judicial power was suspended in Tunisia. Two French tribunals of the first instance were established, one at Tunis and the other at

Sousse. Originally six justices of the peace were sent; later the number was increased, and in 1887, by decree, the civil controllers, who performed the duties of the justices of the peace, were named temporary justices.[58] This system was associated with the Court of Algiers, and although no courts of appeal were created in Tunis, cases could be appealed to the Algerian court.

Since no commercial courts existed in Tunisia, the French courts had power in civil and commercial matters concerning the French and Europeans. Like the consular courts, the French tribunals originally exercised power only when a European was the defendant, not when he was the accuser, but a decree in 1884 abolished this distinction. It made French courts competent in all cases to which a European was a party, with two exceptions: (1) cases concerning personal statutes or inheritance rights of Tunisians, Muslims, or Jews, (2) cases concerning property which was not registered under the Land Law of 1885.[59]

In penal matters the jurisdiction of the French courts was established by an 1892 law. Article One of this decree stated that French courts recognized "infractions of all kinds, that is to say of all crimes, misdemeanors and infractions committed in Tunisia whether by French or French protégés or by the subjects and protégés of the other non-Muslim states and countries, or to their prejudice."[60] To instill respect for French justice Tunisians could be tried in certain instances in French courts. Cases to reprimand Tunisians for infractions against the French magistrates were under the jurisdiction of French courts, and Muslims were obligated to testify and could be punished for perjury. More specifically, Tunisians could be punished for offenses against the police, railroads, post offices, and telegraph lines.

Some judicial reforms were instituted by the protectorate, among which were the rulings that no arrest could be made without a warrant and that the accused must be questioned within forty-eight hours of his arrest.[61]

The *ouzara* tribunal was invested with the power to abolish slavery, which persisted despite an 1846 manumission decree and the Anglo-Tunisian Treaty of 1875 outlawing slavery. The English consulate at the entrance of the souks in the Arab medina became a refuge for escaped slaves. In June, 1880, the British consul reported that five Negro slave women had taken refuge in the consulate.[62] An observer at the time of the French invasion explained:

> Although the sale of slaves has been prohibited for a long time and the markets closed, slavery continues to exist, and the traffic of men, but mostly the traffic of women, is carried on in Tunisia—we have irrefutable proof.[63]

Negro slaves were usually brought into Tunisia from the south disguised as rich Tunisians traveling by caravan. An inquiry revealed that about ten thousand slaves were held in Tunis and environs. Complaints reached the *ouzara* court telling of the brutal beating of fugitive slaves, as well as their mutilation by having their small toes cut off.[64] Resident-General Justin Massicault, desirous of closing the slave markets, had the Bey issue a decree in 1890 which inaugurated a system of penalties against anyone having bought, sold, or held a human being in slavery. Nevertheless, slavery was not eradicated in Tunisia but continued to be a problem.

Prison reform also demanded attention. The prison of Tunis consisted of one foul-smelling room in an ancient building, the windows of which looked out upon a noisy and bustling marketplace. Prisoners had to furnish their own bedding and clothing.[65] Chained prisoners working on the docks at La Goulette were a common sight. Most convicted Europeans served their terms in Algerian prisons and were glad to escape the board and room of the Tunisian holes. Laws regulating the prison of Tunis were passed in 1888.[66] The following year a penitentiary administration was organized and a service of prison inspection established, but the first inspector was not named until 1891.

The French approach to judicial problems was clear. Nothing should be done to deny the Muslims the right to their religious courts in personal matters. At the same time, however, Europeans should have the benefit of French courts. This was the bargain that France had made when the European powers agreed to abandon their capitulation rights. Two legal systems existed side by side, but when they conflicted, the French courts had the power of decision.

Land Ownership and Use

The complex Muslim system of land ownership presented another problem to protectorate officials, a situation which had to be handled cautiously because the system was dictated by Qur'anic law.

Four systems of land ownership existed. First, *melk* land, or property held by the owner in the same relationship that predominated in Western Europe, consisted mostly of small farms in the Sahel coastal region. Second, collective lands owned by the tribes and located in the parched semidesert of central and southern Tunisia were used by nomads and seminomads for grazing land. The third type of property was the public domain held by the state. Last, and most troublesome, was the system of *habous*, or land governed by the Muslim religious rites.[67]

The *habous* type covered from twenty-five to thirty per cent of the Regency and included much of the fertile Medjerda Valley. *Habous* was the Tunisian legal expression for the Middle Eastern Arab term *wakf*, meaning to protect a thing, to prevent it from becoming the property of another person.[68]

Two types of *habous* existed, the public and the private. The public *habous* consisted of property given for the construction of public buildings, mosques, schools, hospitals, fountains, bridges, etc. Qur'anic law considered the donation of these lands a pious work and affirmed that such land was inalienable. A group called the *djema'a* administered the public *habous*, reserving them for religious purposes.[69]

Private *habous* was land which had been donated to some religious foundation, but the donor's family enjoyed the income from the land until the family was extinct, at which time the land reverted to a religious foundation. An article in a Tunisian newspaper explained the process:

> When a head of family fears that his heirs will only dissipate the property that he will leave to them, he constitutes the property "habous"—set apart. Only he declares by solemn act that the revenue of these lands will be collected by such or such members of his family, and that at the extinction of his male line, these lands will revert to some mosque or to some religious institution.[70]

An excellent way too for owners to place their property beyond the power of the Bey, *habous* lands could not be taxed. A person could also declare his property *habous* to keep it out of the hands of his creditors.[71]

The private *habous* was administered by overseers, or *mokhaddems,* who enjoyed the right of exploiting, exchanging, or renting but could not sell the land. A French traveler in the Regency who visited the *sharaa* court explained how some *mokhaddems* took advantage of their position, "I have seen two rich families, of which the revenues amounted to forty million francs, enter, reduced to poverty because, for seventeen years, their *mokhaddems* did not give them a centime, and refused ever to furnish them the latest account. And not the least recourse was possible!"[72]

Understandably, the lands of *habous* were referred to as "estates of the dead hand," and the government searched for ways to free the land and make it more productive. Several methods were used to circumvent the inalienability of these lands. The malekite rite authorized perpetual renting, and a contract of *enzel* was established whereby the land could be rented for an indefinite period upon the payment of an annual fixed rent.[73] The use of *enzel* was the most effective method for putting *habous* into production. While both Tunisians and

Europeans could rent the land, usually the Tunisians were too poor. The procedure was as follows: a request of *enzel* was given to the president of the *djema'a;* during a delay of a month a magistrate of the *sharaa* tribunal decided on the merit of the request, and if accepted it was published in the *Journal Officiel Tunisien.* Auctions were held on the fifth Thursday after the first announcement, with the highest bidder given the privilege of renting the land.[74] In 1888 a decree reaffirmed the procedure of public auction for disposing of *habous* land, and anyone renting by this means had to register the land under the Land Law of 1885.

The second method of putting *habous* into circulation was by exchange. An 1898 decree made possible the transfer of *habous* in exchange for money or more land, a practice the hanefite rite recognized. But if the land was exchanged for money, another piece of ground had to be purchased in its place and given to the religious foundation. The process did not really decrease *habous* but made it possible to obtain land valuable because of location or fertility in exchange for less productive property. Exchange requests, like *enzel* requests, were sent to the president of the *djema'a* and could stipulate exchange either in kind or in money.[75]

The final method of using *habous* land was instituted by still another decree in 1898 providing for long-term leasing. The usual term of lease was ten years, but a lease could be renewed twice, giving a maximum of thirty years, after which time the land reverted to its original *habous* status.[76] While these methods were partially successful in putting *habous* into production, Muslim opposition to the violation of sacred land remained firm.

Religious lands were not the only factors confusing the Tunisian land problem. When the protectorate was established, determining what property belonged to whom and for what reason was virtually impossible, since there was no definite system of land registration. Old property titles consisted of a description of the land but provided for no survey. Upon change of ownership a notation was placed on the title by notaries under the control of the *sharaa* tribunal, but often the papers were lost or destroyed, and many replacements were inaccurate. With the consent of the magistrate the landowner produced evidence of his possessions before the notaries, who gave him an *outika* presumably confirming the lost title, but inevitably a great deal of overlapping and vagueness prevailed. Because in Tunisia tens of thousands of individuals had the same name, and because a large part of the population was nomadic, the confusion was intensified.

Consequently, European colonists could never be sure of their land titles. It was exasperating for a colonist to discover that he purchased land which had already been sold to another settler. And it was doubly embittering for the Tunisian to lose land he had considered as family property handed down by his forefathers. Resident-General Cambon wanted to end the confusion by public land registration, but first there had to be government investigation and authentication of property rights. The Arabs were already so excited about French interference in their traditional land policy that Cambon felt it was wise to make registration optional.

A commission was created to draw up a land law. The actual nature of the resulting law rested on a peculiar circumstance. A series of articles had been written about an Australian land law drafted in 1858 by Sir Robert Torrens, a governor of southern Australia. Paul Cambon was convinced that a similar law could be applicable in Tunisia. The Land Law of July 1, 1885, patterned after the Australian law, established a land registry in which the property would be inscribed. Registration was optional, and both Tunisians and Europeans could avail themselves of the service, although the expense of registration discouraged some from participating. The cost was six francs, sixty centimes per hectare, of which the government paid two-thirds and the applicant the remainder.[77] Since land registrations did not keep pace with the expected figure, large reductions had to be made in the cost.

To register the alleged owner filed a request, which in turn was published in Arabic and French in the *Journal Officiel Tunisien.* Forty-five days later a second notice was printed announcing the date when the land survey was to be made by the newly created Topography Service. After the survey a delay of two months allowed all persons in disagreement to file claims.

To judge the case and decide whether to accept or reject the request a special tribunal was created, which consisted of a president, vice-president, and reporter, who were all French magistrates, and six judges, of whom three were French and three Muslim. If the parties were French or European, the three French judges decided; if they were Tunisians, the Muslim judges made the decision. However, if the parties were mixed, two French and two Tunisian judges heard the case.[78] The decision of the tribunal was final. If the verdict was favorable, the guardian of landed property registered the land. He made two titles in French listing the land rights that the tribunal recognized. The owner received a copy, and the government's pledge to guarantee the land had the effect of increasing the value. The property then passed under the jurisdiction of French law and escaped the rule of the *sharaa* courts. Both French and Tunisians saw the advantage of a clear land title and hastened to register their land.

Another government method to place more land in cultivation was the sale of public-domain lands. In 1885 a decree defined the public domain and charged the Director of Public Works with its administration. The domain included rivers, lakes, ports, aqueducts, public wells, irrigation projects, public utilities, roads, streets, railroads, tramways, and all parts of Tunisia not susceptible to private appropriation. Some of the domain lands of the south which were suitable for olive culture were sold to colonists for ten francs a hectare. One-half of the total price had to be paid immediately and the remainder in four years.[79] By avoiding *habous* regulations and allowing use of the public domain, the government opened Tunisia for colonists.

Lack of Opposition

Strangely enough the administrative, judicial, and land reforms met no serious opposition from the Tunisians. The French occupation army was reduced first to a division and then to a brigade. Even French opponents of the protectorate could not point to disorders with which to taunt the cabinet. Tunisia seemed lethargic and docile. The annexationists in France opposed the protectorate not because it was unable to maintain order but because they felt that pure annexation would give the French colonists and businessmen the power they deserved. One annexationist, Camille Pelletan, simply could not understand the principle of a French occupation army existing alongside the Bey's government.[80] Setting up a protectorate containing Tunisian officials was a blow to French pride. Other partisans of outright conquest considered the establishment of a Tunisian post office antipatriotic. How, they asked, did it happen that before the French protectorate there was a French postal system, but now, after the proud French nation had conquered, there was a Tunisian postal system?[81]

Why was the protectorate accepted so complacently? At least four reasons accounted for this: (1) the policy of using Tunisian officials and the respect for Muslim institutions, (2) the absence of good means of communication, (3) the civil control system, and (4) the lack of any organized nationalist opposition.

French officials, especially Paul Cambon, repeatedly emphasized that the protectorate must preserve and respect as much of the Bey's government as possible. If this factor was ignored, they warned, revolt would break out as it had in Algeria. A small but elite group of Tunisians, many of whom sent their sons to French universities, were kept as officials of the protectorate. For example, approximately half of the personnel

in the Ministry of Finance was Tunisian. Many of these officials were not merely pro-French, but actually French apolo-
gists. One author summarized, "The original feature of the
rule. . .lay essentially in the outward maintenance of the
old machinery of government, upon which a new framework
and new institutions were merely superimposed."[82] Also, domination was nothing new to the Tunisians. Foreign intervention
had already existed in the financial and judicial spheres.[83]
France, to a certain extent, merely formalized a condition that
already existed.

Second, communications of all types were very poor. Not
only were the means of physical communication primitive, but
press and publication laws were passed restricting criticism
through the written word. By a decree in 1884 the Bey applied
the principles of the 1881 French press law to his country. All
newspapers and periodicals were held responsible for any
incriminating article against France, the Bey, or the Muslim
religion. An article against the Bey, his family, the Muslim
faith, or the powers of the French in Tunisia brought a fine of
one hundred to three thousand francs.[84] The editors of political newspapers guaranteed the payment of bonds that were
forfeited in the case of infractions, and fines were levied in
addition to the loss of the bonds. In 1897 Resident-General
René Millet further "suppressed the liberty of the press in
Tunis and submitted all the local papers to a guarantee of
6,000 francs each owing to some violent attacks against his
administration."[85] With the high rate of illiteracy added to
the situation, concerted organized action against the protectorate was obviously very difficult.

Another reason for the lack of opposition was the civil control system. The controllers demoted the most independent
caids and exercised the right of close surveillance over the provincial administration. However, the very need for press laws
and civil controllers suggested the existence of dormant trouble.
Moreover, the trouble in March and April of 1881 had been
instigated largely by the Kroumir and other western tribes. Not

only had their ardor been dampened by the French army, but the tribe had been assessed a special tax for their skirmishes into Algeria. After this the tribes avoided open conflict with the French.

The protectorate harbored Tunisian critics, but as yet the discontents lacked an effective organization. There was at this time no effective nationalistic or pan-Islamic movement. The origins of pan-Islamism are extremely vague; however, most writers agree that the feeling of Muslim nationalism was evident in the latter half of the nineteenth century.[86] Many scholars consider the movement to be a reaction against Western policies in the East. Pan-Islamism took on a different character from the Western conception of nationalism.

> The orientalists have clearly shown that its ultimate objective was the "realization of the Islamic ideal, the unity of the world in Islam, the central direction under a leader (imam) of the world community," and that the basic concept from which thought and action sprang was religious rather than racial or national.[87]

The Tunisian situation in 1881 tended to confirm this statement. From their headquarters in the holy city of Kairouan the Tunisians called for a "holy war," or, as one author labeled it, a "crescentade" against the French.[88] As pilgrims returned from Mecca through southern Tunisia, many evidently carried weapons beneath their cloaks. After a brief stop in Kairouan the smugglers took the weapons and ammunition to insurgent Tunisian and Algerian tribes—in spite of a provision against arms smuggling written into the Treaty of Bardo in 1881. One function of the civil controller was to detect any arms smuggling in his area. The pan-Islam movement was small and did not emerge as a definite organization with a program until the twentieth century. When a vociferous organization appeared in the first decade of the century, it was called the Destour, or Constitution, Party. It was led by the "Young Tunisians," who had been in contact with the democratic ideas of France and who set up a program asking for a parliament elected by the Tunisians under universal suffrage, government offices open to all, and freedom of press and assembly.[89] In his book on the protectorate Paul Huc attributed the origin of the Young Tunisian movement to the period of 1881-1900, when the educated young men came into contact with Western society. He concluded that "the Tunisian awakening was born of this comparison made possible by the development of education."[90]

The administrative, financial, and judicial problems arose as a result of contact between two separate political, economic, and social systems, those of the West and East. Neither system emerged unadulterated, but each held power under a relationship of half-sovereignty. Many of the solutions to these problems, in time, brought their own difficulties.[91]

Economic Problems

The land, parched and eroded, was the basis of Tunisian economy. "Water is the best governor," according to an old Arab proverb. European colonists rapidly moving into the tillable one-sixth of the land in a country with an agrarian economy presented an explosive situation. At one time North Africa had been the granary for the Roman Empire, but a gradual period of dessication and over-grazing had taken its toll.

The principal cereal crops of Tunisia in order of production and exportation were wheat, barley, and oats. By 1903 the area planted in cereals had increased to 936,000 hectares, but still Tunisian cultivation was inefficient in comparison to European agriculture. One observer noted that even on very fertile land only about seven bushels of barley or wheat were gleaned from each acre.[92] First of all, the Arab plow merely scratched the land and did not penetrate the soil properly, laying open deep furrows. Accordingly the protectorate officials offered tax reductions for those who adopted the French plow. The French author Guy de Maupassant explained how the Arab method of plowing also accounted for the low yield:

> The furrow of the Arab is not a good furrow deep and straight as that of the European worker, but a sort of festoon which rambles whimsically even with the ground around the clumps of jujube shrubs. Never does this nonchalant cultivator stop or stoop in order to pull up a parasitic plant sprouting before him. . . . His fields are thus full of clumps of shrubs, of which several are so small that a simple exertion of the hand would be able to weed them. The view alone of this mixed culture of bushes and cereals so offends the eye that one has the urge to take a pickaxe and clear the land where spreads, across the savage jujube shrub, the fantastic triads of camels, plows and Arabs.[93]

One reason for laziness was the poverty of the agricultural worker plagued by heavy taxes. Land was usually farmed in one of two ways, by *khammes* workers or by short-term renting. *Khammes* peasants worked for a landowner and received only one-fifth of the harvest in return. This type of contract was common throughout North Africa. The owner furnished the plow, yoking team, and seed. To keep the *khammes* peasant alive at a mere subsistence level the owner usually gave him some wheat and barley every month plus clothes and a little olive oil.[94] Harvest time brought little relief for the *khammes* worker because one-fifth of the yield was seldom sufficient, especially if he had a family. His nude children lived in squalor, and often the *khammes fellah* had to borrow money from his landlord, and consequently became bound to the soil through debt. To supplement his income the laborer would often hire himself out as a dayworker to harvest for others. For this work he usually received between 1 franc, 50 centimes and 1 franc, 80 centimes per day, while a Sicilian worker received 3 francs, and a French agricultural laborer from 4 to 5 francs a day.[95] Despite the fact that they worked for less pay, the Tunisians had to compete with an influx of Europeans. One writer deplored the system of trying to replace native agricultural workers with Europeans. He urged French landowners to use Tunisian labor to improve conditions and establish the nomad on the soil.[96] However, most owners preferred Italian, Maltese, and French tenants. As Tunisians observed the people around them enjoying a higher standard of living, they began to look for a more remunerative type of farming. When public-domain land was sold, most Tunisians, lacking the money, watched enviously while Europeans purchased the land.

Olive trees were cultivated extensively in Tunisia during Roman times. In a distance of twenty-one miles, which separate the towns of Kasserine and Sbeitla in central Tunisia, ruins of thirty-two ancient Roman olive-oil presses exist.[97] Many Arab authors agree that on the eve of the Arab invasion of the seventh century, "one could walk in the shade of an uninterrupted line of villages from Tripoli to Tangiers."[98] Even with ample allowance for exaggeration, this observation indicated a much more extensive olive cultivation than existed in 1881. When the protectorate was established, around 170,000 hectares of olive groves existed—approximately eight million trees, of which 360,000 were in the coastal region around Sfax. Since then olive cultivation has increased at the rate of 220,000 trees each year.[99]

Zitoun, the Arab word for olive, meant money to Tunisia, for many were engaged in either olive growing or the olive-oil industry. The nutting of olives began in November and ended in February or March, with the heaviest harvest in December or January. Tunisian olive trees reached their full vigor after twenty years, and a tree that gave twenty-two quarts of olives in eight years, forty-four quarts in ten years, would normally yield eighty-eight quarts in twenty-years. There was usually one good harvest in three years. A three-year cycle developed in this order: a good harvest, a mediocre harvest, and a poor one.

The harvest period was a festival time, and the gatherers camped in the olive groves beside their equipment, which consisted of a large linen cloth, a wooden bat, and a coffin. The laborer simply beat the branches until they surrendered their olives, which fell into the cloth, were gathered in wooden coffins and transported by donkeys or camels to the oil factory. This crude approach was nearly fatal to the stubborn branches, which were often broken or mutilated before they yielded their fruit.[100] Around Sfax the workers placed rams' horns on their fingers to keep them from becoming raw while they picked with their fingers by combing the branches. The protectorate gradually persuaded many of the bat-wielding harvesters to adopt this more sensible method.

An important increase in olive production was instituted by Paul Bourde, the former editor of *Le Temps,* who was appointed as Tunisian Director of Agriculture. This energetic man was convinced that the production of olives could be extended to the territory from El Djem to Gabes.[101] His opportunity came when the vast domain near Sfax, which had been held by the Siale family for over a hundred years, became public domain. These so-called "Sialine-lands" were sold at a modest price to both French and Tunisians in 1892. The lands were put into cultivation through *mgharca* contracts, which used European capital and Tunisian labor to make the "Sialine-lands" fruitful. According to the agreement the owner furnished the land, about two or three francs for each olive tree, the expense of a well, and essential improvements on the land. The planter provided plants, tools, and labor. In fifteen or sixteen years, when two-thirds of the trees were productive, the worker paid without interest the sum that was advanced for his support during the unproductive years. At this time the plantation was divided equally between proprietor and farmer.[102] This relationship was much better than the one between *khammes* worker and owner, but even to enter the *mgharca* contract the farmer needed some money and tools. Nevertheless, some small Tunisian farmers recognized a good opportunity under the *mgharca* contract and became prosperous.

One of the most important commercial products of Tunisia was alfa or esparto grass, which grew wild in practically all of the central and southern areas of the country. It flourished in the wide altitude range of sea level to six thousand feet, but would not prosper where the annual rainfall averaged more than twenty inches.[103] The whole plant was, depending on age, twenty-four inches to a yard high, and the length of the leaf averaged from twenty to thirty inches. The leaf or blade was only slightly attached to the plant, hence easily removed. Arabs harvested the crop and were able to pick about four hundred pounds (green) a day.[104] Certain properties of the leaves made them commercially valuable. When the plant was young the leaves were convex, the undersurface curved, and the top flat. The top was characterized by eight longitudinal grooves caused by the prominence of seven fibrous veins. With age the top surface contracted, resulting in the edges rolling toward the center, forming a cylindrical leaf. The abundance of internal fibrous tissues made the leaf very strong and hence desirable in basket- and mat-weaving.[105]

Commercially the most important use of alfa was in papermaking. The cellulose of alfa necessary in paper manufacture was obtained by treating the leaves with steam pressure and caustic soda. England imported the greatest quantity of alfa for paper, and long before the protectorate British consuls had secured alfa concessions from the Bey.

The nomads and seminomads who gathered alfa lived in poverty.

> When one sees passing before his eyes the small load that is transported by donkeys and camels, each of them led by his owner, one cannot understand how such an industry can make a living for those engaged in it. The value of alfa is from 5 to 7 piasters for 100 kilograms [220 lbs.], about 3 francs 50 centimes, and the native is only allowed to sell up to 10,000 tons; . . . what costs him is not the gathering of the load . . . but transporting it to the port of export. Fortunately, in this mild and favorable climate beasts and people eat only what is necessary to live, and time has never been considered as money.[106]

The profit in alfa obviously was not collected by the Arabs or Berbers who gathered and transported it.

"These trees must have their feet in the water and their head in the fire."[107] This old Arab proverb accurately explains the conditions necessary for date palms. Date palms are found throughout the country, but the edible fruit was produced in the oases of southern Tunisia. The Djerid district, composed of four oases—Nefta, Tozeur, El Oudiane, and El Hamma—contained over 35 per cent of the fruit-producing palms. It was in this locale that the famous *degla-en-nour* date was grown, surpassed in quality by none.

Keeping the palm's head in the fire was no problem in sun-baked southern Tunisia, but keeping its feet in water was a constant problem. Water was a precious element, aptly described in the Arab saying, "A drop of water is worth a piece of gold."[108] Beginning in 1885, the company of Ferdinand de Lesseps sank artesian wells that gushed forth at the enormous rate of 300 cubic meters per hour. An agricultural society sank eight artesian wells around Tougount, putting into production 400 hectares of land dotted with 42,000 date palms.[109] Date palms could be planted at a cost of about four or five francs a tree. Fortunately, the palm had no known enemies like the phylloxera scourge on grape vines. Nevertheless, it took nearly ten years before the palm tree reached its productive period.

European colonists, noting that the Tunisian climate was ideal for vineyards, began to increase vine cultivation. There was an extension of European-type vineyards from 100 hectares in 1882 to 5,159 hectares ten years later.

Cattle-raising also attracted European capitalists, since the land could be left uncultivated with only a small area cleared for pasture, and neither elaborate buildings nor many workers were needed. In his article on French colonization in Tunisia Leroy-Beaulieu stated that investors in cattle were able to realize an interest of 12 to 15 per cent on their capital.[110] Cattle farms were confined almost exclusively to the northern part of Tunisia, where more abundant pastures prevailed.

Tunisian forests in the northwest had some commercial

value. Of all northern Tunisian trees, the cork oak was the most important. The outer layer of bark furnished cork and tanning material.[111] The evergreen oak (zeen oak) of the north was used for railroad ties, mine props, and lumber. In the central region Aleppo pines and green-oak trees were found. A little farther south were the junipers of Phoenicia and the gum trees that grew along the desert's edge. Aleppo pines and juniper produced a pitch which the people collected from the dead timber. Struggling for bare subsistence from the dry land, women, camels, and donkeys carried huge bundles of sticks on their backs. The pitch was sold for various purposes; some Tunisians rubbed it on their camels to prevent spring mange, or perhaps waterproofed a goatskin to carry water, or sealed a boat with it.[112]

Heavy industry requires power, an element that Tunisia lacked because she had no coal, and the water supply was too uncertain to be used as hydraulic power. Industry had not advanced beyond the stage of extractive industry such as the mining of phosphate ore, iron ore, lead, and zinc, and simple industries such as olive-oil factories, flour mills, tanneries, and handicraft work.

The early protectorate was the formative period of Tunisian industry. Indeed, until after 1886, most of the olive oil was the product of old oil-presses run by hand or animal power. The period of industrial growth coincided with the introduction of European capital into Tunisia. By 1892 the principal industries in terms of export value were olive oil and fishing, respectively. However, by this date most of the mining concessions had been awarded, and ten years later mineral products became the most valuable of all Tunisian exports.[113]

Before the protectorate no public-works agency existed. However, some income from *habous* was used for public projects considered worthy of the funds. The only accomplishments the Tunisian government could point to were a road from Tunis to the Bardo Palace and to La Goulette, some government buildings, and four obsolete lighthouses. The result of a feeble attempt to develop the silted harbors at Porto Farina and La Goulette was unsatisfactory; no really modern ports existed. The Europeans realized that business and commerce could not grow without railroads, roads, and ports, so the early period was devoted to the improvement of transportation. A veritable revolution in transportation was launched as the young protectorate devoted a major part of its expenses to public works.

A decree in 1882 created a Directorate of Public Works with a former French engineer as director. Ninety-five per cent of the personnel were French, and five per cent Tunisian. It was difficult to find Tunisians who had the necessary technical education to fill many positions in the service.[114]

The protectorate began a series of projects, which included acquisition of water, railroads, roads, harbors, lighthouses, public buildings, and municipal public works. French construction companies received profitable contracts from the protectorate; these agreements were usually accompanied by a concession allowing the company to exploit the project for a long period after its completion. The companies recruited their skilled laborers mostly among Italians, with some Maltese, but the unskilled worker was usually Tunisian. Italian semiskilled and skilled craftsmen worked in the Regency for less pay than their European colleagues. Labor was cheap, and as usual the Tunisian worker received a franc less per day than a European doing the same work.

It was evident that the economy would be developed by and for the colonizers. Few Tunisians would be able to purchase available land or have the capital to develop land already in their possession. The emphasis on railroads, roads, and harbors would benefit the European investors, not the Tunisians. The Tunisian role in most of the development was an indirect and subservient one. Tunisians were like guests in their own house.

3

Impact of French Culture

The blending of Tunisian and French cultures had a profound influence on the future of the North African country. Under the protectorate Tunisia not only experienced the results of European technology but was brought in contact with the thought and institutions of Western civilization introduced by French colonists, clergymen, and educators. A strange situation resulted: on the one hand, the protectorate judiciously avoided offending Tunisian custom and tradition; but, at the same time, Tunisia was in more intimate contact with European ideas and institutions than at any previous period in history. It was ultimately this relationship with the political concepts of France that enabled the Tunisian nationalists to establish a party and a program leading to eventual independence. The nature of the French cultural impact can best be seen through a discussion of colonization, religion, and education.

Colonization

An official of the French protectorate summarized French objectives in Tunisia:

There is no doubt that the final purpose of our installation in the Regency is the colonization of this country, that is to say the development of our influence among the indigenous population, the establishment and diffusion among them of progress and of colonization, the creation of a flowing commerce between the Metropolis and Tunisia, and finally the settlement of our nationals on the soil and the exploitation with our capital in order to aid the growth of the national wealth.[1]

Part of this "final purpose" was accomplished: for instance, a flowing commerce between France and Tunisia was a reality.[2] Certainly the period was an active one for French imperialism. However, one part of the objective moved haltingly—the "settlement of our nationals on the soil." In 1881 there were 20,000 Europeans in Tunisia, only 500 of whom were French.[3] Before the occupation France engaged in commercial activity rather than agriculture in the Regency. In fact, for many centuries Europeans could not possess private property, but when the Bey needed money he sold land concessions. After the protectorate was created, land speculation societies purchased land for resale to colonists.[4]

Although many French agricultural workers were brought to Tunisia in the nineteenth century, there was a change in official French attitude after the turn of the century. The French decided not to sanction government sponsored colonization because of the failure of such a policy in Algeria. Instead the government announced that colonists in Tunisia would have to buy the land. The plan seemed preferable to the one used in Algeria, whereby the government purchased land for distribution, with the result that farm failures obligated France to loan money to bankrupt farmers. There was no room for charity in the colonial policy in Tunisia, and Frenchmen without financial resources were expected to stay out of the country. Since the French could not compete in the industrial labor market with the Maltese or Sicilian workingmen, laborers were not attracted.[5] Consequently, Tunisia was colonized by French capitalists who bought large estates in the fertile North. The Enfida domain, containing around 222,300 productive acres, was sold by the Society of Marseille in holdings of 5,000 to 12,000 acres, and in more numerous lots of 1,000 to 2,500 acres. Many of the landowners lived in Tunisia only part of the year. Young people with fortunes, retired military men, professors, and officials created an educated group in the country.[6]

In general the French have been poor colonists. They hated to leave their homes, and many considered it unfortunate that even conscripted soldiers were sent to the colonies. In his book on French colonialism J. B. Piolet gave several reasons why his countrymen were reluctant to emigrate to their colonies: lack of a colonial tradition; ignorance of colonial affairs; tastes and national character; and a weak merchant marine by comparison with those of England and Germany.[7] When the problem is evaluated in relation to Tunisia, more specific factors are discovered. First, the colonists had to have money to buy the land, construct a house, and exist until the vineyards and olive trees were in production. Second, many owners of large estates hired Tunisians, Maltese, or Sicilians because they worked for a lower wage than French nationals.[8] Third, the French government took no major steps to encourage emigration to Tunisia until 1900. As a result, the Italians in Tunisia in 1891 outnumbered the French 38,000 to 18,000. Of these Frenchmen about 5,000 were merchants, 3,000 were officials of the protectorate, and less than 3,000 settled on the land.[9] The French, nevertheless, held far more land than the more numerous Italians; by 1897 they owned or held on concession nearly two million acres, about one-sixth of the available land. The Italians, in contrast, owned only 96,330 acres, mostly in small farms because they evidently lacked the capital for extensive purchases. Consequently, many Italians worked as laborers; it was a case of Italian manpower and French money.

Finally, the Franco-Italian Convention of 1896 established a relationship between the two groups of nationals. By the agreement Italy relinquished her rights of "most favored nation" in Tunisia and abolished her postal system. In return France guaranteed the following Italian liberties: the right to sit on juries; immunity from capital punishment (such as Italians enjoyed in Italy); the privilege of becoming lawyers or entering other professions; freedom to maintain their schools; and the right of children of Italian immigrants to retain Italian citizenship.

The attitude of the French government toward colonization changed gradually and was brought about partly by the geographical societies, which cautioned that Italian emigration to the Regency endangered French influence. The protectorate began to establish institutions to aid the French colonists, three of which were the Agricultural Chemical Laboratory, the Service of Agriculture and Viticulture, and a Veterinary and Breeding Service. The chief of the last service, called an Inspector of Agriculture and Breeding, was charged with "visiting the centers of production, to put his instructions and advice at the disposal of the native populations and the colonists."[10]

An interesting campaign was begun to bring more French colonists to Tunisia. One propaganda booklet told the French that if they visited Tunisia twenty years from that time they would find a well-run colony lacking nothing, but it warned:

> then a person will not be able to acquire a hundred hectares of land for 10,000 francs. It is necessary to make haste if one wants to profit from the sacrifices of the state in a colony having its own way of life, its autonomous government, similar to the English colonies and where, thank God, the colonists, absorbed by their work, are scarcely preoccupied with politics.[11]

In case the opportunity to escape from politics failed to entice colonists, the Bône-Guelma Railroad reduced its rate 50 per cent for them and transported 220 pounds of baggage free of charge.[12] The Directorate of Agriculture and Commerce published detailed plans for low-cost farm homes. One plan, labeled "economic house for colonists," provided for a kitchen, dining room, and two bedrooms and was priced at 2,300 francs. For 800 francs more a shed could be added to serve as a stable.[13] As Italian immigration into Tunisia increased, the French government's policy toward colonists became less casual. In 1907 a fund of seven and one-half million francs was approved for encouraging colonization. Despite a more active government policy the French still concentrated more heavily on the economic development of Tunisia as late as World War I.[14]

Another way of increasing the number of French nationals in Tunisia was by naturalization. A decree in 1887 stated that after attaining twenty-one years of age the following Tunisians could obtain French citizenship: those who had resided in France, Algeria, or Tunisia for three years; and those who had served France for three years in the armed forces or administration of the protectorate. The period of duration of residence and service was later reduced to one year. The applicant for citizenship presented his request to the civil controller in his district, who conducted an inquiry and reported the results to the resident-general, who in turn obtained authorization for citizenship from the French foreign minister. For those who were not in the service of France there was a charge of fifty francs for the authentication of citizenship.[15] During the first five years the decree was in operation the following became French citizens:

Italians	49	Greeks	6
Anglo-Maltese	33	Spanish	6
Germans	10	Alsatians	4
Tunisians	9	Others	20
Swiss	6		
		Total	143[16]

After 1899 the delay of one year was no longer required in certain cases, but this feeble naturalization program was hardly a successful answer to Italian immigration.

A Frenchman traveling in rural Tunisia noted the wide gulf that existed between Arabs and French. He recognized that the difference of religion and manners was too great for any large degree of assimilation, and he predicted future trouble if relations did not improve.[17] The degree of French influence through colonization showed little positive effect; in fact, the contact seemed to accentuate the differences between French and Tunisians. French colonization in Tunisia was not widespread enough to bring a high degree of assimilation, but was enough to create resentment.

Religion

One man, Charles Allemand-Lavigerie, was largely responsible for the influence of the Catholic Church in North Africa. He was born at Bayonne in 1825, the son of a customs collector. As a young man he was ambitious, intelligent, and authoritarian. Two pious servants directed Charles toward a religious career; in 1848 he was ordained, and he later received a doctor of theology degree and taught at the Sorbonne.[18]

An event in 1855 was destined to change his life and the history of French North Africa, for he was chosen as head of an organization dedicated to the spread of French Catholic influence, through education, to the Middle East. Lavigerie became directly involved in events following the Turkish massacre of Syrian Christians in 1859. France organized a military expedition to the East, and Lavigerie launched an appeal which brought in three million francs to help the Christians in Syria. He then traveled to Syria to administer the relief money.[19] Greatly impressed by the experience, he concluded his report by stating there was something "which no human voice is able to express, it is the impression of horror and pity which seizes the soul at the sight of the general horror. . . ."[20] On his return from the East he saw Pope Pius IX and expressed the need for a greater effort to save the Orientals from their curious pagan rites.

Three years later Abbé Lavigerie was appointed Bishop of Nancy. One day, while at the tomb of Saint Martin in Tours, Monseigneur Lavigerie fell asleep and dreamed that he was "in a faraway, unknown country, where human beings, with swarthy or black faces and having a barbarous language, appeared before him. . . ."[21] Four days later the Bishop of Algiers died and Lavigerie was appointed to the post, which was raised to an archbishopric. With much enthusiasm he entered this "dream-come-true world" in 1867.

His early message to Africa showed his great zeal and referred to a providential mission:

> To make of Algeria the cradle of a great nation, generous, Christian, another France, in a word, daughter and sister of ours, and content to progress in justice and honor beside the mother country; gather around us, with this ardent initiative, which is the gift of our race and our time, the true light of a civilization of which the Gospel is the source and law; to carry these ideas beyond the desert, with the caravans which cross it, and which will lead you, one day to the center of this continent plunged in barbarity. . . .[22]

After some years in Algeria the archbishop realized that no rapid spread of Christianity was possible and changed his approach from that of direct missionary effort, as described above, to one more subtle. Gradual adoption of Christianity was to be accomplished in two ways, through schools and through Christian charity—"for the children, French schools, for all, a discrete preaching, prepared by a great diffusion of benefits from Christian charity."[23]

When in April of 1868 Lavigerie announced his plan to establish schools and dispensaries, the governor of Algeria, Marshal MacMahon, opposed the educational plan and held to the doctrine of the Gospel for the colonists and the Qur'an for the natives. Both the governor and the archbishop went to Paris to plead their case, and the archbishop came back the victor. Monseigneur Lavigerie felt that pride prevented the Arabs from accepting Christianity; therefore, the Christians must get closer to the people by adopting their ways. For this purpose he founded the *Société des missionnaires d'Afrique*, who soon became known as "white fathers" because of the white habits they wore. To staff the dispensaries he recruited some ladies in Bretagne to form the *Soeurs missionnaires de Notre-Dame d'Afrique,* popularly known as "white sisters."[24]

The Shrine of Saint Louis at Carthage gave the prelate and his missionaries an opportunity to extend their influence to Tunisia. The shrine had been neglected, and when Archbishop Lavigerie visited it in 1875, he found the sanctuary in a state of ruin. "It was at the time of this first visit that I began to understand the obligations of France,"[25] reported Lavigerie. He related the state of confusion evident in the administration of the shrine:

> They had, in effect, by a curious confusion, sent to Tunis the statue of King Charles V (the Wise), in place of the statue of Saint Louis. To this statue were harnessed, as one still recalls in Tunis, two hundred Muslims of La Goulette to drag it across the fields and footpaths to the summit of Byrsa, exclaiming, "France fed its kings so well that they became very heavy!"[26]

The prelate went to Rome to plead for French ecclesiastical control of the Carthage area. After his plea the Pope smiled and said, "I grant what you ask—it is just that the French take away, even if they found it at Rome, the sanctuary of a king of France."[27] Lavigerie immediately sent two "white fathers" to the sanctuary.

Outside the Carthage area the Italian Catholics had predominated since 1841, when Pope Gregory XVI created an apostolic curacy in Tunisia staffed by Italian Capuchins. However, in 1881 an 86-year-old man of the Capuchin order, Monseigneur Fidele Suter, asked to be allowed to retire to a convent in Ferrara. The Holy See accepted the request, thus leaving three Italian Capuchins in line for the position. In the meantime France had conquered the Regency, and Roustan asked his government to intervene in Rome to persuade Pope Leo to appoint a Frenchman. The Pope named Mgr. Lavigerie, Archbishop of Algiers, on condition that he would not prejudice the work of the Italian Capuchins in Tunisia. After receiving the confirmation Lavigerie sent a communiqué to the clergy of the diocese of Algiers:

> It is not my duty to compliment here the political events which were recently accomplished in Tunisia: they are foreign to my ministry. All that I want to say about it is that the flag and name of France are engaged in such an enterprise, that it finds among us only hope for its success. Praise to God that this triumph of France grant the final victory of the Christian civilization in the barbarian countries![28]

He concluded that the French conquest made it necessary to introduce French clergy into the Regency alongside Italian. The Pope was bitterly criticized by some of the Italian Capuchins but refused to alter his decision, and transferred the principal complainers elsewhere. Italian newspapers, the *Riforma* in particular, attacked Lavigerie, asserting that his presence in Tunisia was more valuable to France than her army.[29] Apparently the accusation was partly true, because the archbishop took the initiative of introducing French spiritual annexation before France had completely conquered the country. In a tribute to Lavigerie one author wrote, "this protectorate could have been completed earlier, if they had listened to him, and with a notable economy of men and money. . . ."[30]

The papacy continued to shower favors on Lavigerie. In March, 1882, in the Chapel of Saint Louis at Carthage Mgr. Lavigerie received the cardinal's hat and henceforth held the titles: Cardinal Lavigerie, Archbishop of Algiers, Apostolic Delegate of Tunisia. Upon hearing of Lavigerie's appointment as cardinal, the Italian newspaper *Nazione* accused the Pope "of having, by such a nomination, made an affront to Italy, a menace and a damage to her interests in Africa."[31] The Pope's newspaper, the *Osservatore Romano,* replied that Lavigerie was promoted to cardinal two years after the basic French-Italian rivalry over Tunisia had been resolved in favor of the former. A short time later the new cardinal wrote to Pope Leo XIII:

> The most beautiful day of my life will be that when, after having endowed this Vicariate [of Tunisia] of all that is necessary in institutions, in men and money, I will be able to go and prostrate myself humbly at the feet of Your Holiness to ask you to raise again the See of Saint Cyprian and to revive the great church of Carthage, in giving to it a bishop after 1,000 years of dormancy.[32]

The Pope consented to Cardinal Lavigerie's wish and restored the See of Carthage and extended the archdiocese to include the entire country. Cardinal Lavigerie now held the auspicious title of His Eminence the Archbishop of Carthage and of Algiers, Primate of Africa. Through his efforts the cathedral of the Archdiocese of Carthage on the hill of Byrsa was opened in honor of Saint Louis on May 15, 1890.

In Tunisia as in Algeria Cardinal Lavigerie did not hesitate to enter political affairs. He became a trouble shooter for the protectorate and acted as a good-will ambassador to the Europeans and Muslims. Baron d'Estournelles de Constant observed that Sicilians, Italians, and Maltese were fervent Catholics, more attached to the Cross than to the flag, and grouped themselves around Cardinal Lavigerie, their veritable sovereign, who kept them sympathetic toward France. Cardinal Lavigerie and Paul Cambon were old friends, and the resident-general appreciated the power that the cardinal exerted over the Europeans in Tunisia.[33] The cardinal's sympathy toward French republicanism also made him popular with protectorate officials. During a dinner for the French Mediterranean Naval Squadron in 1890, Lavigerie proposed a toast to the French Navy and to the union of all political parties for the benefit of the fatherland. Then pupils of the "white fathers" rose and sang the *Marseillaise*. Strong criticism was hurled at the cardinal from the clerical and monarchial political factions, but Lavigerie felt secure since he had the support of his friend Pope Leo XIII for the republican form of government.

In January of 1882 the cardinal negotiated with the populace of Sfax, who were in trouble because they had resisted France so bitterly the previous summer. An indemnity of six million francs was imposed on the Muslim population, and the principal city officials were to be held as hostages until the sum was paid. This was the price Tunisians paid for defending one of their cities. The last payment was due and they did not have the money.

Lavigerie:	Do you repent?
Muslims:	Yes, yes, we repent: we recognize that we have done wrong, that we have acted as the insane. The Bey is our master, France is strong, and we are weak.
Lavigerie:	. . . at this moment the old chief of your revolt, Ali Ben Khalifa, boasts that you promised him to revolt again, in the spring. . . .
Muslims:	He lies! It is a lie! We do not want to revolt against you. It is we who have been the victims.
Lavigerie:	. . . swear to me that you will not revolt any more against the Bey, who is your legitimate sovereign, nor against France, who is your ally and your protector.
Muslims:	We swear it! We make the promise. . . .
Lavigerie:	In that case, I want to hear you and to intercede for you. Tell me now what you want![34]

He heard what he expected. They could not pay at that time and wanted an extension so that the Tunisian hostages held by the French would not be deported and their property confiscated. Mgr. Lavigerie announced that he had already obtained a delay from the government. A celebration followed as the prelate blessed the city.

One of the prime objectives of Lavigerie's policy was to keep all foreign nationals contented and loyal to the protectorate. His first pastoral letter in Tunisia gave benedictions, "without distinction of nationality and origin. . . ."[35] He established homes for the aged, which included Maltese and Italians, and reminded European nationalities that they were all brothers in Jesus Christ.

When Italy battled flood waters in 1882, Mgr. Lavigerie waged a campaign in Tunisia and Algeria to collect funds for the flood victims. In the fund-raising letter he mentioned that a great many Italians "came to establish themselves in Algeria to form a common people with us. A greater number yet found themselves in the parishes of Tunisia."[36] Even some Muslims helped in the campaign, and Lavigerie sent over six thousand francs to the editor of the *Osservatore Romano*. The gesture helped moderate anti-French tirades of Italian newspaper correspondents in Tunisia.

Nevertheless, more tension developed in the Italian community in Tunis. In 1884 the Capuchin church in Tunis burned to the ground. The next day the *Sentinella,* an Italian newspaper in Tunis, charged, "Some are saying that, in this event, is shown the hand of God. But ninety-nine of one hundred say that in this event is shown the hand of the Cathedral."[37] Immediately Lavigerie started collecting money to build a new church; and the newspaper, condemned by the French tribunal in Tunis, ceased to appear. Three years later Cardinal Lavigerie learned that the Italian Capuchins in Tunisia were to be disbanded for lack of funds. The cardinal traveled to Rome and obtained an order from the Holy See stating that all Italian religious orders would be maintained in Tunisia.

Keeping the French, Italians, and Maltese friendly toward the protectorate was not the cardinal's most challenging task. His monumental and frustrating duty was the conversion of Muslims to Christianity, a task which would try anyone's patience and ability. When Lavigerie first came to Africa, he spoke of a great wave of conversions. A little later he talked of assimilation through schools and charity, and finally he warned his missionaries not to expect any definite results for at least a thousand years.

No official Tunisian policy hindered Christian work; in fact, there was a long tradition of Islamic toleration of monotheistic religions. By treaties in 1824 and 1830 the Bey confirmed Europeans' privileges, among which was freedom of religion. In 1857 the Fundamental Pact extended freedom of religion to the Jews, and the Constitution of 1861, which confirmed the pact, stated in Article 105, "A complete freedom is assured to all the foreigners established in the Tunisian states in regard to the exercise of their religions."[38] In the presence of the Bey's two sons Cardinal Lavigerie raised a toast thanking the Bey for his generosity toward the Catholic religion.

While Muslim law presented no legal obstacle to the practice of the Christian religion within its jurisdiction, it did raise difficulties for Muslims wishing to accept Christianity. The traditional Muslim punishment for apostasy was death by stoning. Certainly the French protectorate condemned this penalty, but the convert could not be sure that his neighbors, particularly in a remote village, might not carry it out. In any event, conversion to Christianity would probably lead to ostracization from the family.[39] It was easy for a Muslim to accept medicine from a Christian dispensary, but adopting a new faith was a serious matter. Two verses from the Qur'an particularly discouraged conversion:

> And the Jews will not be pleased with thee, nor will the Christians, till thou follow their creed. Say: Lo! the guidance of Allah (Himself), is Guidance. And if thou shouldst follow their desires after the knowledge which hath come unto thee, then wouldst thou have from Allah no protecting friend nor helper.[40]

> O ye who believe! Take not the Jews and Christians for friends. They are friends one to another. He among you who taketh them for friends is (one), of them. Lo! Allah guideth not wrongdoing folk.[41]

It was abundantly clear that any Muslims converted to Christianity cut themselves off from Allah's guidance and protection. No exact figure for the number of Muslim converts exists for the period of the protectorate, but a fair estimate seems to be in the low hundreds.

Above all, the protectorate government wanted Christian missionaries to avoid action that might cause Muslim fanaticism. Therefore, when his missionaries were accused of fanaticism by anticlerical politicians and newspapers, Cardinal Lavigerie quickly responded:

> I declare that I would consider as a crime or as madness to overexcite, by acts of an unwise proselytism, the fanaticism of our Muslim populations: as a crime, because thereby I would add thus a new difficulty to all those which France has to overcome at this moment; as madness, because instead of attaining the objective, we would perhaps lose it forever.[42]

Lavigerie reminded the critics that none of his missionaries had established themselves outside of their parishes, none had been massacred, and "all are surrounded by the respect of the natives themselves."[43]

The seemingly good relations between the Christians and Muslims were strained by the Eucharistic Congress of the Catholic Church held in Carthage in 1931. To please the French, both the Bey and the Sheikh-el-Islam participated in the opening ceremony. A young Tunisian lawyer, Habib Bourguiba, later stated that this Christian crusading in Muslim Tunisia launched him into a career of nationalist agitation.[44]

About fifty thousand native Jews lived in Tunisia, nearly half of whom were living in Tunis. In addition a number of European Jews lived in cities of the Regency. An economic and social split developed between the European Jews, who constituted a more wealthy professional and business class, and the Tunisian Jews, who were mostly poor artisans. The first group had a separate *caid* and religious organization, but both groups were ruled by Mosaic law in all cases relative to personal affairs. For all other cases the Jews, like the Muslims, used the *ouzara* at Tunis and the regional courts. Conditions affecting the Jews were not so favorable in Tunisia as they were in

Algeria. The French had naturalized the Jews as a group in Algeria, but the same action in Tunisia would have taken away the Bey's power over the Jewish community. A strong anti-Semitic feeling among the French colonists in Tunisia aggravated the situation further.[45]

Education

In comparison with the rest of North Africa, Tunisia had an advanced system of Muslim education. On the primary level instruction was given in *kouttabs,* which were "schools of the Qur'an." Writing in 1891, d'Estournelles de Constant listed the number of these schools at 971 with over 17,000 pupils. In Tunis alone the number of *kouttabs* increased from 50, in 1877, to 113 by 1890.[46] D'Estournelles wrote that in the village children gathered in a house, on the lawn, or perhaps under a tent, facing their master with their slippers lined up behind them. At a distance the children, sitting on their haunches, looked like a flock of birds. D'Estournelles warned that France must not suppress these schools, for if they did, the masters would teach their pupils hate. The masters, who were trained in religion, commonly cursed parents who failed to send their children to school. France, in the opinion of the baron, did the right thing by not interfering in Muslim education, because in return the Muslims did not prevent their children from learning French. As a result of this moderate approach the highest Tunisian religious dignitary, the Sheikh-el-Islam, lamented, "I regret that my great age no longer permits me to begin the study of your language; I would be the first to follow your lessons; but I will send you my sons."[47]

The Tunisian educational system consisted of the *kouttab* schools, Collège Sadiki, and mosque theology schools such as the one in Tunis called the *Djama'a Zitouna,* meaning mosque of the olive tree. Collège Sadiki was created by the Bey in 1876 to educate men for government service. Because the institution had economic problems, the French financed and recognized it.

In the early years of the protectorate both French and Tunisian professors taught one hundred and fifty students per year, who paid nothing and were given free lunches. A third of the students received free lodging and clothes.[48] The theology school *Djama'a Zitouna* was directed by the Sheikh-el-Islam. In this school were professors of hanefite and malekite systems of religious law, whose curriculum by 1890 included grammar, rhetoric, literature, ethics, logic, theology, interpretation of the Qur'an, law, arithmetic, geometry, algebra, and astronomy. Instruction was conducted in the expansive hall of the mosque, where the students grouped around their professor.

French and Italian schools had existed for many years before the protectorate. Italian Sisters of Saint Joseph of the Apparition established the first school for girls in 1843; this order worked among the Maltese and Italians, and soon Italian schools were located at Tunis, La Goulette, and Sousse.[49] The first French school open to all nationals was founded at Tunis in 1845 by Abbé Bourgade. Here were taught French, Italian, geography, history, and mathematics. Many European children attended, but beset by financial difficulty, the school was closed in 1855.

Mgr. Lavigerie founded the Lycée Saint Louis in Carthage, which provided secondary education for Tunisians and Europeans. Located on the hill of Byrsa, the school had fifty pupils in 1881, when its name was changed to Collège Saint Charles. Two years later it moved to Tunis, and with the approval of Cardinal Lavigerie it eventually became entirely secular. Finally, in 1894 the name was changed to Lycée Carnot, and the instruction was similar to the lycées of France.[50]

It was not Cardinal Lavigerie and his white fathers, however, who were primarily responsible for the spread of French education, but Paul Cambon and the *Alliance française* movement. During one of his visits to France, Cambon established the alliance, modeled on *l'Alliance israelite universelle,* to promote the teaching of French in the Regency. By 1884 seven hundred people had joined, each subscribing 5,000 francs to the cause.[51] Unlike the Israelite alliance, the French one was entirely secular. The committee administering the project included a strange combination of a general, Cardinal Lavigerie, the president of the Protestant synod, the Grand Rabbi of France, and geographer who was secretary-general.[52] The movement acquired legal status and used its funds to promote the teaching of French throughout the world. Tunisians showed little prejudice against French education; in fact, the richest sent their children to the lycées in Paris. Others received French education in Collège Sadiki, where they learned to speak and write French. Two of the best scholars were sent each year to Versailles, at the expense of France; on graduation they were capable of teaching French in their fatherland.[53] Although the Italian schools still instructed almost twice as many pupils as did the French because of the great predominance of Italians in the Regency, the French actually were educating more Tunisians than the Italians were.

After the creation of the Directorate of Public Instruction, Tunisia began to advance in two educational areas—education of women and vocational education. In Tunisia it was felt that even the Qur'an urged education of all Muslims regardless of sex.[54] Twenty-one primary schools and one secondary school for girls admitted Muslims in 1889. All but five were public schools receiving government funds.

Facing foreign competition, the traditional Tunisian handicraft industries began to suffer, and public and private vocational schools were established to produce a more competitive product. This was a departure from the traditional religious education. In addition to handicraft schools several agricultural institutions appeared. The Jews opened a Farm and Apprenticeship School, and the white fathers founded an agricultural school at Thibar. In 1902 a group of enlightened Tunisians organized an agricultural colony for abandoned children. The administration of *habous* ceded 1,200 hectares for the colony plus an annual payment of 15,000 francs. The government matched the sum, and soon sixty Muslims were attending.[55] Tunisians were intelligent and studious and took advantage of their opportunities. From 1885 to 1912 more than three thousand Muslims had attended French schools.

Certainly one of the most important contacts between Tunisians and French was established through the educational system. After leaving French lycées in Tunis, if they had money or a scholarship, students usually went to France for their university education. Gradually, a well-educated group developed who came back to Tunisia and entered government service or professions. These students, proficient in French and conversant with French republicanism, later formed the core of the Destour Party with its rising national aspirations. Eventually, the University of Paris created an institute in Tunis which gave instruction in law and administration, science, literature, and history. By 1952, 953 students were attending the institute.[56] France felt that Tunisians could be better controlled through European education, but this very exposure was to foment an impulse to nationalism and future trouble for France.

Public Health

Public health and public health education were woefully neglected in Tunisia. Open sewage ditches spread like tentacles from the old Arab city (medina) to the Lake of Tunis. The stench of the stagnant lake was notorious, but an old saying claimed that "Tunis is healthy because it smells so terrible that the flies and mosquitoes have left."[57] In comparison with the rest of the Regency Tunis was healthy. From 1887 to 1890 the city had a lower death rate per thousand inhabitants than the French cities of Marseille, Reims, or Toulouse.[58] This was no doubt due to the personal cleanliness of Arabs and to favorable climatic conditions—for example, the strong northwesterly winds that prevail most of the year.

There was about one doctor for every 40,000 people in the rural areas.[59] Cholera and smallpox struck devastating blows.

The death rate from cholera climbed until the protectorate decided to impose sanitary measures in Tunis. A primary menace was a cemetery in a crowded district of the city, where the dead were buried so shallow that dogs dug them up. It was discovered that cadavers were flooded by water that later seeped into open sewers running through the crowded districts. Old cemeteries were closed and new ones were opened outside the city. Unauthorized burials without a doctor's certificate were forbidden. Some Jews, wishing to use the old cemeteries, refused to abide by the regulations, closed their shops, and came into the streets shouting "Down with France! Long live Italy!" Troops had to be used to restore order.[60] The British consul reported in 1885 that during the summer and early fall two or three deaths from cholera occurred each day, and during the zenith months of the epidemic seven or eight died daily.[61]

Smallpox struck with frightful regularity. It appeared every five or six years, afflicted large numbers, then disappeared until the immunity wore off, when it descended on the populace again. During 1888 a smallpox epidemic in Tunis was responsible for 1,645 of 5,807 deaths, whereas in the next year only thirty-nine died of smallpox. Despite the terrible consequences of the disease few Tunisians lined up outside the dispensaries to be vaccinated. Madame René Millet, whose husband became resident-general in 1894, organized the Union of the Women of France, whose members went into the Arab homes to vaccinate whole families.[62]

Hospital facilities were scarce and far from adequate. In 1842 Abbé Bourgade opened the first French hospital in the Arab medina, where Sisters of Saint Joseph of the Apparition gave medical care to the poor. Sadiki Hospital was opened in Tunis in 1879, supported by *habous* funds. However, Sadiki was little more than an asylum housed in an old army barracks. A French professor described his visit to this hospital in 1881:

> In one of the first rooms that they opened for me, I saw a
> blind old man, sleeping on a humid mat covered to the waist

with an old wool cover. On the paving stone, at his door, a bowl in which they had carried his pittance.

Several other rooms of the first floor, likewise unhealthy as the first, contained those struck with marsh fever, in a lamentable state of cachexia.

I did not see either linen or a laundry, M. Kaddour [the doctor] would be embarrassed if he was obliged to take care of surgery which needed repeated dressing.[63]

Finally, steps were taken that led to the establishment of the Pasteur Institute. Resident-General Millet asked Dr. Louis Pasteur to send an assistant to help improve wine making in Tunisia. This assignment initiated a bacteriological laboratory, then an institute for antirabies treatment. The institute in turn inspired a vaccine production center, which led, in 1895, to an antidiphtheria center. The centers were combined in 1900 to form the Pasteur Institute.[64] In 1903 Dr. Charles Nicolle was named head of the institute, where he served for the next thirty-three years. Fierce typhus epidemics gripped Tunisia until Dr. Nicolle discovered in 1909 that the body louse carried the disease; immediately he started a sanitation campaign, and his experiments finally led to a vaccine.[65] For his research on typhus Dr. Nicolle received the Nobel prize.

Public Welfare

Poverty was no stranger to Tunisians. Alongside the Sicilian, Maltese, and Jewish laborers lived the poor Tunisian, or *meskin,* in conditions similar to the poor *fellah* of Egypt. Usually the *meskins* held temporary manual jobs; often they were scullions or street porters. The Tunisian laborer thanked Allah if he had a cloak to keep him warm. He ate a thin barley cake baked under the cinders of a fire, and if he could save a few piasters, he had mutton sprinkled with olive oil on holidays.[66]

France made little direct effort to ameliorate poverty. In fact, she abolished the inadequate Tunisian program of assistance to the poor without offering a substitute program. For many centuries the Tunisians had the *rabta,* a store of grain accumulated by a tithe in kind levied on the cereal growers. Those living outside the northern grain areas paid a tax corresponding in money to the grain levy. The grain and money was used for the poor. Under the rule of Ahmed Bey the system was organized, and 150 silos existed. While reorganizing the tax structure the French abolished the *rabtas* but offered no alternative solution.[67] Although the government did organize societies for agricultural assistance which loaned seed to farmers after a bad harvest year, such help was inadequate. The Consultative Conference in 1897 called for the institution of public assistance.[68] No effective system was created, and distress continued. Writing early in the twentieth century, Victor Piquet concluded his chapter entitled "Condition of the Natives" as follows:

> In a recent year of distress, one saw several unusual personalities make vain efforts in order to move French opinion. At the same time it was discovered that a catastrophe had put a Sicilian town into mourning, and soon considerable sums were collected to aid the unfortunates. One can only applaud, certainly, the gesture which led France to aid generously a sister nation, but the natives of Tunisia—where Sicilians are numerous—have looked with amazement at the protector nation moved in favor of the former and remaining so harshly indifferent to their own misery.
>
> . . . France still forgets too often her obligations which go along with her interest.[69]

Piquet's was a fair comment on the French attitude toward Tunisia, which was neither surprising nor unusual in an era when colonies were advertised as an aid to the economy of the mother country. Ideally a colony was not supposed to be a millstone around the neck of its protector. All colonial policy was weighted on the scales of "material advantage": if the policy increased trade and investments, it was good. One of the strong arguments for the establishment of the French protectorate in Tunisia had been that it would not be a drain on the mother country but would enrich it.

4

Politics, Nationalism, and World Wars, 1900-1949

Internal Politics

From the turn of the century until the outbreak of the Second World War the protectorate government effectively kept tight control of the Regency while pretending to transfer more political power to the Tunisians. No reforms of the period deviated from this basic principle. In its infancy Tunisian nationalism was an ineffectual opponent of the protectorate. The people who forced the government to institute changes in these years were not the Tunisian nationalists but the French colons.

Before 1900 French private capital in the form of investment companies, like the Société Marseillaise, had benefited from the purchase of large tracts of land along the Sahel. For example, the Enfida Domain and some of the Sialine Lands were developed by large expenditures of French private capital. The small French farmers complained that they were treated as orphans by their fatherland and subjected to excessive financial burdens. In 1902 a Commission of Colonization was established to alleviate this situation. With the coming of Gabriel

Alapetite as resident-general in 1906, more progress was made. New incentives to French colonization were introduced:

> All these measures, payment of the price of the lot in twenty years, schemes for the equipment of centers, credits for land development at reduced rates, loans redeemable at long terms, mutuality and agricultural cooperation, reveal that the colonist, far from being abandoned to his lot, received very considerable aid from the state during the difficult initial period.[1]

The number of French in Tunisia grew from 34,000, in 1906, to 144,000 at the end of World War II.[2] Tension mounted between the increased number of French in rural areas and the Tunisian *fellaheen*. Not only different methods of farming but a wide divergence in modes of behavior contributed to the estrangement.[3] While French colons were being settled on fertile soil, there was a feeble effort to settle Tunisians on the arid soil around Nefta in the extreme south.

One of the chief problems of the protectorate was to preserve the French flavor of the country in the face of immigration. For economic reasons France welcomed European farmers but feared the possible political dangers. In 1914 under the system of *jus sanguinis* all individuals born of a Tunisian father were Tunisian, but in 1921 the French rule of *jus soli* was applied in Tunisia. This meant that if one of a child's parents resided in Tunisia the child took the citizenship of that parent: French if the parent was under French judicial jurisdiction, Tunisian if the parent was in the jurisdiction of Tunisian courts. Foreigners in Tunisia could obtain French naturalization. The problem of the Italians was covered by a special convention, but the new system allowed many Maltese and other Europeans to become citizens.

When analyzed, the specific political reforms of the protectorate reveal a clever design to give token concessions to Tunisians while keeping French power supreme. The Consultative Conference was reformed in 1905, opening the way for an additional change two years later. Three colleges comprised the conference: one represented agriculture, another commerce, and the third contained citizens engaged in neither. The French in Tunisia chose their representatives to the colleges by universal suffrage. The conference was allowed to review the budget, and a few trusted Tunisians could observe the deliberations. Later a Tunisian section was created to which the resident-general appointed sixteen members, one of whom had to be Jewish.[4] It was significant that membership in the Consultative Conference was on the basis of commercial, not political, representation. Even the French in Tunisia did not enjoy political democracy; the real political center of the protectorate always remained in Paris.

The political changes of 1922 fitted the same pattern: the Tunisian section of the Grand Council, which replaced the Consultative Conference, contained twenty-six members, two from each of the five regions plus representatives from the Tunisian Chambers of Agriculture and Commerce, and one Jew.[5] Although the Tunisians voted for these members, the protectorate officials controlled the list of candidates. The main function of the Grand Council was to examine the budget. If both sections agreed, the Council could force budgetary changes. However, the government had cultivated and could count on the support of the more wealthy Tunisian landowners from the elite families and the more prosperous merchants.[6] Increasingly these Tunisians were attracted to French lycées and collèges in Tunis, and it was they who were usually elected to the Tunisian section of the Grand Council.

Political control so firmly based could withstand any pressure for radical reforms that the Tunisians could exert in this era. Even after the establishment of the Destour (Constitution) Party, the nationalists called for cooperation with the protectorate. The following declaration of loyalty that the leaders of the Destour Party were asked to accept in May, 1936, illustrates the control:

> The parties concerned affirmed that they have never fought against the principle of the protectorate, that their political ac-

tivity does not have and was not intended to have any violent character, that they had always asked for, with total disinterestedness, a regime of widening justice and liberty and a political association with the Protector Nation. They added that they put their entire confidence in the representative of France to follow a free and humane policy, only inspired by the general interest and that they were ready to make their contribution to such a task.[7]

A period of cooperation between Destour leaders and France ensued, but the firm French control brought on a greater schism in the ranks of the Tunisian nationalists.[8] The internal policy of the protectorate subordinated political to economic interests. Only French and Tunisians having financial power shared in political decisions. This policy, which worked so well in the late nineteenth century, would soon have to bend under the unusual pressures of the following century.

Economy

Consistently with the pattern already established, France enlarged its economic role in Tunisia during the twentieth century. The mining industry, transportation network, and land and forests were developed. By 1904 the Banque d'Algérie opened a branch in Tunis as an inducement for private investment. A twelve-year economic program was financed by a French loan of seventy-five million francs to complete railroads under construction and build new ones, to establish a road system, and to purchase land for colonization.[9] The port of Bizerte was developed and later proved a valuable French military base during World War I.[10]

By economic development France clearly meant progress through French capital and technology to the exclusion of any other power. In answer to a searching query from American businessmen the United States vice-consul reported discouragingly that there were no free ports within the Regency.[11] The internal tax structure was controlled by France, a situation resulting in frequent Tunisian protests. Bank credit was so severely controlled by the government that even French investors complained.[12] Resident-General Etienne Flandin had clearly called for an economic buildup based on "a large influx of French capital and colons. It is indispensable to increase in considerable proportion the number of French citizens in Tunisia. It is both an economic and a political necessity."[13] Spurred on by the number of Italians, France sponsored a program to attract more of her own nationals to Tunisia. After trying various means, a commission of colonization was able to settle over three thousand French families in the protectorate. After a visit to Tunis in 1903, French President Emile Loubet called for a renewed effort to increase French emigration to Tunisia.

Neither the influx of French money nor colonization was an overwhelming success. An economic slump plagued Tunisia, and scarcely had a partial recovery begun when the worldwide depression of the thirties plunged the country into economic despair. The American consul reported in 1926 that no major economic developments had occurred in the last five years,[14] and the following year French Resident-General Lucien Saint complained, "It is useless to hide the truth. It is a lean year."[15] Social unrest, labor strikes, and economic grievances were the Tunisian pattern. Inflation burdened the land. After students protested the conditions, French authorities gave one-year prison terms to the leaders despite their age; and six alleged Communists, all members of the labor syndicate, were banished from French soil.[16]

The American consul candidly reported one of the major Tunisian complaints:

> France has never pursued a firm, constructive policy with Tunisia. It has forced upon the country an army of civil servants, just under 10,000 to administrate for 54,000 French, 100,000 foreigners, and 1,900,000 natives. Out of a budget of 225,000,000 francs the civil servants received 130,000,000. The result is that there is little left for improving and developing the country.[17]

For six years the French had promised a reduction in administrative personnel, but the numbers only grew. The problem was never solved during the protectorate.

Italian Policy

Although various agreements regulated Franco-Italian affairs in Tunisia, friction was aggravated by the large number of Italians in Tunisia and by the general Italian policy in North Africa. While Italy, along with the other European powers, had renounced consular jurisdiction, because of their many nationals in the country, they enjoyed certain privileges that counteracted French power.[18] By the Convention of 1896[19] France was able to reduce Italian influence and establish a *modus vivendi*, but violent antagonism was renewed in 1911 during the Italian Tripolitanian War with Turkey. After the Italian conquest of Tripoli in 1919 the delicate task of delineating the border between Tunisia and Tripoli was undertaken. New tensions developed with the advent of Italian Fascism and Mussolini's expansionist foreign policy. The visit of Mussolini to Tripoli in 1926, emphasized in Tunisian newspapers, was followed by great excitement over the visit of Italian Undersecretary of State Italo Balbo to Tunisia, where he made strong Fascist speeches. After the defeat of France in World War II, the French Vichy regime resisted, as much as possible, German and Italian demands on Tunisia.[20] Sporadically, then, throughout the protectorate period, Franco-Italian rivalry became intense. An Italian saying, "Tunisia is an Italian colony policed by French soldiers," was especially apt during the summer months, when many Frenchmen were temporarily pushed out by the withering sirocco wind from the Sahara.[21]

Nationalism

By far the most significant development in the period between 1900 and 1949 was the rise and growth of Tunisian nationalism. This topic can best be understood by an examination of the origin of Arab nationalism and the contributing causes of World War I, followed by a study of how Tunisian nationalism came of age.

Regardless of the contemporary state of a society, if its people can point to an illustrious past, its future seemingly holds promise of a greater age. Arab nationalists in the early nineteenth century spoke proudly of their Umayyad and Abbasid dynasties of the seventh through eleventh centuries. In contrast they reviewed their own age with humiliation. Almost simultaneously in Egypt and Syria-Lebanon movements arose to revitalize Arab culture, art, and learning, which the nationalists claimed had been corroded by mameluke degradation and Ottoman corruption.

Both the educational institutions and the introduction of the printing press furthered the intellectual movement. Napoleon Bonaparte plundered an Arabic press from the Vatican and started a literary movement in Egypt, culminating in the Bulaq printing establishment, which produced Arab nationalist literature. By 1834 an American Protestant press was operating in Beirut, and later the Jesuits brought the Catholic press to Syria-Lebanon. In 1866 American missionaries opened the Syrian Protestant College, which is now the American University of Beirut; the Université Saint Joseph was founded eight years later. Intellectuals educated at these universities encouraged the growth of the dynamic concepts of nationalism and political democracy.

Contact between Egyptian and Syrian-Lebanese nationalists was strengthened by Egyptian conquest in 1831 of the territory under Muhammad Ali. When Ibrahim, the son of Muhammad Ali, withdrew from Syria-Lebanon and Ottoman power returned, Beirut and Damascus became even stronger centers of nascent Arab nationalism.

By the late nineteenth century French policies in Algeria and Tunisia and British penetration in Egypt had engendered an anti-Western attitude among the Arabs. There was hope of cooperation between Young Turks and Arab nationalists;

however, with consolidated effort and with an intensified Turkification program, the Turkish government drove the Arab movement underground. Secret societies such as the *al-Kahtaniva* tried in vain to revive Turko-Arab cooperation but lost support to the Young Arab Society known as the *al-Fatat*, with headquarters in Beirut and Damascus. The *al-Fatat* called for full Arab freedom unfettered by Turkish control. Although close cooperation between Turkish and Arab nationalists was impossible, the Young Turk movement did serve as a great inspiration to nationalists throughout the Arab world.

The role that religion would play in the nationalist movement was uncertain. The late-nineteenth-century Islamic reformer Jamal-al-Din al-Afghani called for the spiritual unification of all Muslims under Ottoman power to repel European penetration. Nevertheless, many Arab leaders hostile to the Turkish government conducted independent campaigns against the West. While in theory the Islamic world was one community, in practice the most articulate Arab leaders criticized their religion for being politically conservative. Moreover it was convenient and popular to blame Ottoman rule for contemporary political, economic, and social problems. Orthodox Muslims formed a brotherhood which supported anti-Western policies but not the establishment of independent Arab states.

Until after World War I the Arab movement struggled with internal conservatism and lack of direction. The postwar dismemberment of the Arab world, with England and France supplanting Turkish political power, gave the nationalists targets they could attack with passion. Particularly they felt that England and France had backed out of wartime promises of Arab independence. In the Arab world stretching from Morocco in the West to the Iraq-Iran border in the East, only Saudi Arabia and Yemen had escaped direct foreign control, a fact which gave strength and relevance to anticolonialism. When Western support of Zionism is added to the situation, the West could hardly escape becoming the villain in nationalist propaganda.

Tunisian nationalism had much in common with the Arab nationalist movement in the Eastern Mediterranean; several Tunisians had become confirmed nationalists during their travels in the Eastern Arab lands. In the prewar period the nuclei for a Tunisian national movement were found in the old Sadiki Society and among the intelligentsia of the Grand Mosque Zitouna in Tunis. In Collège Sadiki many of the early nationalists received their secondary education under Arab and French instructors who taught French literature and culture along with Arabic studies.[22] The *Djama'a Zitouna* was the birthplace of the Zitouna Qur'anic University. Students from Sadiki and Zitouna tried to establish a Tunisian personality or identity around which a nation could develop. An illustrious early nationalist was Bechir Sfar, a graduate of Collège Sadiki, and then an administrator of *habous* lands, who later served as *caid* in Sousse. During his early public career he praised the French for replacing chaos with political order and for bringing modern technology to Tunisia.[23] However, in 1906, when he was director of a hostel for the aged, he expressed the need for employment and political freedom for Tunisians, saying, "It is the policy of colonialism which is threatening Tunisia with poverty."[24] Bechir Sfar became an influential member of the old Sadiki Society under the leadership of Ali Bach Hamba, a lawyer of Turkish origin who also founded the nationalist newspaper *Le Tunisien*. Writing in the newspaper in 1910, Ali Bach Hamba explained the relationship between the nationalist cause and the Muslim faith:

> Every Muslim is a supporter of Muslim union, and the Tunisians, to a man, are partisans of this policy and are attached to Pan-Ottomanism, which is a consequence of such an idea and a magnificent manifestation of it. If our modern education has given us a new mentality, we have, all the same, as Muslims, reserved our strong loyalty to our brethren in every country.[25]

Another member of the society, Abdelaziz Taalbi, destined to become a famous nationalist leader, was editor of the Arab edition of *Le Tunisien*.

Although these early nationalists were exposed to Western culture and the historic development of the state in Europe, they had other inspirations for their movement. The idea of Muslim brotherhood and the Young Turk Revolution of 1908 influenced Bechir Sfar, Ali Bach Hamba, and Abdelaziz Taalbi. They created a group called The Evolutionist Party of Young Tunisians, popularly known as "Young Tunisians." The Italian invasion of Libya disturbed the Young Tunisians, who encouraged their brother Arabs to resist and who helped Turkish officers to enter Libya secretly. One French political observer called attention to the indigenous nature of Tunisian nationalism:

> The great forefathers: Bechir Sfar, Bach Hamba, Taalbi, Zaouche, principal Tunisians fashioned from western culture, have voiced, since 1906, a sentiment exclusively Tunisian. . . . They were the emulators of the Young Turk Movement.[26]

As an early nationalist leader, Ali Bach Hamba had an illustrious career. In 1910 he urged universal elementary education and the reform of Qur'anic schools by the introduction of scientific studies; he tried to persuade the French to introduce these reforms. Although some progressive Frenchmen supported his view, the extremist factions in the French Consultative Council disdained Tunisian nationalists and effectively resisted any change.[27]

Religious tradition and national feeling joined to provoke the Djellaz Cemetery affair of 1911, a violent reaction against European influence. On a hillside bordering the southeastern edge of Tunis is the vast Muslim cemetery. Expansion of a stone quarry endangered this sacred ground, so the European-dominated municipal council decided to survey the cemetery and establish definite boundaries. When it was rumored that inalienable religious land *(habous)* was threatened, the council assured the Sheikh-el-Medina (religious and secular head of the Arab section of Tunis) that no such land would be touched. By this time, however, a large crowd that had gathered around the cemetery faced a strong police force. Stones were hurled, and shots echoed among the tombs on the hillside. An estimated nine Europeans were killed and twenty injured, while the Tunisian casualties were unreported. Although no evidence connected the Young Tunisians with the riot, the incident illustrated how the nationalists could gain popular support by posing as defenders of religious tradition. A rumor that an Italian had fired the first shot, coupled with the Italian invasion of Libya, subjected Italians to sneak attacks throughout Tunis.

An accidental death on February 9, 1912, in which an Arab child was struck down by a tram operated by an Italian, worsened the situation. In anger Arabs boycotted the trams. The Young Tunisians supported the tramway workers' strike against the government-owned facility. The strikers demanded that no Italians be allowed to drive trams and that equal pay be given for equal work regardless of nationality. More bloodshed resulted, and French Resident-General Alapetite issued an ultimatum that the strike be ended within forty-eight hours. When the time had expired without compliance, leaders of the Young Tunisians were seized. Ali Bach Hamba and Abdelaziz Taalbi, along with two colleagues, were labeled Communists and deported; the rest were imprisoned. Nationalist newspapers were suppressed, and a state of emergency was proclaimed that lasted until 1921.[28] Thus was set the framework of French response that would be repeated many times in the future. French prisons supplied a continuous line of martyrs for the cause of Tunisian nationalism. Under these pressures the nationalist cause remained clandestine and impotent until after World War I.

No Tunisian grievance was represented in World War I, yet the Regency had no choice but to support France against the Central Powers. Tension was inevitable for the Tunisians since their old protectors and Muslim brothers, the Turks, were now an enemy. The French war effort was aided by Tunisian soldiers, workers, and agricultural products. Of the 63,000 Tunisians who fought for France 10,500 were listed as killed or missing in action.[29] The large lake of Bizerte served as a submarine-free rendezvous for Allied convoys going to and from the Eastern Mediterranean campaign. War came to southern Tunisia as a result of events in neighboring Libya, where Arab chiefs, spurred on by the Turkish Sultan's Holy War, pushed the Italian army from the barren frontier. The chief of the revolt, Khalifa Ben Asker, decided to invade southern Tunisia and lead the desert tribes in an uprising against France. In 1915 Khalifa Ben Asker led an attack against several French border posts. By the following year the insurgents were crushed, but not before the campaign had involved 15,000 men, with 748 French and natives killed, and 1,548 dead from sickness and disease.[30] The French military grip on southern Tunisia held fast.

Modern warfare disrupts a nation completely, and world wars naturally have global repercussions. Hopefully, after World War I, Arab nationalists counted on the peace settlement for recognition of their movement. To solve major political dislocations in postwar Europe President Woodrow Wilson suggested that the principle of national self-determination operate in order that nationalist movements should not be constrained only to explode later. This idea verbalized the aspirations of many nationalist groups, including the Tunisians. Once again the climate seemed favorable for the nationalist cause, and Abdelaziz Taalbi returned to Tunis, where he and his colleagues outlined the following moderate objectives: (1) understanding and cooperation with France, (2) administrative reform in Tunisia, (3) reinstatement of the constitution (*destour*) of 1861.[31]

Throughout the Arab world the Allies had received aid against Turkey, and the nationalists expected to be rewarded with independence. Disillusionment came quickly. The Paris

Peace Conference was a bitter experience for the Arabs, whose cause was well presented by Emir Faisal, the Saudi Arabian leader of the revolt against Turkey. The attitude of Georges Clemenceau of France toward the Arab pleas was especially unyielding, and he insisted upon French military occupation of Syria.[32] Unfortunately, Emir Faisal counted on the United States to protect the Arabs. Although President Wilson had vaguely promised to defend Syrian independence against European covetousness, the failure of his health and the U.S. Senate's repudiation of the League of Nations left the Eastern Mediterranean open to French and British control. In December, 1918, the *Manchester Guardian* prophetically editorialized:

> The old Europe is not dead, the Europe of selfish interests, of "imperialist" ambitions, of diplomatic intrigue, of short-sighted views and moral chaos. It is alive among the nations, just as old Adam is alive among us all.[33]

Once again the nationalist cause was frustrated but not destroyed; it was to organize in the postwar years for the final onslaught on colonialism and traditionalism.

During 1919 the Young Tunisians organized the Destour Party (Liberal Constitution Party) and vainly tried to convince France that it was time for political reform. Social unrest and labor disputes followed in the wake of war. While French authorities spoke of the young nationalists as agitators against the government, the American consul described them as "idealists with a vision of Tunisia under entirely native government."[34] After failing to persuade the French to consider a reform program, the nationalists presented their demands to Naceur Bey. These eight demands were also printed on the back of the Destour Party membership cards: (1) an assembly of both Tunisians and French elected by universal suffrage; (2) institution of a government responsible to this assembly; (3) separation of executive, legislative, and judicial powers; (4) access of competent Tunisians to all administrative posts; (5) equal salary and treatment for Tunisian and French officials; (6) institution of elected municipal governments; (7) privilege of Tunisians to purchase land on an equal basis with the French; and (8) freedom of the press, assembly, and association. Soon a ninth request was added: (9) obligatory educational system. In addition a copy of the program was sent to the French resident-general and published in *La Dépêche Tunisienne* on June 23, 1920.[35] The elderly Bey showed little enthusiasm, but his sons strongly supported the Destourian position and persuaded their father to be amiable toward the nationalists.

Ahmed as-Safi, secretary-general of the new party, presented proposals to the French government in Paris, probably assisted by Abdelaziz Taalbi, who was in France at the time. Support was forthcoming from the liberals and moderates in the French Chamber of Deputies, but even this was largely lost when Naceur Bey sent a forty-eight-hour ultimatum to the resident-general threatening abdication unless the eighteen-point plan was adopted. These nine points represented an addition to the earlier nine points, making an eighteen-point program: (1) the premier will be chosen by the Bey; (2) the premier will preside over cabinet meetings; (3) the Bey will inaugurate the legislative assembly; (4) naturalization of Tunisians should cease; (5) the Tunisian army should fly its own flag; (6) all kinds of *waqf* (land consecrated for religious purposes), public and family, should be respected; (7) university education should be established; (8) the Tunisian family should receive more attention and care; (9) the royal family should be accorded the respect commensurate with its tradition, prestige, and position. Strange circumstances surrounded the Bey's threat. An interview with the monarch appeared in a Tunis newspaper quoting him as saying that a constitution was not necessary for his country. Denying the statement, the monarch demanded a retraction and was refused, whereupon he threatened abdication. The French had little time to act, since French President Alexander Millerand was soon to arrive in Tunis for a formal state visit. Once again, as in the past, a strong show of French military muscle broke the Bey's resolve; and President Millerand visited the protectorate from April 27 to May 3, 1922, acting as if nothing had happened. In the course of the president's visit a reporter questioned Resident-General Lucien Saint about the nationalists, and the official replied:

> During the war, the young Tunisians, who have taken from our contact a taste for liberty and independence, have become— by following influences hostile to our authority—accessible to Wilsonian ideas, especially the one which proclaims the right of people to govern themselves.

Furthermore, he asserted, they want an elected parliament and a responsible government, "two requests inadmissible and contrary to the Treaty of Bardo."[36] President Millerand traveled through the kasbah of Tunis hearing shouts of "Vive Millerand! Vive le Bey! Vive la France!" and a few isolated brave voices crying "Vive la constitution!" Realizing that he could not completely ignore Tunisian sentiment, the president called for mild reforms permitting more Tunisian participation in the government. The loyalty of the Bey was the key factor in Millerand's program to discredit Destourian agitation. "Without the support of the crown, the Destour Party, which one knows attach themselves to the Soviets, appear to all without authority," stated the president.[37] Summarizing the visit, various reporters cautioned against overoptimism. Thousands were marching with demands to the Bey, and Communists were trying to convince the Arabs that nationalism and Communism were synonymous. Another observer concluded, "The situation is grave, but not alarming, because the countryside is calm and the peasant indifferent."[38]

When the French Chamber of Deputies debated the Tunisian question, it was obvious that they would not accept the eighteen demands. In July the chamber voted "to maintain in all circumstances the authority and rights of France in Tunisia, to encourage French colonization on the small and the medium scale [as opposed to the creation of large estates owned by absentees], and to carry out broad measures of political reform."[39]

The ensuing reforms were largely administrative and did not shift the power of government from France to Tunisia to the degree that the nationalists had hoped. One decree created the Grand Council, replacing the Consultative Conference, which was composed of a French section and a Tunisian section.[40] This council could not discuss issues of a political or constitutional nature, and even its financial powers were sharply curtailed. An arbitration commission was established to compromise differences between the two sections. Tunisian councils of the *caidat* were formed to study local economic problems, and French and Tunisian regional councils composed of representatives from the council of *caidats,* municipal councils, and the Chambers of Commerce and Agriculture discussed regional economic issues. A civil controller appointed by the French resident-general presided over the regional councils.[41] The post of secretary-general, always held by a Frenchman, was abolished. The real control of internal affairs was not transferred to Tunisians but was now directly controlled by the resident-general. The nationalists were disappointed with the reforms of 1922, and their press criticized many inadequacies. Nevertheless, the new Bey, Muhammad al-Habib, was in favor of accepting the reforms and seemed offended by Destourian opposition.

Despite specific postwar setbacks for the nationalists some encouragement was to be found in the general atmosphere in the Middle East. Italy granted Libya a constitution and Egypt revolted against England, gaining a degree of independence in 1922. Uprisings in Iraq led to an Arab monarchy and mandate status under England with implied independence for the future. In addition Turkey scored a victory against the Greeks, signaling to the Tunisians the revival of Muslim power. Syria became an independent constitutional monarchy in 1920, with

King Faisal on the throne, although France later stepped in and crushed this government. The Middle East was stirring; and although the Tunisians had appealed to President Wilson and the Versailles Powers, they were convinced that their situation called for bilateral negotiations with France.

It was in such an atmosphere that the controversial book *La Tunisie martyre* was published in Paris. Although it was published anonymously, the name Abdelaziz Taalbi is usually associated with the book. Certainly, whether or not he was solely responsible, he had a great deal to do with the work. Habib Bourguiba, a young man who would eventually lead Tunisia to independence, was greatly influenced by the book.[42] During hospitalization for a lung ailment, Habib Bourguiba stated, "I slipped it under my covers and read it surreptitiously, very moved. These figures, these words, this poverty, this humiliation to be colonized. . . . I wept in secret. . . ."[43] The book, which explained the aspirations of the nationalists so well, became the bible of the resistance movement until the Destour Party split. Even today the book is still highly revered by some. After listening to several Tunisian intellectuals criticize the current government for being authoritarian, I was handed a copy of *La Tunisie martyre* with the comment, "This is what we believe" Tunisia, as Taalbi explained, had been humiliated by the creation of the protectorate. The Treaty of Bardo ruined Tunisian power and integrity.[44] In addition, the liberties guaranteed under the Fundamental Pact of 1857 were abrogated by France by press laws that crushed all free journalism.[45] The book concluded with ten requests asking for a political democracy sustained by all the basic freedoms.[46]

A conservative group in the Destour Party, led by Hassan Guellaty and Muhammed Numan, attacked the book for being too radical, but these critics represented a minority and their attacks only strengthened Destourian efforts. The French retaliated by arresting Taalbi in 1920 and sentencing him to prison for plots against the government. Fearing that they would make Taalbi a Tunisian martyr, they released him in

1921, and he left Tunisia in 1922 to further pan-Arabism, not to return to his homeland until 1937.[47]

The French socialist newspaper *L'Avenir Tunisien* supported the book, referring to the nationalist struggle as righteous. Using familiar tactics, the resident-general in Tunis called the nationalists Communists, when in fact the only proven similarity between the two groups was that they were both violently anticolonial. Nevertheless, by 1924 events forced a closer cooperation between Destourians and Communists. A new Tunisian delegation presented its case in Paris, hoping that the coalition of the left *(Cartel des Gauches)* would be receptive. General apathy concerning North Africa and lingering resentment over Naceur Bey's abortive ultimatum weakened support in the mother country, and only the French Communists gave support.

Tension grew in Tunisia in the 1920's until, as the American consul reported, "Never has the native of Tunisia been so independent as at the present time."[48] The rumors that spread when the Egyptian royal yacht visited Bizerte illustrate the high pitch of excitement: it was reported that the Egyptians and Tunisians were preparing to ally against the French.[49] Uneasiness reigned as the Tunisians watched the war between the Riff tribes and the French in Morocco, jubilant when the Riffs, led by Abdel-Krim, scored victories over the French army. It was even rumored that the Riffian leader was going to marry a princess in the Bey's household.[50]

Tunisian nationalists were also concerned about an attempted meeting of the French rulers from Morocco, Algeria, and Tunisia to establish for the area a common government with the capital in Algiers. This possibility seemed remote in the face of the Riffian war in Morocco, but the Destourians acted to protect their own nationalist cause. Arms had been smuggled into Tunisia from German submarines during the war, and the trackless Sahara was ideal for smuggling more weapons, which were often stored in mosques, forbidden territory to the non-Muslim. France cracked down on this illicit trade but never completely stopped it.

In such an atmosphere France unveiled a statue of Cardinal Lavigerie at the entrance to the Arab medina in Tunis. With an uplifted Cross in one hand and a Bible in the other Cardinal Lavigerie marched with flowing robes onward toward the Grand Mosque. No greater affront to the Muslims could have been conceived if it had been carefully planned. Four thousand Tunisians demonstrated while French soldiers encircled the monument.[51] The major accusation that the French hurled at the nationalists was that they were Communists, a charge designed to have a great effect back in France, where this ideology was considered a current threat to Western Europe. While most of the Destour leaders were not Communist, the labor syndicate had been infiltrated, as the following newspaper plea indicates:

> Workman! You must use force, you must reply with force. To the violence of the bourgeois, the proletariat must oppose violence. This force will be organized, will be disciplined so as to be ready for the cause of the proletariat. For that, we call upon the workmen of this country to rejoin their proper organizations of the communist party.[52]

Communist influence in Tunisia was exerted among the working class in the labor syndicate, the *Conféderation Générale des Travailleurs Tunisiens* (CGTT), founded in 1924; however, the leader of the syndicate, Muhammed Ali, was not a Communist. Sympathy of the CGTT for nationalist uprisings in Syria and tribal revolts in Morocco brought charges of Communism, until Muhammed Ali and five others were sentenced for plots against the security of the state.[53] When Muhammed Ali was exiled for ten years, the CGTT was dissolved. For a time he lived in Egypt and then went to Saudi Arabia, where he died in 1932.

Obviously French authorities saw only the Communist threat

and underestimated the extent of nationalist feeling. "As to the political situation, the Young Tunisian movement never existed," claimed Resident-General Lucien Saint; "but," he added, "there flourished in Tunisia a Communist movement which was fairly dangerous. As everywhere, revolutionary internationalism was the animator of a primitive and semi-religious nationalism."[54] His attitude allowed Saint to ignore the fact that the 1922 reform plan was too mild and that legitimate national agitation existed outside the Communist movement. Repression was the resident-general's answer. Political leaders were imprisoned, newspapers closed, and films censored, especially if they portrayed revolution. Admittedly, with both Taalbi and Muhammed Ali absent nationalist agitation in Tunisia was lethargic. The so-called "villainous decrees" stymied the press and political activity. In fact, by 1928 the American consul reported that there were no distinct Communist or nationalist movements in operation.[55] The disheartened Destour Party slowed its activities and waited for a more favorable time, which came in the 1930's.

Indeed, the thirties proved to be a crucial period for Tunisian nationalism. A new newspaper, *La Voix du Tunisien,* was started, with the young nationalist Habib Bourguiba joining its editorial staff. When French President Gaston Doumergue arrived in Tunis in 1931 for the fiftieth anniversary of the protectorate, the *Voix* greeted him with an angry editorial. During his six-day stay in Tunisia President Doumergue praised the work of France but completely ignored nationalist demands and never mentioned reform.[56] By now the world economic crisis was felt in North Africa, and the Destourian press intensified its attacks. However, a new press law required every newspaper published in a European language to have a French editor; and in the case of *La Voix du Tunisien,* which published in French and Arabic, two editors were required— one French and one Arab.

After two years on the *Voix* Bourguiba and his friends founded their own paper, *L'Action Tunisienne,* which pledged to go beyond the old Destourian position and plead the case of all Tunisians regardless of religion. Indirectly this was an attack on the party leadership for being too narrowly Muslim in interest and for ignoring the Jews and poorer European workers. The newspaper promised to search for a remedy for the great economic crisis.[57] Before the crushing blow of French suspension in May of 1933, *L'Action Tunisienne* published strong appeals for solidarity in the face of colonialism: "The people are much more menaced by the divisions which weaken it than by the slump in oils or the fall of the grain market."[58] More than any previous newspaper *L'Action Tunisienne* stressed unity to destroy French rule:

> And the voice of the people will be heard. Neither the gen-
> darmes, nor the machine guns, nor the assault cars, nor General
> Noguès arriving in person to supervise the operations, nor even
> the brutalities of the Senegalese, nothing will be able to silence
> this great voice.[59]

A new resident-general, Marcel Peyrouton, replaced François Manceron with instructions to be less timid in the face of the Arab peril.

It was becoming apparent that a more militant group was emerging within the Destour Party, a group led by Habib Bourguiba and his colleagues who had worked on the news-paper. Because of their connection with the paper these ardent nationalists were called the "Action Tunisienne" members of the party. They attacked the former party leaders for their policy of gradualism and inactivity. No reconciliation was possible, and in March, 1934, at a conference in Ksar Hellal the Neo-Destour Party was formed with Dr. Mahmoud Materi as president and Habib Bourguiba as secretary-general. While Dr. Materi gave dignity and prestige to the new party, it was Bourguiba who formulated the ideas and the program.

The Ksar Hellal meeting took place in a private home with sixty delegates present. Bourguiba insisted that only constant and persistent pressure could make France release Tunisia.

After all, Bourguiba reminded his followers, even the well-stone is grooved by the rope in time. The first open friction between the two party factions came in September, 1934, at Moknine, when one policeman and many Tunisians were killed. The Old Destourians severely criticized the methods of the "Neos," claiming that they only produced more French oppression.[60] In turn Bourguiba zealously attacked the Old Destour for failing to gain popular support for the coming struggle with France. The Neo-Destourians were committed to "the struggle in the street to obtain the independence of Tunisia by opposing French imperialism and colonization which was responsible for the misery into which the country is plunged."[61] Fearing the effectiveness of the new program, the French seized Bourguiba along with seven other party leaders and sent them to prison at Bordj le Boeuf on the edge of the Sahara. The final ascendancy of the Neo-Destourian faction over the old party was delayed until 1937.

In general the nationalist cause brightened when the liberal Popular Front came to power in France. This bloc of liberal parties included the only friends the Tunisians had in Paris. Armand Guillon replaced Marcel Peyrouton as resident-general in the spring of 1936, and Bourguiba and his colleagues were released from prison. At the second national congress, held in the fall of 1937, Bourguiba spoke of improved relations with France and announced telegrams of support for Tunisia from Senegal, Indochina, Antilles, Morocco, and Algeria. The French undersecretary of state for foreign affairs, Pierre Vienot, represented the Popular Front on a trip to Tunis and called for closer cooperation between the two countries in the struggle against underdevelopment. The undersecretary encouraged the Neo-Destourians with his condemnation of certain "private interests contrary to the general interest of Tunisia."[62] He also accused a previous French government of favoring certain private companies that were given concessions in Tunisia. Just as Neo-Destourian hopes were raised by the liberal approach, the fall of Léon Blum's Popular Front threw them again into despondency. At the next national council the party pledged itself:

> To continue the struggle with more force than ever for a coordinated action of the Tunisian masses in order to hasten the coming of a politics of understanding and comprehension which can be created only by the abolition of inequalities and privileges based on race or nationality.[63]

During the Popular Front period Abdelaziz Taalbi was permitted to return to Tunisia. A great ovation greeted him, but soon it was evident that Neo-Destourian opposition to the leader of the Old Destour was violent. As a price for reconciliation the Neo-Destour asked that the older group expel some of its leaders for cooperating too closely with the French. Taalbi refused, stiffened his opposition, and wrote an article in *L'Irada* accusing the Neo-Destour of violence and terrorism against the Old Destourians. Riots broke out between the two groups in Mateur and Beja, and three people were killed.[64]

The Old Destour then launched a verbal attack on the new party, accusing it both of duplicity when it called for independence and of collaboration with the French. Some Old Destourians labeled the Neos radical, uneducated, and violent. On October 3, 1937, the front page of *L'Irada* featured a cartoon entitled "The Naked Truth," showing Bourguiba and Dr. Materi with bloody hands. The decision to continue physical attacks on the Old Destour offended Dr. Materi, who withdrew from the party. Other moderates also withdrew, leaving the militant nationalists in complete control.

The more moderate Destourians clung to hopes based on the Paris Peace Conference and on French and British promises of eventual independence for the Arab states in the Eastern Mediterranean. The radical Neo-Destour called attention to the emptiness of promises by the so-called Western "liberators" of the Middle East. The Neos also criticized the conservative alliance between the Old Destour and Muslim religious leaders and called for secular nationalism directed against Western

European colonialism. Frustration over the failure of Vienot's policy and the belief that the Old Destour was incompetent drove the Neo-Destourians to a revolutionary policy marked by strife and bloodshed. The split between Old and New Destour became complete.

Open conflict between Tunisia and France characterized 1938. The year began with a riot in Bizerte over the firing of an Algerian worker. Elements of the Neo-Destour and the revived CGTT led the protest, which ended in bloodshed when the mob got out of control. More labor unrest followed when the CGTT openly resisted the influence of the French *Confédération Générale des Travailleurs,* with which it was affiliated. When the French resident-general once again dissolved the militant Tunisian labor syndicate, riotous demonstrations occurred. The revolutionary tone in the aims of the Neo-Destour Party is evident in the complaint of Salah Ben Youssef, an influential party leader:

> The French arrive in Tunisia in tatters and rapidly make a fortune. . . . They take everything from you and give you nothing. Your money is used as graft to pay the officials to buy your rightful land from you. You are then forced to retreat to the mountains, to the deserts, among the scorpions, in arid regions, where you are reduced to the level of beasts, you are forced to eating grass.[65]

These tensions came to a horrible climax in the bloody affair of April 9, 1938, a day now celebrated as Martyrs' Day in Tunisia. After demonstrations before the French Residence protesting repressive measures, a mob dispersed only to regroup the next day when the French took one of the popular leaders, Allala Belhaouane, to the Palais de Justice for trial. This time thousands of people pressed in on government troops, which fired into the crowd, killing 122 and wounding 62. A state of siege was proclaimed, schools were closed, and French police started closing Neo-Destour cells and arresting party officials. The leader of the Msaken cell exhorted an angry mob to "avenge the murder of women and children."[66] He was promptly sent to prison. The French military leader in the Sahel, General Abadie, issued a tough proclamation:

> I will not discuss the objectives followed by the Neo-Destour, but I guarantee that you will never attain these objectives by violence and revolt. . . .
> I give you forty-eight hours to disperse your groups and re-establish complete calm in the entire Sahel.[67]

The Neo-Destour Party was temporarily outlawed by France. Bourguiba wrote an article declaring that a complete rupture had developed between the party and France. Sabotage, arson, mutiny, and bombings followed as once again Habib Bourguiba and his colleagues went to prison. This time the Neo-Destour was strong enough to keep up pressure secretly even after the wholesale arrest of its leaders. The militants who were still free decided that the French would not condemn Bourguiba to death if they realized the resistance went on and they might have to negotiate with the Neo-Destourian leader in the future. Habib Thameur headed the aggressive group with the assistance of Hedi Saiki. Not only was the group able to get news items broadcast from Radio Berlin during the war, but it also had a secret communication network leading to Bourguiba himself. Neither French oppression nor World War II destroyed the party's efficient underground organization. Two days before the Allied armies entered Tunis Dr Thameur and Hedi Saiki went into exile in Germany until the end of hostilities, when they met Bourguiba in Egypt and founded the Bureau of the Arab Maghreb, dedicated to the expulsion of France from North Africa.[68]

A new resident-general, Eirik Labonne, arrived in the fall of 1938 faced with the rapid deterioration of Franco-Tunisian relations, but France advanced no positive program for Tunisia and remained preoccupied with the problems of Europe, where the Spanish Civil War and the Austrian Anschluss cast ominous shadows.

With the possibility of world war imminent the new official concentrated on strengthening the economy and defense of Tunisia, since war would probably cut communications between France and her protectorate. With Tunisia precariously close to Fascist Italy the Italians in the protectorate presented a threat. After war broke out, the Italians around Bou Fica (47 miles south of Tunis) built a country villa for Mussolini. Tunisian nationalists, who worried about the Italian menace, preferred the continued presence of France to Italian Fascist domination. Seizing the opportunity, Resident-General Labonne tried to improve relations with the Neo-Destour, but the French military refused to cooperate.[69] French forces in Tunisia were braced for an Italian attack from Libya after Mussolini declared war on France. Although Italian planes attacked targets in Bizerte and Tunis, Italy decided to wait for a German victory and gain Tunisia without an invasion. The French retaliated with air strikes against the Libyan frontier post at Naloub and Italian bases in Sicily. Italians in Tunisia were deported to desolate camps in western Tunisia or Algeria, emerging after the war more bitterly anti-French than ever.[70]

Warfare with all its destruction and horror was only postponed for Tunisia. The Allied invasion of North Africa in 1942 and the British Eighth Army offensive in Libya eventually pushed General Erwin Rommel and the German Afrika Korps into bitter last-ditch battles on parched Tunisian soil. The desert sands became the scene of some of the bloodiest battles in history.[71]

During the early war years Habib Bourguiba was imprisoned in the Basses-Alpes Department in southeastern France, not far from the Italian border. He was liberated by the Axis invasion of southern France and sent to Italy. The Italians hoped that Bourguiba would cooperate with them and help stir up Tunisian opposition to the Allies. He did not choose to do so. Just before the Allied landings in North Africa,

Bourguiba sent an important letter to Dr. Habib Thameur, the titular head of the Neo-Destour:

> Give to the militants the order—under my responsibility and even under my signature if it is necessary—to enter into relations with the Gaullist French of Tunisia (there are bound to be several there: certain of our socialist friends for example) to arrange if possible our clandestine action with theirs and leaving aside for after the war the problem of our independence. . . . Our support to the allies must be unconditional. . . . I repeat it to you: it is a question of life or death for Tunisia! And if in spite of all that I say you are not convinced, obey! It is an order that I give you. Do not debate it! I will take the entire responsibility before God and before history. . . . All our action should be based on that. All should be looked at from this angle . . . and a day will come when you will give thanks to God that I had seen correctly and that I had spared our dear native land the greatest catastrophe of her history.[72]

A most prophetic statement, considering that it was sent before the Allies had invaded North Africa and before the British Eighth Army was able to take the offensive against the famed Afrika Korps. Meanwhile in Rome the Italians allowed Bourguiba to broadcast to the Tunisian people, still hoping that he would support the Axis cause. Although he remained faithful to his announced position, he was allowed to return to Tunis in time to see the last phase of the battle for North Africa.

In the meantime (1942) a nationalist, Moncef Bey, became the Tunisian monarch, informing the startled French that he intended to rule his country. In vain the Bey requested the Vichy government under Marshal Philippe Pétain to grant major reforms. These included: (1) a consultative council with a large Tunisian representation; (2) more Tunisians in public office; (3) equal treatment and salaries for Tunisian officials; (4) Tunisian control of the central administration; (5) limitation of the power of the French civil controllers; (6) use of the

Arab language in the schools; and (7) government control of utilities in the public interest. The Bey told the Tunisian *caids* that they were the "only representatives in the country," and that if the French civil controllers interfered with their duties, "not to hesitate to come to me."[73] A sharp dispute in 1943 between the French resident-general, Admiral Estéva, and the Tunisian minister of justice resulted in the Bey's request that Estéva be recalled. Although the French ignored the Bey's demand, the occupying Germans forced Admiral Estéva's return to France. When the Axis Powers were expelled from Tunis, the commander of the French forces in North Africa, General Alphonse Juin, became acting resident-general.

The fate of Moncef Bey was about to be decided. The French accused the Bey of collaborating with the Axis during the occupation and conferring the order of *Nicham Iftikhar* on enemy personalities.[74] If the Bey did this, it was surely under the pressure of the Vichy government. The real grievance that France had with Moncef Bey was that he supported the Tunisian nationalist position. On orders from Algiers, General Juin went to the Bey to ask for his abdication; when the monarch steadfastly refused, he was flown to Laghouat in the Algerian Sahara. The throne was immediately given to Sidi Lamine, who would cooperate with France. Only after the exiled Bey sent a letter of abdication was he moved to more comfortable quarters on the coast. This treatment of the legitimate ruler stirred up more hatred of French rule; the deposed Bey became a national martyr and "Moncefism" a new weapon in the nationalist arsenal. Later, General Juin viewed the affair as an unnecessary mistake of the government in Algiers and an affront to a monarch who was not proven disloyal.[75] The deposed Bey's martyrdom was complete when he died in 1948, never having been restored to his throne.

The exile of Moncef Bey and the death of the Old Destour leader Abdelaziz Taalbi on October 1, 1944, left Habib Bourguiba the undisputed leader of the nationalist cause. When Bourguiba was allowed to return to Tunis, he expected favors from the Free French for the aid that Tunisia had given during the war. Instead, General Juin ordered that Bourguiba refrain from political activity, live in Tunis, and not leave the city without authorization.[76] When, with the aid of the American consul, Hooker Doolittle, Bourguiba asked to see the resident-general, he was told that the only person he would be able to see was the director of the French police.[77] A close friendship developed between the American consul and the Neo-Destourian leader, resulting in repeated French requests for the transfer of Hooker Doolittle: later he was transferred to Cairo. Unable to hide his disenchantment with France, Habib Bourguiba wrote to President Franklin D. Roosevelt on June 1, 1943:

> On the morrow of the victory in Tunisia, I called on the Tunisian people to collaborate with France in the task of reconstruction, to leave until after the war the solution of political problems. The Residency reacted by forbidding the publication of this appeal, which obviously did not suit its plans, and by ordering my arrest and that of my comrades.
>
> The Party's collaboration was not wanted. Actually it will not be able to collaborate on the basis of the present "reforms," which constitute a brutal retrogression even by comparison with the pre-war status.[78]

But sympathetic though the United States might be, only French action could alleviate the situation, and the Allies, busy preparing for an invasion of Sicily, paid little attention to Tunisia. The following months were frustrating for Habib Bourguiba because it was obvious that France would remain intransigent to Neo-Destourian demands. In spite of its futility Bourguiba agreed to the issuance of the 1945 Manifesto of the Tunisian People asking for complete independence. All the reform groups in Tunisia supported the document. No longer, Bourguiba reasoned, could the issue be localized; the world must understand the plight of Tunisia. For this reason he decided to go abroad and plead his country's cause. The League of Arab States had been recently formed and its support would be helpful. The United States and other members of the United Nations fighting the Axis Powers also needed to be informed.

Denied an earlier request to leave Tunisia, Bourguiba made plans to depart secretly. Late in March, narrowly escaping the French police, he boarded a fishing vessel in Sfax and began his trip to Libya. A difficult pilgrimage had begun. In Egypt he discovered that few people knew anything about North African affairs, let alone Tunisia, and the delegates to the Arab League were preoccupied with Arab-Israeli affairs. Finally he was able to organize a Tunisian nationalist office in Cairo, controlled by three Neo-Destourians, Doctor Habib Thameur, Taieb Slim, and Rachid Driss.[79] These men began a propaganda campaign designed to break through Arab indifference.

Bourguiba's trip to Syria and Lebanon was equally frustrating. News from Tunis that fifty leaders who had signed the independence manifesto had been arrested and sent to prison was discouraging. The critical situation encouraged establishment of liaison between the small Tunisian Communist Party and the French Communist Party, both of which shouted "Death to colonialism!" The Neo-Destourians viewed the liaison with disfavor since they feared and opposed Communist power or that of any nationalist group outside their own party.

Meanwhile, Bourguiba decided to take his case to America, and after much effort he received a visa from the American consulate in Egypt and began the arduous trip to the United States. This, too, proved to be discouraging. It seemed quite evident that the large powers could afford to ignore a small country like Tunisia, and Bourguiba was still only a humble pilgrim.[80] At a party given by the Ambassador from Saudi Arabia Bourguiba was introduced to Secretary of State Dean Acheson and at least talked briefly about Tunisian affairs. Later Tunisia established an office in New York City and presented her case more fully to the United States and the United Nations.

Bourguiba returned to Egypt by way of Amsterdam and Geneva. The whole mission had consumed two years, but support was still weak for the small country. Eventually reports from the famine-ridden land helped to attract world attention. Perhaps, Bourguiba thought, more attention would now be given to the plight of all Northwest Africa (the Maghreb). Hopefully, he sent a message from Cairo to Ferhat Abbas, the leader of *L'Union Démocratique du Manifesto Algérien,* stating, "A solid union of the three North African peoples forged in the blood of our martyrs, in the tears of our widows, we reconcile ourselves singly to our ideal."[81] The eventual cooperation of Morocco, Algeria, and Tunisia was an ideal that had intrigued Bourguiba early in his political career, but talks with the Moroccan nationalist leader, 'Allzl al-Fassi in Cairo offered little encouragement. Each of the Maghreb states wanted complete control of its own nationalist struggle, and North African unity was but a remote possibility.

In a letter to his son, who was currently finishing his legal studies in Paris, Bourguiba summarized his mission:

> The advice, the orders, the direct commands I have given, have not had any result. Nobody wants to risk his liberty, still less his skin. It is the peculiar quality of condemned people. They want very much to be free, but they wait for liberation from a miracle from outside. This miracle will not come if they do nothing from within.[82]

Clearly he saw that he must return to Tunisia and organize for a more effective internal struggle against the French.

In Bourguiba's absence Salah Ben Youssef assumed the leadership of the Neo-Destour Party. On the sacred occasion of the 27th of Ramadan (August 23, 1946) Ben Youssef harangued the crowd, "Are you unanimous in proclaiming the total independence of Tunisia?" The shout "Independence! Independence!" rang out.[83] After observing the vigor and ambition of Salah Ben Youssef, many people predicted his future struggle with Bourguiba for party leadership. Although Bourguiba knew of Ben Youssef's ambition, he received a visit from him in Egypt without comment or incident.

Partly encouraged by the Indonesian victory against colonialism and desirous of stirring Tunisia to greater opposition to France, Bourguiba finally returned to Tunis. Although French colonists in Tunisia opposed his return, certain French officials hoped that Bourguiba's arrival would split the Neo-Destour Party. On September 9, 1949, he was back in Tunis ruling as the undisputed leader of the party despite the Youssefist faction. Salah Ben Youssef would choose a more propitious time for the power struggle.

The nationalist movement nurtured in the interwar period grew steadily after the Second World War. Much had been tried but little accomplished; the French remained adamant. Far greater pressure than France imagined was growing among the normally docile Tunisians and no ephemeral or feeble reforms could contain it. Strong Tunisian nationalism had clouded relations between the protector and the protected. The positive and constructive period in Franco-Tunisian relations had given way to humiliation and frustration. To hold the territory France had to repress the Neo-Destour. No longer could French officials take pride in bringing technology and progress to a backward land; now they had a hated police function that began to eat away at their own morale.

5

From Hope to Disillusionment and Bloodshed, 1950-1953

Labor Organization

The Tunisians had no effective economic weapon with which to belabor France until they organized the labor movement. Ferhat Hached and an old school companion, Habib Achour,[1] resigned in disgust from the French labor syndicate, *Conféderation Générale du Travail* (CGT), in 1944 when Communists became influential in the organization. Hached became secretary-general and Achour an assistant secretary of *L'Union des Syndicats Autonomes du Sud Tunisien*. This organization and a similar one in northern Tunisia were merged to form *L'Union Générale Tunisienne du Travail* (UGTT) in 1946, with Ferhat Hached as its able secretary-general. Soon the UGTT applied for membership in the World Federation of Trade Unions, but it was not accepted, on the ground that it discriminated against European workers in Tunisia. After realizing that the main French syndicates had local branches in Tunisia which recruited the European laborers, the world

131

federation then admitted the UGTT, but again the Tunisians became disturbed at the Communist influence in the federation and resigned to join the International Confederation of Free Trade Unions. Ferhat Hached became well known and highly respected in the ICFTU. In Tunisia the small Communist-affiliated *Union Syndicate des Travailleurs Tunisiens* became so weak by 1956 that it dissolved itself; from that period on the UGTT was unopposed.[2] France could no longer accuse the Tunisian labor movement of Communism. The Neo-Destour was the most potent Tunisian political institution, and it augmented this power by an alliance with the UGTT, creating an indispensable coalition for Tunisian nationalism. Political pressure now sustained by the threat of general strike gave France a much more formidable opponent than it had faced in the interwar period.

By 1950 the UGTT had endured some severe trials. In 1947 a strike in Sfax over wages ended in violence as gendarmes fired on the workers, killing thirty-two and wounding two hundred, while the leader of the Sfax syndicate, Habib Achour, was arrested. The "Enfidaville Affair," when workers at the *Societé du Domaine* asked for higher minimum wages, was also a supreme test for labor. Although Minister of Social Affairs Mohammed Badra requested the company to delay action until the government council could decide, the company brought in other laborers and rioting erupted. French gendarmes were met by a hail of stones, and after an ensuing fusillade six Tunisians were dead, sixty wounded, and one hundred and sixty-six arrested. Ironically, several hours later the council modified the wage scale.

Habib Bourguiba first met Ferhat Hached in 1949 and immediately liked him. During his sojourn in Paris in 1950 Bourguiba boasted, "Our great central syndicate, the UGTT, by the voice of its secretary-general, Ferhat Hached, has brought to me from this sector, even to Paris, the support of the Tunisian proletariat."[3] Secretary-General Hached passionately expressed the plight of Tunisian workers as he attacked the French colonists in the newspaper *Mission* for seizing the good land and living in comfort beside the "unspeakable misery in which the Tunisian laboring population is totally confined."[4]

Cooperation between the Neo-Destour Party and the UGTT offered Bourguiba the chance to maintain pressure on France, a policy he had advocated since 1934. After three years' absence Bourguiba returned to Tunis in September, 1949, to lead the independence movement. He had decided that the time was ripe to press the struggle on the home front, however bitter the price.

> Prepare to organize fellaghas, to hold the thickets and the mountains. Do not fear either the machine guns, or the tanks, or the airplanes. You will thereby give the United Nations the occasion to intervene, and the historic day will come when the tricolor will be replaced by the Tunisian flag.[5]

For this total effort the labor organization supplied effective weapons: work stoppages and general strikes to plague the French by paralyzing the economy.

Schuman's Thionville Speech

Tunisian hopes for independence were greatly encouraged by France in 1950, only to be dashed to the ground by the reversals of the following year. In the spring Bourguiba was back in Paris helping organize Tunisian students. He presented a seven-point program which would revive Tunisian executive power and greatly weaken French surveillance. Seemingly these requests were ignored until, during a speech at Thionville, France, in June, French Foreign Minister Robert Schuman made a statement that had little effect on his audience but was heard clearly in Tunisia.[6] Speaking of the newly appointed resident-general in Tunisia, he declared, "M. [Louis] Perillier in his new functions will have as his mission to understand and to conduct Tunisia toward a full expansion of its riches and *to lead it toward independence, which is the final objective*

for all the territories at the heart of the French Union."[7] Here
was the opportunity that Tunisian nationalists were waiting
for, and they were determined not to allow France to forget
this promise. Bourguiba was elated by the news and predicted
that France would realize a conquest of hearts infinitely more
effective than the possession of Tunisian territory.[8] Resident-
General Perillier arrived in Tunis with promises of new steps
in the evolution of Tunisia.

Evolution is a relative and ambiguous word, and when the
actual reforms were announced, Tunisian hopes fell. The general principles of a three-point program announced by the
resident-general were: (1) the administration will be opened
to a selected group of Tunisians; (2) the population will participate in municipal organization; (3) Tunisian institutions
will be adapted to modern life.[9] In making the announcement
Perillier failed to mention Robert Schuman's speech. Although
Schuman had warned the Council of the Republic that France
could not indefinitely keep an administration in Tunisia,
pressure mounted in French official circles for moderate reform.
When the reforms were implemented, the old Tunisian Council of Ministers, or cabinet, was changed from an equal number
of French and Tunisians to nine Tunisians and three French.
The Tunisian prime minister, and not the French secretary-
general, presided over this council.[10] However, France still
controlled finances and foreign affairs and retained the right
to close surveillance over Tunisian officials.

The real issues remained unsettled. In August of 1950 a
new government was formed in Tunisia under Prime Minister
Sidi M'Hamed Chenik, who dedicated his ministry to advanc-
ing Tunisia by successive stages toward internal autonomy.
Many nationalists argued that internal autonomy was a long
way from independence and debated Robert Schuman's use
of the word "independence." Apprehension mounted when
France seemed to be retreating rapidly from the foreign minister's position. To keep the issue alive the Chenik government
worked on a reform plan to be presented to France in the fall.

The important Tunisian organizations that pressed for independence were the UGTT syndicate, the Neo-Destour Party, the Destour Party, the Socialist Party, and the Communist Party. Although a very close relationship developed between the Neo-Destour and the UGTT, the others appeared to agree only on Tunisian independence as a vague goal. There was a wide range in methodology, resulting in intrigue and much in-fighting.

The Chenik government, which included members of the Neo-Destour Party, decided to present reforms that would establish internal autonomy. At the same time the French colons, working through their agricultural organizations and representatives in the French National Assembly, called for the preservation of the Grand Council, which guaranteed them equal representation with Tunisians. The French in Tunisia pleaded for France to maintain the principle of cosovereignty and to allow only mild reforms—certainly not internal autonomy or independence. When the French government announced the reforms in February, 1951, cosovereignty was obviously the objective. More civil service positions were available for Tunisians, and orders of the Tunisian prime minister no longer had to be countersigned by the French secretary-general, although the resident-general had to sign them. A seven-seven split between French and Tunisians was maintained in the Grand Council. One key provision was that "the control of personnel and of public expenses remain exclusively under the jurisdiction of the French secretary-general."[11]

These first reforms pleased nobody. In France the Rassemblement and Radical Parties complained against the whole concept of cosovereignty by boycotting the Grand Council. In May the Bey sent a note to the French protesting the concept of cosovereignty. Surely this doctrine was one of the most awkward in political history. Who could define it? How could there be cosovereignty when the Treaty of Bardo in 1881, at least verbally, recognized Tunisian sovereignty? Salah Ben Youssef, secretary-general of the Neo-Destour and minister of justice in the Chenik cabinet, accused the French of scheming "to weaken the power of the Neo-Destour and its participation in the government." Further, the French did "not have any right to a say in nor to administration of public affairs."[12] It was clear that Salah Ben Youssef wanted full independence for Tunisia, and as tension grew, French Resident-General Perillier complained that Ben Youssef had adopted a demogogic attitude in public. A confirmed nationalist naturally looked aghast at the idea of cosovereignty. A deadlock resulted as the Chenik government arduously worked on a reform plan based on internal autonomy to present to France. Another prominent party official, Hedi Nouira, described the French February reform as "only a preface, a springboard. The essential remains to be done."[13]

Tunisian Reform Plan

After sending their plan to Paris on October 31, 1951, the nationalists anxiously awaited a reply. An editorial in the Neo-Destour newspaper, *Mission,* outlined the nature of the plan, asserting that no sovereignty but Tunisian would be acceptable. In addition, "the executive can only be exclusively Tunisian and only a representative (in an assembly) is conceivable if he conforms to these conditions."[14] As the Chenik delegation presented its case in Paris, the *Mission* asked that there be no agreement compromising basic Tunisian rights, which, after all, were simply rights of all mankind.[15] These statements indicate that the Tunisian nationalist movement was organized, dedicated, and certain of its goals, that it had reached maturity. When organizations representing the French colons demonstrated against the Paris talks, the Neo-Destour called a one-day general strike to protest the actions of the vociferous minority.

The atmosphere in France was so unfavorable toward the Tunisian plan that Foreign Minister Robert Schuman and Resident-General Perillier were obliged to retreat from their liberal positions on Tunisia. M. Colonna, a senator representing the French in Tunisia, traveled to Paris in November and participated in the interpellation of Minister Schuman before the Senatorial Commission of Foreign Affairs. Senator Colonna cautioned the commission against any relaxation of French power, to which the foreign minister replied, "It is not a question of abandoning the prerogatives of France in seeking a more close cooperation with the Bey's government."[16] The following month the *Rassemblement Français de Tunisie* held a banquet in Paris to discuss the role of French colons. Here, M. de Klugueneau, representing the RPF in Tunisia, listed the great accomplishments of France in Tunisia in seventy years and called for "a public life in which France and Tunisia meet again in more and more intimate association."[17] On the contrary, the two antagonists were becoming more estranged as the Tunisians pushed toward independence and the French stubbornly clung to their power in Tunisia. After reviewing the situation, the secretary-general of the Arab League told the press, "It will not be our fault if the French government once more falls short of realizing that it cannot maintain in the middle of the twentieth century a hundred-year-old colonial policy."[18] A serious conflict was developing as one of the Tunisian party leaders, Mongi Slim, warned, "The patience of the Tunisian people has attained its limits and the Political Bureau of the Neo-Destour will not be able to prevent them from attaining by themselves their liberty and independence."[19]

The French reply on December 15, 1951, was a shock to even the moderate Tunisians. After flatly rejecting the Chenik plan, the note concluded:

> The French government instructs her representative in Tunis to constitute next January a mixed Franco-Tunisian Commission to study the provisions of a representative system, which can replace the Grand Council. . . .[20]

Although modifications would be made in the present government the note strongly asserted the rights of the French in Tunisia. Robert Schuman bluntly replied that "One can not prevent the participation of the French in the function of political institutions in Tunisia."[21] The Tunisian delegation considered the response "a rupture of negotiations." A change to a more conservative French parliament and the lack of Socialist representation in the cabinet were largely responsible for the unexpected, harsh reply. Dislodged Socialist Party leaders warned against "the dreadful consequences" of the French note.[22] Even the moderate Tunisian nationalist General Saadallah called it a step backward by creating a cosovereignty which was a violation of the Treaty of Bardo. Disillusionment spread like a disease in Tunisia. "France having shut the doors, what can be done?" asked a leading Arab newspaper.[23] Departing from his usual optimism, Habib Bourguiba lamented that "the response of France has ended the Tunisian experience, which was a tendency to conciliate, in peace and amity, the hopes of the Tunisian people for independence. France opens a crisis similar to those of 1934 and 1937."[24]

Animated debate took place in France. Chenik, there to present his government's case, had been optimistic on the eve of the French response; now he was shocked and discouraged. A cabinet spokesman for the Neo-Destour, Salah Ben Youssef, accompanied Chenik to Paris, called for a Tunisian boycott of the mixed commission, and dejectedly told the French, "To affirm as a necessity the presence of Frenchmen at the heart of the Tunisian government is purely and simply to turn the back on promises solemnly taken."[25] Once the original shock had worn off, outright defiance set the tone of nationalist comments. Bourguiba told the press, "The exasperated Tunisian people, deceived, driven out of patience, must show proof to the eyes of the world that they are ready for liberty."[26] This statement was the first indication of how, through the United Nations and trips abroad, Habib Bourguiba planned to inform the world of Tunisia's plight. The policy proved to be a wise and helpful one for Tunisia in the future. The most defiant response to France was made by Hedi Nouira:

> We still remember the words of M. Robert Schuman when he assured the United Nations Assembly that they need not question the liberalism of France. Our ears always resound with the

profession of French faith to conduct people to the full capacity to govern themselves. . . . Then, the change of direction, comes the letter of December 15. This made the twist to sharp assertions, to unilateral commands of "You move and you submit." Ah well, no! We will not move and we will not submit.[27]

An internal French squabble over Tunisia took place in December. The French political leader Michael Debré criticized France's Tunisian policy and suggested a plan that would gradually provide for the departure of France but would still retain a strong French economic and cultural influence. Officially as early as May, 1950, the French Socialist Party had approved a plan drawn up by the Socialist Party in Tunisia which called for:

1. Setting a date for the end of the protectorate and the independence of Tunisia.
2. Reforms protecting everyone in Tunisia from the exploitation of capitalism and feudal servitude.
3. An immediate treaty giving sovereignty to Tunisia.

The Socialist report cautioned that Arab nationalism could not be stopped at the Libyan border.[28] In general the attacks on the government blamed it for being blunt and undiplomatic and carrying on an unimaginative policy in Tunisia. Conversely, French conservatives accused Robert Schuman of being soft on Tunisia, to which he replied that his policy was "not guardianship but supervision."[29] About this time the press announced that Libya would gain its independence on December 24; no such Christmas present was in the offing for Tunisia.

Destour vs. Neo-Destour

Although following the Second World War its influence had diminished, the Old Destour Party still carried on a press campaign against what it called the radicalism of the Neo-Destour. The Destour had dedicated itself to Tunisian independence as early as its proclamation of 1933, but it often differed with the methods of the Neo-Destour. In 1949 the Destour voiced its program through *La Nation Tunisienne* with the motto "Union, Action, Independence."[30] The paper called for a national front. At this time the Destour supported Habib Bourguiba as the most important nationalist leader. However, in 1951 a new newspaper, *Indépendence,* was created as an *"hebdomadaire d'union nationale pour l'indépendance et contre la collaboration."*[31] The significant change was in the phrase "against collaboration." The new group was accusing the Neo-Destour of close cooperation with the French. After the rude French rebuff of December, 1951, the old Destour redoubled its anticooperation line in an "I told you so" frame of reference:

> The Old Destour seeks only unconditional and complete independence; it has never been partisan to a policy of progressive steps, nor the negotiations engaged in by the Chenik Ministry.[32]

The Old Destour, which had branded the Neo-Destour radical, was now taking the more radical position. Actually this was a political maneuver by the Old Destour to regain the strength it had lost since 1937—a last effort to turn the French rebuff of 1951 into disaster for the Neos.

The proposed national front that the Destours wanted never materialized, and soon they turned to editorial attacks on the Neo-Destour Party. The militant action of the Neo-Destour was strongly denounced in the *Indépendence* in February, 1951:

> The president of the Destourian cell of Tebourba was attacked and wounded this week by the Neo-Destourians. At Sousse at the time of a private reunion of the Destour, "Neo" elements pretended to stop the reunion. It was necessary to drive them from the house by force. . . .
>
> It demonstrates clearly however, that Tunisians refuse to follow the Neo-Destour in the great dupery of governmental collaboration and of reforms which reinforce the protectorate.

It demonstrates why the sane elements like Doctor Slimane ben Silimane or Rouissi condemn the Neo-Destour and have quit its Directory Committee.

It demonstrates why Emir Abdel Krim and the representatives of the Arab Maghreb have rejected this new politics. . . .

It demonstrates why the fourteen thousand students of the Grand Mosque and their professors rose up against the attitude of this party. . . .

It demonstrates why numerous nationalist newspapers in Arabic or French point out the very grave dangers of the policies of the Neo-Destour.[33]

When analyzed, the old Destour criticism of Neo-Destour collaboration with the French proves to be weak. After all, the Neo-Destour was represented in the Chenik government and had to deal with the French if a solution was to be found. How could anyone have foreseen the French rebuff of December 15? Also, Neo-Destourian action was consistent with Bourguiba's policy of exerting pressure on the French but, at the same time, keeping the lines of communication and compromise open.

Unfortunately, more bloody conflicts developed between the two Destourian groups. The schism was widened when the Old Destour criticized the negotiations with the French and called for a national front including the Socialist and Communist parties. The leaders of the Neo-Destour feared a coalition most of all, because they believed that a multiplicity of parties would destroy the nationalist movement. "I am particularly impressed in the bad sense by the instability which characterizes the political life in France," said Bourguiba some years later in reference to French political parties.[34] Furthermore, according to Neo-Destourian thinking, both the Socialist and Communist parties of Tunisia were influenced by their respective parties in France, opening the door to ruinous factionalism. So the struggle with the Old Destour became a fight to the death. Internal unity was a necessity in order to defeat the French, and debate among Tunisian parties was a luxury that the Neo-Destour considered disastrous.

The Destourian intellectual and journalist Dr. A. Ben Milad launched the most damaging charge against the Neo-Destour in an article entitled "Fascism in Action."

> The methods that Bourguiba employed in order to create the split in the midst of the Destour in which he came to adhere, as well as the campaigns of lies which he did not cease to keep up in order to launch his party, were only copies of Fascist and Nazi methods. Also compatible with the Fascists were aggressions against individuals which the "Neos" used as weapons against their adversaries. And a few democratic Tunisians issued the cry of alarm of 1934. . . .
>
> Harassments, imprisonment of the members of the Zitouna committee under the benevolent eye of the Minister of Justice Ben Youssef, when this was not ordered by him. Aggression against the sheikhs in Tunis; against students at Sfax, at Kairouan, at M. Saken and this week at Bab Souika and at Carthage.
>
> The incident was endowed with the same strategy of April 9; with this difference that the oppressors were the "Neos" and not the police.[35]

There were more accounts of attacks on students, and on May 31, 1951, Dr. A. Ben Milad concluded: "The Tunisian people have not ceded to colonialism. They will not cede to the Neo-Destour. . . . Of origin national or foreign, tyranny is tyranny."[36] This stormy period in Tunisian internal affairs caused apprehension; after all, how does one justify violence among his own countrymen? Educated in the Western European democratic tradition, many Neo-Destourian leaders respected democracy and a permissive political system. Deputy secretary-general of the Neo-Destour Party Hedi Nouira explained:

> It is not by exclusions and mental restrictions that one will provoke the psychological impact capable of rallying around a well conceived program, the vital forces of a country. . . .

The only means to command nature is first of all to follow it, said Bacon. This is the secret of all the British success in matters of colonial politics, not in vexation or appearances.[37]

In periods of extreme crisis expediency often overrides cherished democratic principles. The French used press censorship and police-state methods against the nationalists, who increasingly began to act in the same manner. The independent Arab newspaper *An-Nahdha* accused the Neo-Destour of rationalizing its lack of democratic principles by having its political writers point out defects in democracy and "exalt the principle of unity of view in public opinion, in a country where a powerful authority rules."[38] In *An-Nahdha,* stated the Neo-Destour, "declarations are in contradiction with party acts. Also party militants ask themselves, with embarrassment, if they aren't really democrats, even if they affirm the party, or if they participate in neutralization of the opposition in order that in the country, nothing is expressed but the voice of the party."[39]

An ambiguous relationship developed between the Tunisian Communist Party and the Neo-Destour. When the UGTT, which was closely affiliated with the Neo-Destour Party, withdrew from the CGT because of its alliance with the French Communist Party, many Tunisian Communists blamed the Neo-Destourians. The Communists charged that the Neo-Destour had fallen "in the Fascist snare, and that its strikes, its movements are directed by Mussolini."[40] Despite these differences the Communist Party supported the nationalist fight, representing it as a struggle against colonialism and imperialism. Although it has been claimed that some members of the Neo-Destour cooperated closely with Communists, the real hope of the Tunisian Communist Party was to join a national front in cooperation with the old Destour.[41] Both the Old Destour and the Communist Party condemned the negotiations with the French. In 1951 the Communist Party declared,

"Struggle and not negotiations, that is the path of victory."[42] The Tunisian Communists were happy to see the problem internationalized, and they sent a delegation to the United Nations in 1952 to help speed negotiations. However, Communist interest in internationalization inevitably ran counter to strong Neo-Destourian nationalism. During imprisonment, Bourguiba expressed his views on Communism to a reporter for *Tunis Soir:* "The best barrier against Communism is constituted by the UGTT on the social level and the Neo-Destour on the political level."[43] Bourguiba was convinced that the Muslim faith alone was not an effective obstacle to Communism. After all, the Soviet Republics of Azerbaijan and Turkmen were Communist Islamic states. The only true answer was "a nationalism resolutely committed to the path of progress. . . ."[44]

The Tunisian Socialist Party also supported independence and expressed interest in the proposed national front. In January of 1952 there was a congress of the *Fédération Socialiste de Tunisie.* An editorial reporting on the conference stated the Socialist viewpoint of negotiations with France under the title, "To the Rear! March!"[45] Regardless, the Socialists enjoyed a better relationship with the Neo-Destour than the Communists, and several Socialists served as government ministers.

Bourguibism

Habib Bourguiba was not a political theorist but a political pragmatist. After studying political theories advanced by Aristotle, Plato, Mao Tse-tung, Lenin, Trotsky, and Khrushchev, he decided that Neo-Destourian socialism could not be imported. "The theory matters little to us; what matters is the ultimate goal."[46]

A compromise strategy, which became known as "Bourguibism," was developed by the leader of the Neo-Destour. This method necessarily involved negotiating with the French and not refusing anything that would allow Tunisia to move closer to independence, no matter how feeble the agreement. While accepting meager steps, Bourguiba prepared for a new victory which would bring him closer to his goal: such basically was Bourguiba's answer to Old Destourians, Communists, and Socialists who accused him of collaboration. In October, 1961, during a two-hour speech after the Bizerte crisis, Bourguiba expressed his strategy again, "Such is 'Bourguibism'; one must assimilate in a war the positions where it is a question of progress toward the final objective occupying one by one the positions of the adversary, but always keeping the less vulnerable positions, the most favorable in relation to the positions of the other."[47]

Since Bourguiba was convinced that Tunisia would need the support of world opinion, especially if the issue were taken to the United Nations, he again traveled extensively to create foreign support. The second trip abroad was more successful than his earlier journey and proved to be one of the most fruitful aspects of Bourguibism. Writing in the *Mission*, Bourguiba clearly and decisively outlined his program.

> Our movement is a serious movement; the entire world knows it. We are strong because we are moderate. We want an understanding with France. We have always said it and I repeat it, but that which is impossible today, is to begin to finesse anew. It must be admitted that the Tunisians have the right to govern Tunisia. If this principle is recognized, we will recall the appeals to the United Nations, to the Security Council, and to the Arab League, because it is in (bilateral face to face) negotiations that we wish to regulate our dispute. We are a western movement in the French style.[48]

Another feature of Bourguiba's political program was that ultimately a new relationship could be established with France. In 1964 Bourguiba seemed confident that the new relationship with France was imminent: "We were deeply convinced that, by its very nature, colonialism was destined to be left behind, through the creation of a new style of bond between the two peoples, based on a deeper knowledge enabling freedom of choice and unhampered development."[49]

When a reporter for *Le Monde* asked Bourguiba about the use of violence, he denied that his program was based on violence but added that "the recourse to violence is the only outlet left to men whom one has driven to despair."[50] Although it would take the French some time to realize it, by 1952 Bourguibism was triumphant and the Neo-Destour Party was the only group that could bargain for the future of Tunisia. The Old Destour group had lost most of its following, and too many influential Tunisians had decided that they would not tolerate the status quo.

Struggle for Independence

The years after 1952 were the critical period. There could be no turning back for the Tunisian nationalists. For the French either the nationalists must be dealt a death blow or negotiations must be opened. Each side pursued its aims with firm determination. Bloodshed, murder, rape, terror, and imprisonment were the result of the impasse. The strain was too great, the points of view too diverse for anything but chaos to result. The status quo could not be retained for long. Which side would retreat? Cosovereignty and internal autonomy were already outmoded doctrines for the Tunisians; their cry was "independence." In the shadow of the goal of independence, compromise measures were obsolete.

France replaced Resident-General Perillier with Jean de Hautecloque, who came determined to restore French prestige. He was convinced that Tunisia could be subdued and was naive enough to say that the people had forgotten Habib Bourguiba. But they had forgotten nothing, and soon the resident-general had earned the nickname "Jean le Terrible."[51] Pressure was exerted on Lamine Bey to dismiss the Chenik government and appoint one more friendly to France, when Bourguiba arrived in Tunis after an absence of nearly a year.

He immediately sensed the tenser atmosphere. Prospects of a settlement were dim, and nationalists looked aghast at French insistence that 300,000 Europeans have equal representation in the Tunisian government with the 3,000,000 natives. Bourguiba announced a rupture of relations with France and convinced the Chenik government and the party leaders that they must appeal their case to the United Nations. A secret meeting of the outlawed Neo-Destour Party was being held when French police broke in, arrested Habib Bourguiba, Mongi Slim, and four other party leaders, and sent them, along with six Communists, to prison. Rupture and arrest brought violence, but the party cells were ready and organized for action. The UGTT called a general strike, and crowds shouting "Bourguiba" filled the Avenue de France and the area around the French Residency. At Nabeul three were killed and twenty wounded, the railroad from Tunis to Sfax was cut, and eleven died and thirty were wounded at Sousse. New arrests were made, but the violence increased.[52] The situation was grave; France had nearly 30,000 soldiers on "police action," but an army cannot fight a dense populace. Guns, dynamite, and homemade bombs can easily be hidden under burnous and robe. The terrorists had an ample supply of German and Italian arms abandoned during the hasty Axis retreat in World War II. Old German and Italian antitank mines were a good source of gunpowder for homemade bombs.

In January a group of intellectuals, mostly Old Destourians, published an appeal for the end of violence, but an angry climate gripped Tunisia. Gasoline fires, bombings, assassinations, general strikes, and protest marches all punctuated the Tunisian appeal to the United Nations. Salah Farhat, the leader of the Old Destour, in a rare display of Arab unity, published a condemnation of French action and placed the support of his party behind the United Nations appeal.

France went through a series of cabinet crises in 1952, and finally, after René Pinay established a government in March, the United States urged him to settle the Tunisian problem outside the United Nations. Any hope of an early settlement waned with the new instructions to the resident-general demanding that the Bey dissolve the Chenik cabinet, establish a curfew for Tunis, and assign Colonel Schmuckel as commander of the French forces in the Tunis area. The Bey named as prime minister Salaheddine Baccouche, whose only claim to fame was that he enjoyed the title "Tunisian King of Coca Cola" through investments in the company. Suddenly France declared the crisis over and announced reforms which gave autonomy to Tunisian ministers, increased the number of public offices to be held by Tunisians, and established assemblies which were representative of local interests. When Resident-General Hautecloque arrived in Paris on April 18, he announced, "The situation in Tunisia is now satisfactory."[53]

Indeed, nothing had been accomplished as far as the Neo-Destour was concerned. Tunis and La Goulette were under a tight curfew, bloody riots broke out in the streets, and an explosion at the central post office wounded thirteen people. One day a funeral procession slowly winding its way through the twisting streets of the Arab medina of Tunis was surprised by a group of police. The pallbearers hastily put the coffin down and fled. Upon opening the coffin the police discovered that it was filled with knives, clubs, and bottles full of gasoline.[54]

Terror and Death

From January 28 to February 1, operation "Mars" was ordered as a punishment for Tunisian nationalists. This "mopping-up of Cape Bon" was a brutal and systematic attack on the people and property of the area immediately south of Tunis.[55] The men that Resident-General Hautecloque made responsible for this terror were General Garbay, known as "the pacifier of Madagascar," who was the superior commander in Tunisia, and Colonel Schmuckel, the commander in the

Tunis area. The troops were paratroopers destined for Indochina and a battalion of the Foreign Legion composed mainly of German soldiers, many of whom were veterans of the North African campaign of World War II. Cape Bon was chosen for several reasons: its proximity to Tunis offered little risk because it could easily be cut off from outside communication; it was an area in which Tunisian terrorists were numerous; it was a region of some property wealth. At seven A.M. the troops moved in, pillaging, wrecking, beating, and raping.

With communications cut some time passed before the horrible story was told, but a full investigation was conducted by the Chenik government, and a report signed by Doctor Materi and Dr. Ben Salem was made public on March 8.[56] The death toll was not high, but the misery was devastating. Over seven hundred Tunisians were arrested. Babies were thrown to the ground and many young girls and women were attacked. One excuse given by General Garbay for the atrocities was that "It is necessary chiefly not to forget that the local tradition exists that each passage of troop is accompanied by pillages, by rapes. . . . The rapes and the miscarriages are part of Tunisian folklore!"[57] When it did reach the world, the news aided the Tunisian cause in the United Nations. In the *Mission* Hedi Nouira reminded the French that the solution of the current problem "is not military, it is political."[58] Reaction was intense and protest strikes occurred all over Tunisia.

On March 21 Paris gave Hautecloque almost complete freedom to bring order in Tunisia. When asked about the Tunisian terror, Resident-General Hautecloque stated, "Although the Neo-Destour deny all solidarity with the Communist Party, the collusion of the two movements in the terrorist agitation which has shaken Tunisia for three months appears evident."[59] He also linked Bourguiba and Ferhat Hached with the campaign of terror. He quoted from Bourguiba's speech of January 13, 1952, when he declared, "it is necessary that blood flow."[60] These are strange accusations from a resident-general who ordered the "mopping-up" of Cape Bon.

While the problem was under discussion in the United Nations, the situation in Tunisia had not improved. The Neo-Destourians considered the ministry of Ben Mohammed Baccouche only a French puppet government. To Ben Youssef, Baccouche was a "quisling," and Ferhat Hached called him an "old feudal."[61] Furthermore, the circumstances surrounding the deposition of the Chenik government were strange. On March 26, 1952, Resident-General Hautecloque had given police powers to General Garbay, and without trial or regard for protocol, Prime Minister Chenik and many of his ministers were placed under house arrest in southern Tunisia. Although on March 22 the French government had given Hautecloque full power to get rid of Chenik's cabinet, neither Foreign Minister Robert Schuman nor Secretary of State Maurice Schuman thought he would use physical constraint.[62] Speaking of Hautecloque, Maurice Schuman said, "We are concerned about what he will do or mostly what his advisers will ask him to do. We do not want new measures of force, nor the deposition of the Bey. We battle on many fronts against the nationalists and against the 'colonists' and against the residence."[63]

In May the Pinay government sent an emissary to Tunis to urge the resident-general to open negotiations with the Tunisians and present new reforms proposed by Robert Schuman. The Bey, realizing the unpopularity of the Baccouche cabinet, appointed a committee of forty to study the new reform plan. Many influential Tunisian nationalists such as Ferhat Hached, Dr. Sadok Mokkaddem, Tahar Ben Ammar, and Aziz Djellouli served on this committee, which found the reforms ambiguous and advised the Bey to reject them. While the changes were concessions to Tunisian participation and power in the government, the nationalists felt they represented only a slight improvement. When asked about the reforms, even the moderate Prime Minister Baccouche could not be enthusiastic.

> I think that they are clearly insufficient. I do not believe that they are capable of satisfying the said demands.

The program of reforms proposed by France does not constitute a "dictate." It is only a base for amiable and sincere discussion between two friendly countries.[64]

Indeed little had changed; the terror increased during the summer of 1952, strikes were called in protest, and in the U.N. France stubbornly held to her previous position that Tunisia was a national issue beyond the competence of the General Assembly. From May to October seventeen assaults against Tunisians yielded only one arrest, while wholesale deportations of Tunisians followed each death of a European. A secret European terrorist organization called the "Red Hand" operated freely, distributing propaganda tracts, one of which was entitled "Ferhat Hached the American."[65] The year ended with the brutal and shocking assassination of Ferhat Hached, the secretary-general of the UGTT. A labor leader connected with international organizations, Ferhat Hached enjoyed a higher degree of immunity from arrest than other Tunisian nationalists. He was found on a road near Tunis, his body riddled with bullets and his car punctured with bullet holes. He was a martyr in the cause of Tunisian freedom, and his death gave greater drive and determination to the whole nationalist struggle. The American labor leader, George Meany, was stunned by the brutal murder of Hached and requested a U.N. investigation of this "grave threat to peace."[66] The guilty were not apprehended, and in September of 1953 Hedi Chaker, a Neo-Destourian leader, was assassinated under similar circumstances.

Political Prisons

The whole issue of widespread arrests, deportations, and concentration camp methods was raised by the UGTT in a request asking the International Commission against Concentration Regimes to investigate the situation in Tunisia. A letter sent by Mahmoud Messadi, deputy secretary-general of the UGTT, called attention both to the difficulty of getting access to the camps and to the inhumane treatment. The commission wrote to Resident-General Hautecloque for information. In his reply he told the commission that members of the UGTT had been arrested not for syndicalism but only for activities disturbing the political order.[67] Nevertheless, the commission asked to visit Tunisia, and M. Hautecloque consented, but added:

> I want to hope that this visit will be useless because I have the intention that a series of very liberal reforms on which I am working at this moment will be confirmed by the Bey to return to their family circles all the Tunisians who have been imprisoned, with the understandable exception of those under the charge of judicial proceedings for crimes, assaults, or offenses.[68]

On October 1, 1952, he announced that the plan had been implemented, but the "reforms" proved only that the wholesale arrest and detention of political prisoners had been carried on by the French. The assassination of Ferhat Hached speeded up the demand for the inquiry, and on January 17, 1953, David Rousset, president of the commission, arrived in Tunis along with three members of an investigating team. When the report appeared in March of 1953, the commission denied that France ran a concentration state in Tunisia, but it did point out that, to a degree, instances of concentration methods were evident. In some camps the food was very bad and hygienic conditions were terrible. There were cases of illegal arrests and torture. In regard to tortures the report stated:

> These processes are doubtless not sufficient to create a regime of concentration camps, but they give the regime a police or inquisitional character that is scandalous for a democratic nation.[69]

That French methods may not have been as bad as those of the Nazi regime was of little comfort to the Tunisian nationalists. Resident-General Hautecloque's only comment was that he refused to believe the "report of the tortures."[70] Beatings, electric shock, and other ingenious tortures were discovered by the commission. Actually the problem was a judicial one. By issuing a series of decrees France could order arrest for any political action which hindered the protectorate. If a person were jerked from his home in the middle of the night under one of these arrest orders, he had no judicial recourse or protection.[71] Resident-General Hautecloque's policies were not successful, and a long cabinet crisis in France in the spring of 1953 prolonged turmoil on both sides of the Mediterranean. After Sheikh Ahmed Belgaroui, who had cooperated with France, was brutally attacked, the resident-general put new security measures into effect and warned, "In case these measures prove to be insufficient, I have firmly decided to reinforce them as much as will be necessary."[72] He was definitely following his earlier "get tough" policy. These garrison state methods brought more attacks from the nationalists. The first meeting of the *Union Générale des Etudiants Tunisiens* (UGET) in Paris was held in July. This conference asked all young Tunisians, "of all walks of life, students and workers, to unite and to join the national struggle in order to reconquer our sovereignty and to seize our independence."[73] From his prison on the bleak island of La Galite Bourguiba sent encouragement to the UGET and attacked the policies of Hautecloque, which he called "a blow of the sword in water" and "foolish."[74] Bourguiba contended that France must negotiate with the Neo-Destour Party to retain *any* future influence in Tunisia.

Disillusionment clouded nationalist efforts. Tunisian nationalists had been disappointed by the moderate U.N. resolution, which merely called for negotiations. The United States was more concerned about getting France into the European Defense Community than about the struggle in North Africa. Nothing was done to ease the shock of Ferhat Hached's murder. To retaliate, the nationalists began a wave of assassinations. Chadly Kastailli, the moderate vice-president of the city council of Tunis, was slain on the street. Two Neo-Destourians, Hedi Nouira and Mohamed Masmoudi, were arrested and accused of complicity in the affair, although their guilt was not proven.[75] Only twenty-four hours after the Neo-Destour had requested new talks with France, the heir-apparent to the beylical throne, Prince Azzedine Bey, was slain. The party condemned this action, and three men were sentenced to death for the killing. The year 1953 ended with a grave situation in Tunisia.

After traveling in Tunisia during this period, the French writer Roger Stéphane wrote an interesting summary of the situtation.

> And yet, all travelers in Tunisia sense and discover that contact can be renewed: 6,000 prisoners, a leader assassinated [Hached], deaths daily, cities and villages "ravished," in a word the terror has not conquered the Tunisian people. Not vanquished, it has left intact their dignity and their willingness for conciliation. In spite of the incoherence of French policy, in spite of the use of force, the Tunisians are neither submissive nor inflexible. . . . They are still today disposed to speak. But it is necessary to hasten. Each day the irreparable could develop.[76]

The incoherence of French policy in North Africa was a direct reflection of serious political problems at home. As the seasoned French politician Paul Reynaud expressed it from the tribune of the Assembly, "France is the sick man of Europe. . . . She needs more reforms than those of 1789. . . ."[77] A series of cabinet crises plagued the country: from the fall of Henri Queuille's government on July 11, 1951, until the coming to power of Pierre Mendès-France on June 19, 1954, there were five separate governments and one hundred and ten days without a cabinet. The main issue that split France was the treaty of the European Defense Community (EDC), which was signed in May, 1952, but still not debated by the National Assembly, where it ran into all kinds of opposition. Would the plan ruin France's defense establishment? What would be the relationship of the French army to European defense? These and other questions led to heated debate. In his book on the Fourth Republic Jacques Fauvet attributes great importance to this issue.

> The E.D.C. divided the parties and even the men against each other. It helped to "atomize" French political life and, by this fact, to prepare the weakness, then the prostration of the regime, the decline and fall of the Fourth Republic.[78]

At home an internal crisis and labor strikes paralyzed France, and abroad the hopeless war in Indochina and the worsening situation in Morocco and Tunisia nearly forced the governmental machinery to a halt. Prime Minister Joseph Laniel turned his attention to the major problems of the EDC, North Africa, and Indochina, but his government did not submit the EDC to the assembly. In Tunisia he tried unsuccessfully to relax the tension, but in Morocco the deposition of Sultan Mohammed V led to a deterioration of that situation, and although some partition of Indochina seemed certain, the ignominious defeat of France at Dien-bien-phu brought the fall of Laniel's government on June 12, 1954.

Pierre Mendès-France was invested as prime minister on June 18, 1954. He pledged that he would end the war in Indochina, calm North Africa, and develop some accord over the EDC. Actually, the Laniel government had committed itself to the future conference of Geneva before the fall of Dien-bien-phu, but the government of Mendès-France received credit for the resulting accords on Indochina.

In Tunisia the terror continued. Habib Bourguiba, who had been transferred to France by the Laniel government, explained:

> If the Tunisian people are still in the battle . . . if blood still flows in Tunisia, if nuclei of armed resistance appear here and there in the South . . . it is because, in place of internal autonomy that they had been promised, one seeks to impose cosovereignty with the French colony on them, that is to say by the suppression in an indirect way of the Tunisian state.[79]

The United Nations

Frustration attended Tunisia's initial efforts to present its case to the United Nations. The secretary-general of the Neo-Destour, Salah Ben Youssef, and a party colleague, Mohammed Badra, went to Paris to prepare their case. At that time the French delegate, Jean Chauvel, was president of the United Nations Security Council. He said that since Tunisia was not a sovereign nation, only France had the right to represent this country in the world organization. The Tunisian delegates next asked Pakistan to present their case and declared that they were willing to abide by the Security Council decision. France then declared that it would walk out of the U.N. if the Tunisian question were introduced. In addition, France denied Ben Youssef and Badra permission to leave Paris for New York City. In March, after Premier Chenik and three close associates were arrested, Ben Youssef and Badra hurriedly left Paris for Cairo lest they too should be imprisoned. It would be nine months before any U.N. action was taken on Tunisia.

Many international problems clouded the world environment when the Tunisian question was finally brought before the United Nations. Some of these issues helped the Tunisians, but others tended to obscure or hamper their cause. Bourguiba considered the risk necessary and hoped that his years of travel throughout the world had familiarized enough nations with the Tunisian side of the North African question.

A brief look at the world situation will place the Tunisian dispute in its larger context. In the Far East the Korean War threatened to engulf East and West in world war, especially after June, 1952, when Chinese "volunteers" streamed into North Korea. In Indochina France had her own bloody war against Communist forces. The United States attitude on Tunisia strained relations with France. Ferhat Hached had been respected among American labor leaders, and earlier, after an international labor conference in the United States, he told his organization: "Hold fast for three more months. Under the pressure of the United States, France will be obliged to cede, and victory will be ours."[80]

However, France could resist American pressure in a period when the United States wanted above all to keep the NATO alliance strong. In May, 1952, the French ambassador in Washington, Henri Bonnet, told Secretary of State Dean Acheson that a few extremists in Tunisia were using terror to try to break up the relations between France and the United States.[81] By June the United States threatened to abstain if the Tunisian problem were brought before the United Nations General Assembly; and on June 12, 1952, Secretary of State Acheson said the United States recognized the interests of France in North Africa. Geographically speaking, the possession of North Africa by an enemy power would mean that Western Europe was outflanked. After studying statements in the American press, a Belgian journalist concluded that United States observers understood North Africa about as well as French reporters understood the events and conditions in Texas.[82] The United States, while posing as anticolonialist, still favored a bilateral solution of the problem, not wishing to alienate either side during a period of high international tension. In October, 1952, a *New York Times* article attacked the position of the African and Asiatic powers that represented the Tunisian cause in the United Nations.

> The position of France is solid . . . whoever is informed, and loyal, is not able to deny the admirable things that France has done for the Tunisians and the Moroccans and one is not able to refrain from being in accord with the French when they are conscious of the insults and attacks of certain countries of Asia who have refused to grant to their populations the rights and advantages that France accorded to the North Africans.[83]

In addition the American Scripps-Howard newspapers cautioned that France was a vital link in Western defense throughout the world.

Another important international area was North Africa itself. A revolution raged in Egypt, and by July, 1952, King Farouk had abdicated in favor of his son Ahmed-Fouad. One year later an Egyptian republic was established with Gamal Abdel Nasser as the leader of the new regime. Next door to Tunisia, Libya had been granted independence in December, 1952, encouraging Tunisian nationalist aspirations. Algerian nationalism was growing, and the long struggle with France was about to begin. The Moroccan situation had already been introduced into the United Nations. These complex problems were all involved in the internationalization of the Tunisian question.

As early as 1948 Georges Bidault, then foreign minister of France, warned his government not to try to solve the problems of Tunisia and Morocco unilaterally because, "we risk provoking an appeal to the United Nations. This would be madness on our part!"[84] On January 12, 1952, a carefully worded letter from Prime Minister Chenik introducing the dispute into the United Nations was sent to the president of the Security Council. The path of folly that Georges Bidault had predicted was taken. The Chenik letter called attention to the French note of December 15, which demanded "the participation of the French citizens in Tunisia—a foreign colony—in the working of the political institutions of Tunisia."[85] This, stated Chenik, was in contradiction with the provision of the Treaty of 12 May, 1881—which "maintained intact for His Highness the Bey the enjoyment and exercise of domestic sovereignty."[86] Chenik further stated that actions in Tunisia since 1881 clearly violated the spirit of the U.N. charter:

> To develop friendly relations among nations based on respect for the principle of equal rights and self-determination of peoples, and to take other appropriate measures to strengthen universal peace.[87]

Prime Minister Chenik concluded his letter with the request that Tunisia be permitted to participate in any U.N. discussion of the dispute. This led to some of the most fascinating and important debates ever conducted in the United Nations.

In presenting the Tunisian case a group of Arab and Asian members of the U.N. called for the liberation of Tunisian nationalist leaders held in various French prisons and for the immediate resumption of Franco-Tunisian negotiations. During February the Tunisian issue was lively in the United Nations and in Tunisia as well. On the home front street violence and protest strikes kept the French authorities busy, while French colons urged their government to resist Tunisian independence at all costs. As terror increased, French colons worked in the fields protected by armed guards. Dynamite blasts rocked Sousse, and the chief Neo-Destourian leaders in Le Kef and Gabes were arrested.

In March and April of 1952 the Tunisian issue was before the Security Council of the United Nations. Afganistan, Saudi Arabia, Burma, Egypt, India, Indochina, Iraq, Iran, Pakistan, the Philippines, and Yemen asked the council for a discussion of Tunisia, saying that the situation "menaced gravely the maintenance of international peace and security and falls therefore under the influence of article 34 of the Charter."[88] France maintained that it was not within the jurisdiction of the Security Council to discuss Tunisia. Its delegates argued that France's position in Tunisia was guaranteed by international treaty and that any U.N. interference would impair this treaty and encroach upon the legitimate foreign affairs of France. Within the Security Council itself Brazil, Chile, Nationalist China, and Russia said they would vote to put the matter on the agenda, but France, the United Kingdom, the United States, Turkey, Greece, and the Netherlands called for bilateral negotiations between France and Tunisia outside the United Nations. As a result, on April 14 the Security Council refused to place Tunisia on the agenda.

France declared itself willing to accept the idea of internal autonomy for Tunisia if it were accompanied by progressive reforms. When asked about Tunisian independence, French officials expressed doubt about the country's readiness. Robert Schuman cautioned that premature independence would place "in peril not only the legitimate interests of the French and others . . . but the further developments of these same territories [Tunisia and Morocco] that we are not able to turn over to adventure and anarchy."[89] Tunisian nationalists found this charge particularly odious. Bourguiba stated that it was absurd to consider Tunisia less ready for independence than Vietnam, Laos, and Cambodia and His Highness Lamine Bey less qualified than men like Norodom Sihanouk or Bao Dai. In France, François Mitterrand of the *Union Démocratique et Socialiste de la résistance* Party (UDSR), who had long been critical of French policy in Tunisia, blasted the government charge of prematurity in North Africa:

> Tunisia and Morocco—do they have an institutional organization less free than Gabon, or Oubanghi, or Kenya, or the Sudan?
> The French Union will only be a reality if it offers more civic liberty and progress. If not millions of men will look elsewhere for their destiny.[90]

By the summer of 1952 the Arab-Asian nations were joined by Lebanon and Syria, and all thirteen asked to have the Tunisian question discussed in the United Nations General Assembly. Their memorandum of July 20 accused the French of installing a resident-general with full powers as a head of state in violation of the treaties of Bardo and La Marsa. France exploited Tunisian land, colonized the country, then terrorized all who protested. All legitimate attempts to be independent were met with force. The Arab and Asian countries protested further:

> Since April, 1952, therefore, French authorities have not taken any successful step towards either the restoration of civil liberties or the beginning of negotiations. On the other hand, the tension in Tunisia has increased and there is a deep sense of frustration among people in many countries of the world and especially in the Asian and African countries.[91]

Although a special session of the General Assembly was requested, the issue was added to the agenda for the regular fall session. France based her case on the incompetence of the U.N. according to Paragraph 7, Article 2 of the charter, which reads:

> Nothing contained in the present Charter shall authorize the United Nations to intervene in matters which are essentially within the domestic jurisdiction of any state or shall require the members to submit such matters to settlement under the present Charter; but this principle shall not prejudice the application of enforcement measures under Chapter VII (Action with Respect to Threats to the Peace, Breaches of the Peace, and Acts of Aggression) .[92]

The French government decided that it would not allow any interference by the United Nations in the Tunisian and Moroccan problems and ordered its delegation to walk out when the subject was brought before the session. In November Foreign Minister Schuman had a conference with Secretary of State Acheson at the U.N., and the United States adopted the French point of view. Actually the United Nations became so preoccupied with the Korean crisis that North Africa received less attention than the situation warranted. In December the debate on Tunisia was centered in the Political Committee of the General Assembly, where the Arab-Asian motion was rejected in favor of a more moderate Latin American motion. The motion resulted in the first United Nations General Assembly resolution on Tunisia, which was passed on December 17, 1952. It embodied the Latin American motion, which asked France and Tunisia to negotiate their differences and in the meantime to refrain from provocative acts.[93] The resolution implied that negotiations would lead to Tunisian self-government. Dean Acheson and U.S. Ambassador Philip C. Jessup strongly supported the Latin American resolution. In doing so, they claimed to support solutions instead of revolutions and declared that they believed in the sincerity of France in Tunisia.

France persistently refused to recognize the power of the General Assembly to interfere in what it declared was a national affair.[94] This position was based on the contention that the charter of the United Nations does not authorize the General Assembly to recommend the revision of treaties nor examine the treaties of a protectorate. Interestingly enough, both Tunisia and France took refuge in different aspects of the treaties of Bardo and La Marsa. Tunisia argued that the treaties recognized a Tunisian sovereignty which the Regency had never renounced, and France maintained that the treaties gave her a legitimate right in Tunisia, which made the issue strictly a national one out of the realm of U.N. review. Actually both sides apparently realized that the treaties were outmoded and needed to be revised or abolished. The U.N. justified its action on the basis that the Tunisian problem represented a threat to international peace and security. Madame Pandit, representing India, expressed U.N. sentiment as follows:

> In the presence of events so sorrowful as the dastardly assassination of M. Ferhat Hached, it is permissible to state that Tunisia constitutes today an area of trouble which threatens to extend well beyond its frontiers and to constitute a veritable menace to peace if one does not seek to relieve this situation in time.[95]

Shortly after the General Assembly passed the resolution of December, 1952, Bourguiba wrote to Mohamed Masmoudi, who represented the Neo-Destour in Paris, that France had already violated the resolution by attempts to control the Bey. These were provocative acts condemned by the United Nations resolution, concluded Bourguiba.

There was not enough big power support for the United Nations to do more than urge a bilateral solution to the problem. Once again, in the fall of 1953, Tunisia was debated in the Political Committee. On September 19 France walked out of the General Assembly meeting because the delegates were debating the Moroccan and Tunisian issues, and in November the frustrated General Assembly rejected all recommendations on Tunisia.[96] Finally, on December 17, 1954, the General Assembly passed a resolution on Tunisia which turned out to be a permanent postponement of the issue:

> *Noting with satisfaction* that the parties concerned have entered into negotiations and that these negotiations are still in progress,
>
> *Expressing confidence* that the said negotiations will bring about a satisfactory solution,
>
> Decides to postpone for the time being further consideration of this item.[97]

Frustration, stalemate, and lost motion characterized the situation in 1954. In Tunisia the antagonists were deadlocked over the issue of internal autonomy vs. independence; neither side would compromise. The United Nations, preoccupied with other world problems, merely encouraged France and Tunisia to work out their own solution. The deadlock could have lasted a long time had it not been for a bold reform move that grew in France and would eventually be executed by Prime Minister Pierre Mendès-France.

6

From Rapprochement to Republic, 1954-1959

Abortive March Reforms

One necessity for improving Tunisian-French relations was the replacement of Resident-General Hautecloque. "Jean le Terrible must go," shouted the Tunisians. In the face of Parisian indecision Hautecloque and the colons had carried on an independent policy which shocked even the French. The resident-general's policies having failed miserably, Foreign Minister Georges Bidault asked the Council of Ministers to approve Pierre Voizard as the new resident-general. A lively discussion developed in the council, with François Mitterrand, Edgar Faure, and Pierre-Henri Tietgen maintaining that France should have a new reform program for Tunisia and then choose the man to implement it. Nevertheless, Voizard was appointed without a new plan and Mitterrand resigned from the ministry in protest.

In the meantime, however, Voizard was denied broad powers of independent action upon his arrival in Tunis in September, 1953. The reception of the new resident-general was bitter: both French colons and Tunisian nationalists jeered and spat at him. His first task was to reduce tension by lessening the most flagrant affronts of the garrison state;[1] police powers were returned to civilian control, censorship was stopped, certain restrictions on the Sahel region were lifted, and twenty-two political prisoners were released.[2] In January Resident-General Voizard announced that political reforms would save the day before the end of the year. Prophetic as this was, the reforms that finally led to Tunisian independence were not the ones introduced by Voizard but the Declaration of Carthage, which came later.

The first reforms proposed in March seemed to be ill-fated from the beginning. The resident-general left for Paris in February, promising to return with a reform program. Meanwhile, in anticipation of reform, a new government was established in Tunisia under the premiership of Mohammed Salah M'Zali, who had held many government posts since 1918: *caid* of Bizerte, minister of commerce and handicrafts (1947 to 1950), and minister of commerce and industry in the Chenik cabinet (1950 to 1952). His government contained some moderate nationalists but no Neo-Destourians. Upon the installation of this government, Mohammed Lamine Bey told the Tunisian people:

> As the Tunisian government now enjoys our absolute confidence and is determined to devote its every effort and its undivided attention to the public welfare and to our country's future, we call on all patriots to unite with us in order that God may crown our action with success.[3]

This time, however, Bourguiba greeted French promises of reform with skepticism and seriously doubted that France had changed its basic position:

> France will not be able to retain her African position and her world position if she does not refrain from violence on a small

peaceful people who, experience has proven, will not allow themselves to be swallowed up by force *nor by trickery* but experience still proves, is ready to deal freely with France in measures where she is spared her dignity and her sovereignty is respected.[4]

When revealed, the March reforms called for changes in the executive, legislative, and communal structures of Tunisia. More Tunisians were to be brought into the Council of Ministers, over which the Tunisian prime minister would preside, independent of the surveillance of the French secretary-general. A Tunisian assembly having deliberative and consultative power would be elected by universal suffrage; however, for budgetary talks a delegation representing the French in Tunisia would attend and have equal representation with the Tunisians. Provision was also made for provincial, municipal, and local councils.[5] In introducing the reforms M. Voizard warned, "To those who say this is too much, or this is not enough, my answer is that you must judge the tree by its fruit and, in judging this fruit, you will be judging yourselves for it will be essentially your work."[6]

Judged by many people, the reforms were found wanting. Once again the questions of cosovereignty, double nationality, and government by partnership were raised but not settled. The plan created an unequal partnership, with France retaining the reins of power. The French writer André de la Far called the reforms "the best arrangements that we are able to have in the present circumstances."[7] The measures pleased the French and Tunisian moderates, but radical Neo-Destourians and French colons were contemptuous of the plan. The resident-general who later succeeded Voizard, General Boyer de La Tour, declared that the Neo-Destour would have accepted the March reforms if France had not been vulnerable because of Indochina and frequent cabinet crises. General Boyer de La Tour felt that Mendès-France need not have gone so far in making concessions to the Tunisians. Instead he favored a program like the March reforms which "would have been able to accord a respite of several years."[8] The general's claim seems highly unlikely, since Resident-General Voizard had alienated the Neo-Destour, and some Tunisian party leaders had condemned the reforms as early as April 2—over a month before the fall of Dien-bien-phu. "The Tunisian people will never accept cosovereignty with the French colony," announced Bourguiba from a French prison in May.[9] Furthermore, he pointed out, the proposed assembly would have only consultative power; the French still proposed to retain "all the levers of command."[10] The French jurist Carmel Tabone said that the March reforms advanced the thesis of double nationality, which was "a sociological monstrosity."[11]

Once more the situation deteriorated: the reforms were inadequate, the new M'Zali government did not have Neo-Destourian support, and Resident-General Voizard failed to see that only negotiations with the Neo-Destour Party had any chance of success. Chaos broke out. This time the Tunisian *fellaghas* struck with greater intensity throughout the land. From March through July the victims of the terror included 74 civilians killed and 67 wounded, and 21 killed, 52 wounded, and 5 missing among police and security guards.[12] The *fellagha* terrorist movement began in 1952 with the dismissal of the Chenik ministry. Most *fellaghas* were militant and dedicated Neo-Destourians, many of them illiterate. Some were the uprooted who found a cause to fight for; others were ruffians or former brigands. Their leaders were men in various parts of Tunisia able to inflame, inspire, and direct bands. In the Gafsa region the leader was Lazhar Chraiti, a veteran of the war in Palestine, who was the only leader with military training. Sassi Lassoued led *fellaghas* near Le Kef. By 1954 a closer cooperation had developed between the *fellaghas* and the party, and about 1,200 combatants roamed Tunisia distributing propaganda or attacking. If enough arms could have been obtained, the number would surely have been larger.

In a French prison Bourguiba was questioned about the terror by *Paris-Match,* to which he replied, "all the regrettable acts and what will happen in the future are a normal and predictable reaction against the violence of the French authorities."[13] The reporter then asked Bourguiba why he had returned the cordon of *Nicham Iftikhar* given to him by the Bey in 1950. He explained that it was a protest against the Bey's acceptance of the March reforms, which only prolonged Tunisia's agony. Bourguiba made it clear that the Neo-Destour would not accept less than a Tunisian government with its own institutions and an elected assembly to carry out the Destourian program. "Tenacity" was party policy. The Neo-Destour would not accept the March reforms because they were not even a step in the right direction; this was consistent with the theory of Bourguibism. Anarchy threatened as *fellagha* attacks grew in intensity; travel was curtailed; terror lurked at every turn; and Europeans avoided the Arab medinas.

Declaration of Carthage

In 1954 Pierre Mendès-France became the new premier of France. He promptly declared that he would not tolerate delays in the fulfillment of promises made to people who had faith in France. Along with Marshal Alphonse Juin, General Boyer de La Tour (the new resident-general), and Christian Fouchet (minister for Moroccan and Tunisian affairs), Mendès-France visited the Bey and made the Declaration of Carthage on July 31, 1954. This short trip profoundly altered the course of Tunisian history. "The self-government of the Tunisian state is recognized and proclaimed without reservation by the French government," declared the prime minister.[14] However, he called for continued French influence in Tunisia and for a common foreign policy. In addition he asked for conventions to regulate relations between the two countries and concluded, "Immediately after the conclusion of these conventions, self-government will be an indisputable fact, there being no restriction or limitation other than those arising out of the conventions themselves."[15] Mendès-France deplored the violence and bloodshed in Tunisia and warned the Tunisians:

> Like you, I have the right to hope that an end will now be
> put to these acts of violence. If it should become necessary to
> employ further means to subdue them, the French government
> will not hesitate to send all the reinforcements necessary; if it
> should become necessary to have recourse to Draconian measures
> to keep the peace, it will do so with regret.[16]

In a Tunis café a Frenchman was heard to exclaim disgustedly,
"So, just like that, they gave them internal autonomy."[17] Hoping to quiet a storm of protest, General de La Tour reminded
French colons that France had promised Tunisia internal autonomy for a long time. He also pointed out that France had
introduced to the Tunisians the idea of political liberty.

In Tunisia the M'Zali government offered its resignation, a
move welcomed by the nationalists, and the Bey asked a political independent, Tahar Ben Ammar,[18] to form a government
to negotiate the "transfer to Tunisian men and institutions
the exercise of internal sovereignty."[19] Resident-General Boyer
de La Tour, cautious about how much autonomy Tunisia
should have, especially in a period of *fellagha* terror, issued
an order: "The right to requisition for lodging and quartering
of troops will be exercised beginning September 13 in all the
territory of the Regency."[20] Nevertheless, the leaders in Paris
had determined that a political settlement must be reached
regardless of the terror. Bourguiba praised the new government in Tunisia, which was composed of various national
political factions, and concluded, "This ministry of national
union and reconciliation will benefit those who place the
salvation of the fatherland above everything else."[21]

The French National Assembly approved Mendès-France's
Tunisian policy by 451 to 122, but the real success of the pro-
gram depended upon its reception by influential groups in
Tunisia. A number of French intellectuals under the influ-
ence of Dr. Etienne Burnet[22] and two former civil controllers,
Henri de Montety and Charles Saumagne, urged cooperation

between French and Tunisians to implement the reforms. Neo-Destourian leaders also received the proposals optimistically. After studying the Declaration of Carthage, Bourguiba called it a substantial step in the direction of the complete sovereignty of Tunisia. Tahar Ben Ammar's government included four influential Neo-Destourians: Mongi Slim and Mohamed Masmoudi as ministers of state, Hedi Nouira as minister of commerce, and Sadok Mokkaddem as minister of justice. The rest of the cabinet contained five independents and one Socialist. From his exile in Cairo, Salah Ben Youssef expressed confidence in the new government and felt the declaration offered a good basis for negotiation.

Not all voices were favorable. In Cairo the Muslim Brothers accused the Neo-Destour of going back on an agreement to struggle for the liberation of the entire Mahgreb:

> The acceptance of internal government for Tunisia constitutes high treason and a conspiracy against the liberation movement. We are profoundly disturbed by the appeal of Habib Bourguiba to the Tunisian people recommending the acceptance of the Mendès-France program.[23]

It is interesting that later Ben Youssef was also to take this position and to fight within the party to preserve a program for the entire Maghreb. In Tunisia the Old Destour Party, although weak, was skeptical about the Declaration of Carthage, charging that "the range and the substance of internal autonomy" were greatly limited by French demands of close Tunisian adhesion to the French Union.[24] This was an ambiguous and largely unfounded criticism. The French colons also vehemently protested the move by Pierre Mendès-France. Nevertheless, the machinery leading toward internal autonomy would grind over all opposition as the Neo-Destour put its weight behind the plan.

Tunisian-French Negotiations

Prime Minister Tahar Ben Ammar promised to use internal autonomy to establish "a democratic regime guaranteeing justice and security for all."[25] The new minister pleased the French by declaring that "Tunisian sovereignty one and without division was not at all incompatible with French presence in Tunisia."[26] He never expressed the ultimate goal of complete independence that Bourguiba envisaged. Nor did he pose the threat to French influence in Tunisia that the Destourians posed; therefore, he was considered an acceptable negotiator by the French government. When negotiations opened in September, the chief Tunisian delegates were Tahar Ben Ammar, Mongi Slim, and Mohamed Masmoudi.

Pierre Mendès-France was preoccupied with the National Assembly debate on the EDC. Although the president of the Council did not like some aspects of German rearmament, his government was committed to the defense of the EDC treaty. The forces against the treaty were strong, and the debate took on such importance that Mendès-France left Christian Fouchet in charge of the Tunisian negotiations. But because Fouchet was without instructions, little progress was made. When the EDC treaty was rejected, the prestige of Mendès-France's government was weakened, and the forthcoming debate on North Africa would prove fatal to the government.

Algerian nationalists put pressure on France after the defeat at Dien-bien-phu in Indochina, and the Tunisian negotiations encouraged even greater Algerian unrest. After a heated debate the government policy was rejected by a vote of 319 to 273.[27] President Coty realized that the new prime minister must have a liberal Tunisian policy or all North Africa might burst into flame. Mainly for this reason, he asked Edgar Faure to form a new government. With only Communists and Socialists in opposition, the new cabinet was invested on February 23 and negotiations on Tunisia were resumed. Edgar Faure knew Tunisia. During the war he traveled the bicycle paths along the Gulf of Hammamet, and he and his wife had shown sympathy for the cause of the Tunisian nationalists.

Many frustrating obstacles discouraged the Tunisian negotiations. The *fellagha* bands in the Tunisian mountains paid little attention to the Paris talks and continued their terror

against French colons. It was difficult to convince these un-
disciplined hordes that the time for negotiation had come.
Terror and banditry must spend their momentum. Forty-one
killed and thirty-two taken prisoner was the *fellagha* report
for September. In desperation, Resident-General Boyer de La
Tour offered amnesty to the *fellaghas*. Although the Neo-
Destourian leaders denounced individual acts of terrorism,
they cautiously avoided a condemnation of general military
actions. Mohamed Masmoudi spoke of the *fellaghas* as "our
brother combatants, wherever they are found."[28] In the event
that negotiations collapsed, the Neo-Destour had a card to
play—the resumption of terror. It was difficult for the Tunisian
officials to repudiate the *fellaghas* completely without weakening the resistance movement. Finally, concerted Franco-Tunisian action was taken. A committee of forty-four, half Tunisian
and half French, was charged with arranging an amnesty if the
fellaghas would surrender their arms. The twenty-two Tunisians were professional men who had been protesting the terror
for years. Not all of the mountain leaders cooperated, but the
majority did. One such leader, Lazhar Chraiti, issued a statement of reconciliation:

> This accord has been approved by the Tunisian people, by
> the intermediary of the leaders of their party. In our turn,
> we approve the application of the contents of the common
> declaration of the two governments. . . . We have confidence
> in the negotiations of the two governments for our security,
> that of our families and of our liberty.[29]

The winter of 1954-55 saw the *fellagha* movement gradually
disintegrate.

Another period of uncertainty set in for Tunisian nationalists when Salah Ben Youssef in Cairo began to adopt the position of the Muslim Brothers and questioned the sincerity of
France. Ahmed Ben Salah, who was in charge of the Neo-Destourian office in New York, feared precious gains toward autonomy were slipping through the hands of the negotiators.
In Paris Bourguiba's book, *La Tunisie et la France,* became

the center of controversy when Gabriel Puaux, one of the senators representing the French in Tunisia, called it a new *Mein Kampf*. Bourguiba nevertheless remained optimistic, because he felt that internal autonomy would surely open the way to eventual independence.

However, more difficulties faced the negotiators in Paris. The new government seemed less eager than its predecessor to move ahead with the talks. Edgar Faure's government appeared to be influenced more by the French in Tunisia. Disagreement arose over the proposed court of arbitration and the prerogative of using the French language. As the negotiations became more tedious, the newspapers alternately reported breakdown, then renewal, of the talks. Finally, both Bourguiba and Faure took more responsibility, and their meeting on April 21 led to a protocol registering agreement on the main texts under discussion.[30] The details were left for discussion on a lower echelon of the two governments. Groups opposing the accords fought a bitter, but losing, battle. In Tunis French terrorists beat 82-year-old Dr. Etienne Burnet with an iron bar because he supported the talks. In Rome Salah Ben Youssef declared, "The Tunisian people reject these conventions. They decided to stop them by all means in their power. In consequence to sign them or impose them is definitely to make war on him [Ben Youssef]."[31]

After the agreements were ready to be signed, Bourguiba prepared to return to Tunis, but not before he made it clear that his ultimate goal was Tunisian independence. In the following statement we have the essence of the familiar Bourguiba method:

> We know that independence must be reconciled with interdependence between countries linked by permanent and superior interests. In the scrupulous enactment of the conventions, in the respect of the sovereignty of each state and the dignity of each people, we hope to find formulas which will be consecrated, by a free association, to the friendship and solidity of the two countries.[32]

His statement was remarkably free of malice toward a country that had imprisoned him three times for political beliefs.

The negotiations lasted until the Franco-Tunisian Conventions were signed on June 3, 1955. While Ben Ammar led the Tunisian negotiations, Habib Bourguiba played an important role behind the scenes. Held in six different prisons since his arrest in 1952, Bourguiba was finally moved to a supervised residence in Paris, where he was permitted to confer with the Tunisian delegation.

Bourguiba's Return

Tumultuous celebrations greeted Bourguiba's return to Tunis in 1955. As the "City of Algiers" steamed into the channel of the Lake of Tunis, people waving frantically were jammed on anything that could float until the lake became a mass of upturned faces. As far as Bourguiba could see from the bow of the ship the frenzy surrounded him and the piercing "yew, yew, yew" shout of the women echoed across the water. Crowds lined the shores, climbed poles, and carried banners reading "Welcome to Bourguiba," "To Our Supreme Fighter," "To Our Father," "To Our Brother," "To Our President." One local newspaper estimated the crowd at over 400,000 persons.[33] When he stepped ashore, Bourguiba was mobbed, and revelry lasted through June 1 and 2, two days which are now celebrated as national days in Tunisia.

The six conventions forming the settlement between Tunisia and France were signed on June 3, 1955. A primary or general convention established the following lines of authority.

> From the date of the ratification of the present conventions, France recognizes and proclaims the self-government of Tunisia, which shall have no restrictions or limitations other than those resulting from the provisions of the present conventions and of the conventions now in force, it being understood that, in the fields of defense and foreign affairs, the present state of things shall continue and matters shall be dealt with as they have been up until this day.[34]

In retrospect the amount of hardship, frustration, and despair that went into the simple clause "France recognizes and proclaims the self-government of Tunisia" is almost unimaginable. In matters of defense and security France retained power, and any matter of disagreement would be submitted to a Council of Arbitration staffed equally by the two powers. Later an additional member, who could be French, Tunisian, or of another nationality, was added to the council.

A Convention on the Status of Persons protected the personal status of French nationals residing in Tunisia and defined French and Tunisian nationality. France still maintained judicial power in Tunisia in cases involving a French national or a non-Tunisian. In most instances, however, cases involving Tunisians alone came under the jurisdiction of Tunisian courts.

Close cooperation between the two governments was provided for by a convention dealing with technical and administrative matters. It covered the fields of government and private contracts, health and medicine, civil aviation, and radio and television broadcasting.[35]

Education was the main concern of the Cultural Convention. While Tunisia was given the privilege of defining the "objectives, structure, curricula, diploma requirements and administration of education in Tunisia,"[36] the French retained schools for those who wished to use them. A mixed commission composed of three French and three Tunisians was established to administer this agreement.

Last, an Economic and Financial Convention kept Tunisia within the franc area and created a customs union to enhance trade between the two countries. Private investments in Tunisia were also facilitated by this pact.

After the conventions were signed, Bourguiba, as president of the Neo-Destour, made a triumphal tour of southern Tunisia, receiving ovations everywhere. However, the thunder of criticism still echoed in Cairo, where Salah Ben Youssef denounced the conventions as "dangerous and compromising irremediably the future of our nation."[37] This was a hint of a bitter intraparty struggle that would develop after Ben Youssef returned to Tunis. Besides Ben Youssef, others condemned the agreements. Some Old Destourians and Communists complained that Bourguiba cooperated too closely with France, but the most violent opposition came from the French colons. Blaming the United States for supporting the agreement, French terrorists bombed the United States Information Service building in Tunis and tried to blow up the home of Howard Hill, the American vice-consul.[38] Despite opposition, Tunisian home rule passed the French National Assembly 540 to 43. Prime Minister Edgar Faure predicted:

> The days of colonialism are over, but the era of partnership has begun. Our old country, which has accepted limitations on its sovereignty, has sufficient authority to ask the same attitude of peoples that do not yet have their sovereignty.[39]

The final ratification and signing ceremonies for the conventions were held in August. The Tunisian newspaper *Le Petit Matin* dedicated its entire front page to the signing with pictures of the principal figures in the negotiations.[40]

With the abolishment of the office of resident-general, Roger Seydoux was named French High Commissioner in Tunis, a position that did not hold a fraction of the power of the old resident-general. At the same time France announced six billion francs in financial aid to Tunisia. The Neo-Destour Party took advantage of the amicable climate to urge France to allow the return of the exiled Sultan Mohammed V of Morocco. The party appealed

> to the government, to the people of France, and to the international conscience in order that they put an end to a policy of force and put in its place a policy based on negotiation and free understanding.[41]

France announced that a solution of the Moroccan situation was imminent.

Ben Youssef vs. Bourguiba

A full-scale power struggle developed in the Neo-Destour Party after Salah Ben Youssef returned amid ovations in the fall of 1955 and ended with his flight from Tunisia in 1956. "The Neo-Destour, it is I," he boldly announced.[42] Attacks on the conventions and appeals for a program for all of North Africa were the mainstays of Ben Youssef's radical approach. Two able, dynamic, and ambitious men stood facing each other; since neither was accustomed to retreating, a lively battle was inevitable. Ben Youssef wanted a program that would wrest party leadership from Bourguiba. He decided upon an emotional pan-Arabic appeal and a denunciation of the agreements as fragmented and weak. Yet Bourguiba could proudly point to a settlement that brought Tunisia a long stride closer to eventual independence. Bourguiba sought support from the young militants in the party, while Ben Youssef tried to gain influence through the agricultural syndicate, *Union Générale Agriculteur de Tunisie* (UGAT). The experience of each antagonist was reflected in his program. Ben Youssef had been in Cairo, where the whole North African problem was considered as a unit, and Bourguiba was on the "firing line" in Tunisia or in a French prison, where all seemed to hinge on the Tunisian fight with France.

As secretary-general of the party, Ben Youssef took every opportunity to press the attack. In a public address at the Grand Mosque he said that the conventions "in legalizing all that colonialism usurped since 1881 had established the protectorate regime on more solid bases."[43] "Only the people should have the last word, reject the conventions," Ben Youssef told six thousand Muslims, and "remain united in order to obtain the complete independence of Tunisia, Algeria, and Morocco."[44] The Political Bureau of the party dismissed Ben Youssef as secretary-general and canceled his party membership. In spite of the severe reversal he doggedly pressed for a program creating freedom for all the Maghreb. The Youssefists published a telegram that the Algerian and Moroccan delegation at the U.N. had sent to Ben Youssef thanking him for requesting that the Algerian problem be discussed in the United Nations.

In November at Kairouan Buorguiba launched a verbal blow at Ben Youssef.

> We find in the Ben Youssef position the same utopia, the same unrealism and empty extremism of the Old Destourians: the same demagoguery against which he has struggled when he was in our ranks.[45]

The strategy in the battle became quite clear as a party congress was announced for November 15, 1955, in Sfax. Ben Youssef needed a substantial boycott of the congress because he was not strong enough to win a floor fight at the meeting. He therefore struck hard at the party leadership, charging, "The Political Bureau . . . is a band of criminals, gangsters and Fascists."[46] However, Bourguiba's oratory appealed to the strong feeling of loyalty that people had for him, "You know that I do not have any ambition. . . . Our brother Destourians, executed last year on the shores of Lake Sedjoumi, cried in dying, 'Vive Bourguiba.' I will always do everything to merit this confidence."[47]

The Youssefists established their Tunis headquarters at 23 rue Al Djazira on the edge of the medina and organized their attack. They traveled around Tunisia asking various Neo-Destour cells to boycott the congress. Violence erupted at a cell meeting in Melassine, and several Destourian groups published telegrams in the newspapers asking for a reconciliation between the two factions. Not only did the boycott fail, but at the opening session of the congress Bourguiba undercut some of the Youssefist propaganda by calling for a new era throughout North Africa. Salah Ben Youssef presented his ideas to the congress, but his views were not reflected in the action of the party. The congress proclaimed that "implemented in a spirit of free cooperation and in accordance with historical evolution, the June 3, 1955, conventions mark an important step along the road to independence."[48] It was a clear victory for Bourguiba.

After the congress Ben Youssef's position became desperate, and riots erupted wherever he went. Telegrams appeared in the newspapers protesting his visits and asking him to stay away. Violence swirled about his headquarters on the rue Al Djazira. He decided on a last-ditch attempt and requested a new party congress to be held in January. On two counts the Political Bureau denied his plea: first, it came from an illegal party, and second, it would create public disorder.[49] Immediately forty Youssefists were arrested and brought before a special criminal court; Ben Youssef escaped to Libya. Arms were discovered in a raid on his home, Youssefist newspapers were suspended, and about 120 more people were arrested throughout the country.[50] The complete crackdown had come.

Without real hope of success Ben Youssef carried on his opposition from Cairo, where in June of 1956 he was officially recognized as chief of a liberation army by the Tunisian section of the Bureau of the Maghreb. However, in Tunisia Minister of the Interior Mehiri confidently announced, "In two months the last vestiges of Youssefists have been liquidated, and all danger coming from this side has been erased."[51] Refusing to be "erased," Ben Youssef proposed a "sacred union" with Bourguiba in October:

> That because of exceptional, historical circumstances for Tunisia, the Maghreb and the Arab countries, all differences be resolved between the partisans of the opposition and those of the government, from which will be formed henceforth a single patriotic front.[52]

The ruling Neo-Destour saw no reason to accept a possible enemy back in its ranks now that it was free from political opposition. On January 24, 1957, Salah Ben Youssef and six of his followers were condemned to death in absentia for treason. One curious meeting did take place in Zurich, Switzerland, in March, 1961, between Habib Bourguiba and Salah Ben Youssef, but no reconciliation or agreement was reached.

The death penalty was carried out in Frankfurt, Germany on August 14, 1961. Ben Youssef and his wife were in Wiesbaden, Germany, when they received a call to come to Frankfurt. They arrived about 4:30 P.M., and after leaving his wife in a restaurant, Ben Youssef met two men in the hotel lobby. They went to a room from which the two men emerged thirty minutes later, telling the hotel clerk they would return. When her husband had not returned by 8 P.M., Mrs. Ben Youssef was taken to the room, where she found him gasping for breath with a bullet wound behind his left ear. He died later at a hospital, at the age of 51. The two men, plus a third who was an interpreter, left Frankfurt with Tunisian passports and Swiss visas. Herr Wolf, a police official in Frankfurt, has stubbornly refused to identify the men.[53]

This was the end of Salah Ben Youssef but not of the Youssefist movement. In December, 1962, while President Bourguiba was in Le Kef, there was a plot to assassinate him. Captain Kabair Mehrezi, one of the instigators of the plan, was a member of the president's personal bodyguard. He knew the password and planned to lead the assassins to the bedroom where Bourguiba would be murdered in his sleep. At the last minute a sergeant in the army revealed the plot to the authorities in time to save the president's life. Later, speaking of the plot against his life, Bourguiba mentioned the Youssefists as one implicated group. "They do not hesitate before any alliance: sheikhs of the Grand Mosque, East, West, all is good if they find there support for their thesis, support for their work of undermining. Always looking for discontents. Always prompt to exploit the workers of hate and rancor. These men have not disarmed." The president further complained, "The debris of the Youssefist movement are henceforth on our frontiers in Algeria."[54]

After gaining internal autonomy, the Tunisians worked vigorously to fulfill their new opportunities. With Tahar Ben

Ammar as president of the Council, an all-Tunisian ministry was created in September, 1955. Aspirations ran high among the nationalists; the present looked bright and the future promising. The acquisition of internal autonomy meant that Tunisia was one stage closer to complete independence. Actually, internal autonomy lasted only about two hundred days before independence was acquired. France certainly had not contemplated this rapid transition. "Autonomy yes, independence no," said Christian Fouchet, the minister of Moroccan and Tunisian affairs.[55] In speaking of the coming negotiations on Tunisia, Pierre Mendès-France emphatically stated, "This union of France and Tunisia, we want indissoluble. . . ." He assured the government of "our willingness to oppose today, tomorrow and always secession or anything leading to it."[56] During his trip to Carthage Pierre Mendès-France had asked the Bey to approve reforms that would assure the lasting presence of France in Tunisia.[57]

Internal Autonomy to Independence

Various factors generated the climate which made Tunisian independence possible. The French had confidence in Tahar Ben Ammar, who was a moderate nationalist and an owner of large estates. He was not one to act detrimentally to the interests of France. In the French National Assembly debates on Tunisia, Prime Minister Edgar Faure read a statement by Ben Ammar:

> The Tunisia of tomorrow will be a constitutional monarchy. Monarchial power clothed with democratic principle will be this moderate and conciliatory force indispensable for the equilibrium of our young state. . . .
> The front of our institutions will carry the words "Liberty, Tolerance, Social Justice." We go along with the principle of legitimate monarchy, pledged to stability, to the principle of democratic legitimacy, pledged to liberty.[58]

He then urged the assembly to act with confidence in Tahar Ben Ammar and the institutions of Tunisia. The atmosphere of trust led to cooperation on the local level that actually went beyond the conventions in matters of police power. Local negotiations were in accordance with future independence, because internal autonomy and independence were synonymous at that level of government.

Although Youssefists and others wanted immediate independence, Bourguiba made it clear that he was willing to use time and political finesse to accomplish the objective. It is hard to slow extremism in any revolutionary struggle, and impractical as many of the Youssefist ideas were, they had appeal for the uneducated. Also, some intellectuals within the party and the UGTT argued that independence was necessary before radical economic planning was possible. The dynamic idea of a country being master of its own fate was a powerful force, whether its origin was Youssefist or radical Neo-Destourian. Bourguiba, as president of the Neo-Destour, could not move too slowly in the face of Youssefist pressures without forfeiting his role as the architect of Tunisian independence.

The Moroccan situation from 1953 to 1956 had an important effect on the independence movement in Tunisia. The arrest and exile of Sultan Mohammed V in 1953 had created a serious situation. The six conventions signed by Edgar Faure giving Tunisia internal autonomy further aggravated the Moroccan problem. The Moroccan nationalists observed the second anniversary of the sultan's exile by the massacre at Oued-Zem, which took the lives of forty-nine French, including fifteen children. General Boyer de La Tour, his mission finished in Tunis, was sent as resident-general to Morocco to negotiate the difficulty. Prime Minister Faure favored the restoration of the sultan, and finally, on November 16, 1955, two years and three months after his exile, Mohammed V made a triumphant return to Rabat. The important factor in regard to Tunisia was that the sultan and Foreign Minister Antoine Pinay signed an agreement providing for negotiations "destined to give to

Morocco the legality of an independent state united to France by permanent links of an interdependence freely consented to and defined."[59] This pact went beyond the internal autonomy granted to Tunisia and caused the Neo-Destourians to demand equal treatment from Paris. Naturally it strengthened the Youssefist attack on the conventions, putting France in a difficult position. Because France did not want the Youssefists in power, they were more receptive to new agreements with Habib Bourguiba and Ben Ammar. Ex-premier Mendès-France published an article calling for a new look at Tunisian affairs in light of the Moroccan agreement.

France did reexamine its Tunisian policy and drew up the Franco-Tunisian Protocol of Agreement on March 20, 1956, signed by Prime Minister Ben Ammar and French Foreign Minister Christian Pineau. The Protocol called for "complete sovereignty" instead of "internal sovereignty." Full independence arrived as an anticlimax. The Treaty of Bardo was no longer valid, and changes were made in the six conventions to comply with the new situation. In addition, Tunisia gained the right "to exercise her responsibilities in the fields of foreign affairs, security and defense and to build up a national Tunisian army."[60] The protectorate was dead. In rapid succession Tunisia established an army, took control of the national radio, assumed police power on the frontiers, and passed a statute regulating French officials in the country, allowing France to keep troops at Bizerte and a few other bases. The fight for political autonomy was won.

With the advent of autonomy Habib Bourguiba prepared to be the head of state, not just the power behind the state. The exact constitutional nature of the Tunisian state was to be determined by a Constituent Assembly, the first session of which was presided over by Bourguiba on April 1, 1956. Three days later Tahar Ben Ammar resigned as premier. He had served his country well and was more than a figurehead. The confidence in which the French leaders held him was instrumental in the successful negotiations from 1954 through

1956. However, there were some real obstacles to his continuation in office. Ben Ammar was committed to a constitutional monarchy and the party was not. Constant internecine strife in other Arab states worried the Neo-Destour leaders, and they determined to avoid such feuds at all costs. This avowal meant one leader and one party—Bourguiba and the Neo-Destour must be supreme. Tahar Ben Ammar was not a party member; as president of the conservative Chamber of Agriculture he had opposed nationalization and land reform and the fixing of agricultural wages—all policies that the Neo-Destour supported. During the premiership of Ben Ammar his own agricultural workers went on strike protesting his conservative management.[61] It would have been embarrassing to have an elder statesman remain in a high position when his views disagreed so sharply with the party's. Although he served in the Constituent Assembly and the National Assembly, his influence rapidly weakened.

During the struggle with France the UGTT labor syndicate played a prominent role under the dynamic leadership first of Ferhat Hached and next of Ahmed Ben Salah. With the Neo-Destour Party outlawed by France for much of this period, an even greater responsibility fell on the UGTT. After the ban on the party was lifted in 1954, a rivalry developed between the syndicate and the party when each began to discuss economic planning. The able and ambitious secretary-general of the UGTT, Ahmed Ben Salah, saw the problems facing the country:

> It is foolish to believe . . . that the combat for the national cause is going to cease with the acquisition of autonomy; it on the contrary only begins on the internal domain for the realization of social justice and true democracy.[62]

Predicting a strong future role for UGTT, he declared, "Once national emancipation is realized we will fight ferociously against any government which does not pay attention to the aspirations of the workers. . . ."[63] After independence, feeling that the economic problem was paramount, the UGTT brought out a voluminous report entitled *Economic Report of the VIth Congress of the UGTT, 1956*. The enemy was defined clearly as underdevelopment, and drastic economic measures were recommended. A five-day cabinet crisis had been precipitated in April while Bourguiba was first forming a government. Ben Salah wanted the chief economic responsibility in the government and favored the application of stringent economic measures. Bourguiba disagreed, and the government was formed without Ben Salah. When asked if he agreed with Bourguiba, Ben Salah said:

> Fundamentally—yes. But on various details we disagree. We were against the uniform wage cuts which were recently enacted; they affected the low-grade government servants very severely, and the high-grade officials only slightly; it should have been the other way round. We are great believers in social security, complete with adequate health services etc.[64]

It is sometimes argued that Tunisia delayed its economic revolution until 1961, when the plan was finally begun. Perhaps Bourguiba was right in taking more time to erase Youssefist opposition and other elements hostile to extensive planning before the program was started. In any event Bourguiba wanted his name to be associated with the major economic changes, and he wanted the government, not the UGTT or Ahmed Ben Salah, to sponsor them.

The disagreement between Bourguiba and Ben Salah was not only over economic policy; there were political differences. Ben Salah subscribed to the position held by the Youssefists that a general Arab North African response should be made against France, with Tunisia doing much more to aid the Algerians. During the Suez crisis Ben Salah cautioned North Africa, "Tunisia is *not* independent. And Suez is being used as a piece of psychological warfare to maintain the whole of North Africa in a state of servitude or economic impotence."[65] Not only was Ben Salah refused a cabinet seat, but his power in the labor syndicate was undermined. A fight developed in the UGTT national congress with Habib Achour, a strong Neo-Destourian, calling for the formation of a rival syndicate, the UTT (Union Tunisienne du Travail), the nucleus of which was to come from a group of laborers from Sfax.[66] Habib Achour accused Ben Salah of too much political activity in the leadership of the UGTT. The first step had been taken by the Neo-Destour to assure a labor syndicate closely allied with the party. Because of schism at the congress Ben Salah tendered his resignation as secretary-general, and Ahmed Tlili was elected in his place to head a united UGTT created out of the UTT and the old UGTT. Bourguiba and the party leaders were satisfied: the UTT had served its purpose in effecting a UGTT closely aligned with the party. Ben Salah's bid for power had been crushed, and from this time on the alliance remained firm.

Contrary to his earlier bold statement of labor competition with government in October, 1956, at Bizerte, Ben Salah said, "The UGTT and the Neo-Destour are not only a single party. They struggled together for the liberty of the country and will continue to struggle for her success."[67] This change of emphasis was too late to save his position in the UGTT, and he remained conspiciously absent from government circles until given the post of minister of health in July, 1957.

Establishment of a Republic

Habib Bourguiba was gradually assuming sole leadership of newly independent Tunisia. Although he talked of a constitutional monarchy in a speech at Djemmal on March 25, 1956, he was consolidating his own power. Just before the conventions were signed with France, Bourguiba had high praise for the beylical system.

> The Tunisian people are very attached to the beylical formula, which for two and a half centuries incarnated its political per-

sonality. The people do not forget that following the first World War these princes have largely aided the struggle of the nation for her liberty. A reigning Bey is dead in exile for having manifested an active sympathy for the nationalist ideal in a period when the popular movement was practically decapitated. The Tunisian people will not forget that the reigning Bey suffered much from the policy followed by France from December 15, 1951 until July 31, 1954.[68]

Despite these words of homage the Neo-Destour Party decided that the beylical power should be limited until it was at least as innocuous as English royal power. In a press interview in 1952 Bourguiba was asked if the terms "sovereignty of the Tunisians" and "the Bey's sovereignty" were not contradictory. His reply was that the Bey's sovereignty was like that of the King of England or the President of France.[69]

On December 29, 1955, the Bey issued the decree establishing a National Constituent Assembly to meet in April and draw up a constitution. By this act the Bey obligated himself to sign and promulgate a constitution that he had not even seen. At the insistence of the Neo-Destour Party he was weakening his own position. The assembly was to be elected by direct and secret universal suffrage. Bourguiba announced that "The preparation of the lists and their legislative questions will be severely controlled."[70]

The Neo-Destour created a national front list of 98 candidates and exhorted the people to elect those lawyers and professors. Included in the Neo-Destourian list were two Jews, a Socialist named Chadly Rhaim, and the independent Tahar Ben Ammar. Besides party members the national front also included candidates representing UGTT, UNAT (Union Nationale des Agriculteurs Tunisiens), and UTAC (Union Tunisienne de l'Artisanats et du Commerce). The close relationship between the syndicates and the party assured the Neo-Destour of complete control of the assembly. Over 83 per cent of the 762,138 eligible voters cast their ballots. The Youssefists called for a boycott of the election, and it is interesting that only

59 per cent of the voters in the city of Tunis voted, compared to the high national average.[71] The national front received 597,813 votes to 7,352 for the Communist list and 233 for an independent group from Sousse. Although the assembly planned to establish a "constitutional monarchy of which the motto would be liberty, order, justice,"[72] by July 25, 1957, the group had abolished the monarchy and proclaimed a republic. This important step followed a vital joint-meeting of the Political Bureau of the party and the Council of Ministers. Evidently the party had decided early in the spring that the monarchy must be abolished.

While the assembly was in session, various steps were taken to destroy the power of the Bey. In May, 1956, the Bey's appointive power was canceled by the Council of Ministers, reducing the civil list controlled by the throne; one month later the Bey's budget was cut and his property was transferred to the Tunisian state.[73] Last, on July 25, 1957, the assembly gave Bourguiba the title of chief of state until a constitution was established, and the Fete of the Throne, commemorating the anniversary of Bey Lamine's accession, could no longer be celebrated. The Bey and heir apparent were held in house arrest. The monarchy was dead. Bourguiba's power was assured when he formed a council completely controlled by Neo-Destourian ministers.[74] The destiny of the new republic was in the hands of Habib Bourguiba and the Neo-Destour Party.

Total unity through total organization was the goal. Like Communist parties, the Neo-Destour was organized into militant cells in different districts of the cities and in the small villages. These cells had the triple function of political activity, education of the people, and organizational activities. The local cells formed regional federations in the principal centers of Tunisia. The party's National Council is composed of delegates from the regional federations along with representatives from the national syndicates and the Political Bureau. The Political Bureau under the presidency of Bourguiba consisted of ten members, five of whom were ministers in the government. Annually a national congress is held attended by representatives from all the cells. The party gains a great deal of strength from its affiliated national syndicates: UGTT representing labor, UNAT—agriculture, UTAC—artisans and merchants, UGET—students, UNFT—women, plus Young Destourians and Scouts. Party policy and information are published in its newspaper, *L'Action*.

Authoritarian Control

The French historian Ch.-André Julien, a personal friend of Bourguiba, described the party:

> The Neo-Destour conducts its campaigns with a growing dynamism and a modern technique inspired by the Communists and Fascists. Its propaganda utilizes all the proper means to capture the imagination: solemn visits of chiefs to the cities, processions, insignias, young people in uniform, decorated platforms, national hymn similar to the Egyptian hymn, Arab orchestra with copper instruments.[75]

This militancy disturbed the Old Destour group, which had hoped for freer political discussion. The Neo-Destour decided that political discussion should take place only within the party.

In political theory the Neo-Destour originally was not an authoritarian party. For example, Hedi Nouira, who served as minister of finance in Bourguiba's first two governments, described the party in 1954: "Constitutional and liberal, as indicated in the rest of its name, the Neo-Destour is not only inspired by a moderate theocracy but by the principle of Western property rights."[76] He called for the coexistence of two powers, executive and legislative, each independent of the other and both equally powerful. The legislature should make the laws and the executive should execute them. This proposal suggested Western democratic ideas, some of which did appear in the constitution of 1959, although in actual practice they would be ignored.

The Paris cell of the Neo-Destour, historically more liberal than the party at home, periodically called for liberalization. An analysis of the Paris cell meeting in 1955 shows plans for a complex democratic program. Under the heading of "constitutional problems" the report recommended executive power which subordinated "governmental action to law."[77] Legislative power should adequately represent the people, with the assembly having the right to make, modify, or abrogate laws. There should be no government interference in the judicial system. The Paris group wanted a veritable bill of rights to (1) give freedom of political expression, (2) allow freedom of religion and association, (3) assure equality before the law without distinction of race or religion, (4) give equality to women, (5) insure the inviolability of domicile and correspondence, and (6) confirm the right to strike.[78] All private property that was contrary to the general interest could be collectivized, and the church should not be allowed to become a state within a state as it had in Europe. In actuality the government that emerged would be considerably more authoritarian than the Paris cell had visualized.

The Constitution of 1959

When the republican constitution was published on June 1, 1959, it was a presidential document giving almost complete power to Habib Bourguiba, who was certain to be elected as the first president. A clue to the type of republic to come was revealed in a radio interview with Bourguiba in 1957:

> We are orienting ourselves toward a regime which assures a minimum of stability at the head of the state. It is for this reason that we prefer to go toward an American regime, but our constitution will not be a copy of the American Constitution.[79]

Indeed, the constitution went well beyond the American Constitution in bestowing power on the president. The Tunisian president appoints the members of his government, who are responsible directly to him, and makes all other civilian and military appointments. While the president cannot nominate himself for more than three consecutive terms (of five years each), the legislature has neither power of impeachment nor effective impediment to the wishes of the president. When the legislature is not in session the president can rule by decrees, which are submitted to the assembly at its next regular session. Judges are appointed by the president upon recommendation of the Higher Judicial Council. There is no supreme court to decide on the constitutionality of legislation.

In an article analyzing the Tunisian constitution George N. Sfeir wrote:

> In the new states of Asia and Africa which have adopted modern constitutions, one finds the letter of the constitution providing ample securities of individual rights, whereas in the body politic these rights and securities are in fact still being striven for, and the institutions groping for roots. It represents an anomalous situation in which constitutional forms often exist side by side with arbitrary rule, a situation often inviting resort to extra-legal acts in order, truly or allegedly, to reassert constitutional rights and promote more liberal institutions.[80]

The statement describes the constitutional situation in Tunisia very adequately. The party leaders' argument that authoritative power is necessary to carry out badly needed reforms seems to be the most plausible explanation for the monolithic political structure of Tunisia.

In analyzing the 1962 plot against his life, President Bourguiba deplored the lack of unity and civic sense among the Tunisians:

> A democratic regime based on public liberties, as in Great Britain, is desired. But we must be careful. Great Britain and Tunisia are not at all similar. Admittedly, the government is criticized in Parliament and in the press in Great Britain. But over and above these criticisms and divergencies, every English-

man has a civic sense, patriotism, a national awareness, as a result of which the English are united as one man when it is a question of the respect due to the State.[81]

He added that in Tunisia "grudges are put before the national interest." This observation raises the question of how unity and a civic sense can be created. One might argue that England did not develop these qualities through authoritarianism and the police state. How much "civic sense and loyalty" can be imposed on people by the state? It would seem well for Tunisia to move toward greater democracy, because not all presidents might carry their responsibility as well as Habib Bourguiba. If not, democratic institutions might be the only salvation from dictatorship.

Several important domestic and foreign problems occupied Tunisian attention in the formative period from 1956 to 1959. Internally, the steady move to a republic brought about the discrediting of the Bey and his household along with moderate leaders who had favored a constitutional monarchy. The Neo-Destour used the Youssefist agitation in two ways: first as an excuse to attack moderates, thus negating Youssefist charges of conservatism, and second, as a means generally to purge political opponents, including the Youssefists, by alleging plots. The eldest son of the Bey, Chedley Bey, served two years of a five-year sentence for complicity in the disappearance of royal jewels. The former premiers Mohammed Salah M'Zali, Salaheddine Baccouche, and Tahar Ben Ammar were all disgraced and accused of collaboration with the French. Salaheddine Baccouche served six months at hard labor of a ten-year sentence and was released on April 1, 1959, only to die eight months later at the age of seventy-four. Mohammed Salah M'Zali was sentenced to ten years in prison but was released early. Tahar Ben Ammar was charged with complicity in the disappearance of the royal jewels and with other crimes. The National Assembly, of which he was a member, met in March of 1958 and canceled his immunity from arrest, whereupon he was convicted and imprisoned.[82] In general the new Tunisian

Republic acted against the former officials like a frightened and vindictive government unsure of itself. However, the Youssefists were accused with good reason of fomenting a plot against Bourguiba's life with the help and knowledge of the Egyptian government. President Nasser was enraged, called Bourguiba a liar, and asked for a neutral investigation of the plot. Tunisia never consented to the investigation. Fifty-three people were tried for this plot in November, 1958, and by the next October, 128 had been tried, some in absentia.[83] The Tunisian Communist Party headquarters was raided, and Communist power steadily declined.

The period was a tense one in foreign affairs also. Pressed by the radicalism of the Youssefists and by their loyalty to the Algerian cause, Bourguiba insisted upon a settlement of the Algerian war before relations could be normal with France. France, exercising the right to pursue Algerian rebels, had violated the Tunisian frontier, raided Tunisian border villages, and carried out a despicable air attack on Sakiet Sidi Youssef.[84] Tunisia reacted by closing French consulates and arresting French officials working in the post, telephone and telegraph offices, accusing them of spying and wiretapping. Until the republic was constitutionally launched in 1959, internal and external pressures seemed to push Tunisia closer to an authoritarian state. Even efforts to counterbalance the loss of French help with closer American ties were only mildly successful.

When President Bourguiba returned from a visit to the United States, having received very little economic help, he explained the situation:

> The moral support of the United States should not lead us to adopt an unfriendly attitude toward France. If we had thought of United States aid, it was only to the extent that this might be used to complement French aid. We never had any thought of the United States taking over from France.[85]

Although a gala celebration greeted President Eisenhower's envoy, James P. Richards, when he visited Tunis, the United

States clearly considered North Africa within the French sphere of influence. At this time military aid was refused Tunisia, and only three million dollars was granted for economic aid. Beset on all sides with difficulties, the new republic began with uncertainty and after searching desperately for help, found little.

7

Problems of Independence

There is never a moratorium on problems; for a new government, its very immaturity is a problem. Tunisia was challenged in the following areas: (1) relations with France during the Algerian war, (2) Bizerte crisis, (3) economic planning, (4) party organization and loyalty, (5) education and a search for identity, and (6) Maghreb relations. Mismanagement of any one of these areas could have been serious for the new republic; none were ignored. The story of how Tunisia reacted to her problems is an interesting chapter in the contemporary history of emerging nations.

Tunisian-French Relations

Tunisian-French relations dominated the internal and foreign policies of Tunisia for many years after independence, fluctuating greatly up to and through the Bizerte Crisis of 1961. On the eve of the granting of independence several European homes were bombed, and rioting broke out as three hundred French young people carrying the tricolor successively attacked the American Consulate, the American Information Service, and the newspapers *Le Petit Matin* and *El Amal*.

Angry shouts against American support of a freer Tunisia were heard as the American flag was burned by the mob.[1]

In an early spirit of cooperation a series of agreements were signed by Tunisia and France, opening diplomatic representation on the ambassadorial level. The respective ambassadors were in fact given special privileges in the two nations. In countries where Tunisia was not represented diplomatically, France handled the interests of the Tunisian government. No lasting accord, however, was possible because of the seriousness of the Algerian situation. In a May press interview President Bourguiba made it clear that this problem overshadowed all others:

> All depends on the rapid solution of the Algerian problem: the restoration of the internal situation in Tunisia, the economic and social reforms, the settlement of property, of interdependence with France. . . . We cannot refrain from helping our brother Algerians. We certainly do not have the intention of declaring war on France, but if Tunisian volunteers ask to fight in Algeria in the name of Arab solidarity, as those who did during the war in Palestine, I will not oppose them. As for our aid to the French troops to stop the traffic of arms, it is a step that is impossible to take.[2]

It was apparent that all aid short of an actual state of war would be given to the Algerians. An independent Tunisia was valuable to the Algerian rebels, who used it as a sanctuary and a source of arms and supplies. France, too, shuttled troops back and forth across the border until Tunisia announced that the frontier would be closed to French troops.

Relations became critical in October, 1956, when France seized the Air-Atlas plane carrying Ahmed Ben Bella and other leaders of the Algerian *Front de Libération Nationale* (FLN) en route to Tunis for conferences with President Bourguiba and Sultan Mohammed V. The reaction was swift and brutal. Tunisia blocked the movement of French troops throughout the country. New attacks on the French broke out, and in Tunis incidents resulted in fourteen killed and sixty wounded.[3]

A twenty-four hour protest strike was called by the UGTT. Tunisia embarked on a more open program of assistance for the FLN, and France reacted in May, 1957, by suspending economic aid promised to Tunisia amounting to twelve billion, one hundred million francs. Angrily Bourguiba declared, "in renouncing the aid convention, signed a month ago, France has denounced, by this consequence the Financial and Economic Convention of June 3, 1955."[4] Although the situation was eventually reconciled by negotiation, the Algerian problem still remained acute. When Vice-President Richard Nixon arrived to help the Tunisians celebrate the first anniversary of their independence, he spoke in favor of Algerian independence by peaceful means.[5]

A new crisis developed in 1958: since the Algerian war continued without a hint of settlement, the Tunisian workers in French-controlled industries went on a seven-day sympathy strike. Near the border on Algerian territory a contingent of French troops was ambushed, with sixteen killed and four taken prisoner. Accusing the FLN attackers of coming from Tunisian territory, the French sent General Buchalet to Tunis with a protest letter from Premier Félix Gaillard. President Bourguiba refused to see the general under the pretext that he had served during the French protectorate in Tunisia.[6]

Border incidents continued, and on February 8, 1958, the world was shocked by French bombing of the Tunisian village of Sakiet Sidi Youssef. Between eleven o'clock and noon twenty-six French medium bombers attacked the village. Sixty-nine Tunisians were killed, twenty-one of whom were children, and many were wounded. The property damage was devastating. Why was this done on Saturday morning, when many people were crowded in the marketplace and the children were out of school? Although the French government had authorized ground reprisal raids upon government approval, the bombing was neither a ground raid nor a reprisal approved by Paris. That the commanders in the field went beyond all authority in sending the raid against Sakiet Sidi Youssef[7] was of little comfort to the Tunisians as they tried to lessen misery and sorrow in the smoldering village.

The radical act begot radicalism. Bourguiba demanded the evacuation of French troops and forbade all troop movements within the country. Four hundred European farmers were removed from the frontier area, and the French consulate in Tunis was closed. The leading liberal periodical editorialized:

> One thing is clear: In order to be respected in 1958 one can no longer be a friend of the west. In order to be considered and to be favored it is necessary to be a Nehru, Tito or Nasser.
>
> The day when Bourguiba will decide to take the path these have taken since 1952, Tunisia will be no longer slandered and attacked, but solicited.[8]

On February 17 Tunisia and France accepted the good offices of the United States and Great Britain. Tunisia repeatedly refused to accept controls on the border, and when France was about to renounce the Anglo-American good offices, President Dwight Eisenhower sent a message to Prime Minister Gaillard which resulted in an agreement without border controls. The move, however, was a fatal one for the Gaillard government, which was accused of weakness in the face of American pressure and was defeated two months later by 321 votes to 255.[9]

The new cabinet crisis and the subsequent insurrection in Algeria led to the end of the Fourth Republic and the investiture of General Charles de Gaulle on June 1, 1958. Now President Bourguiba would deal with the man of whom he had said, "General de Gaulle, . . . I admired the man during the war, and read his *Mémoirs;* what a writer, what perspicacity!"[10] An accord signed on June 17 provided for the progressive withdrawal of French troops from Tunisia and replacement by Tunisian troops. Unfortunately the issue of the French base in Bizerte was not settled. Bourguiba made a hypothetical proposal to France that they could retain Bizerte if France would find an immediate solution to the Algerian dilemma, a proposal which France naturally rejected. President Bourguiba became more critical as the Algerian war dragged on. The French journal *Réalités Tunisiennes* called attention to the worsening relations with Bourguiba:

> We reflect with sadness that it took years for a good number of our compatriots to understand that the policy of M. Bourguiba consisted in giving the impression that he played the game candidly for the purpose of better arriving at his goals by the path of Oriental detours.[11]

Bizerte Crisis

Repeatedly Bourguiba demanded that the French abandon their military base at Bizerte. Finally, in the summer of 1961 President Bourguiba took the offensive on two fronts, Bizerte and the South. In many respects Bizerte was secondary to the southern boundary issue. Tunisia called attention to a 1910 French and Turkish treaty that placed the southern boundary at Charmes instead of at Fort Saint to the north. The matter was doubly important since oil had been discovered in the Algerian Sahara not too far from the contested frontier. As the Tunisian army marched into the disputed territory, French paratroops were rushed to the scene. At the same time excited Tunisians, urged on by the shrill "yew-yew-yew" yells of the Arab women, crowded around the French military base at Bizerte. In the frenzy a few mortar shells were lobbed into the compound of the base. In both the south and north the French response was explosive. On July 22 heavy fighting erupted with the French using rocket-firing planes. Tough French paratroopers of the Foreign Legion were ordered out of the Bizerte base, and a wholesale butchery of Tunisian soldiers and civilians began. The embattled Tunisians were trapped with their backs to the sea or the lake—there was nowhere to go. Later, Tunisian Minister of Information Mohamed Masmoudi charged that more than one hundred of the dead were found with their hands tied.[12]

In a United Nations Security Council discussion the United

States and Great Britain failed to support Tunisia, a situation that Bourguiba euphemistically called "disconcerting." The response to American indifference was immediate; the United States Information Service library in Tunis was stoned. The United Nations urged a cease-fire, but the damage had been done. Brutal slaughter had been the French response, and Tunisia was in a state of severe shock. Casualties ran into the thousands. Bitterness and stunned disbelief marked President Bourguiba's response: "The American attitude in the Security Council has sounded the knell of the West in North Africa."[13] An American journalist simply explained, "The French troops slaughtered the Tunisians," and attributed the U.S. attitude to a desire to keep French friendship in the face of a Berlin showdown.[14] Later Bourguiba confessed, "I never thought that the French navy, machine-gunning airplanes, and napalm would be the response"[15]—a serious miscalculation and one that might have cost him the presidency. It is strange that Bourguiba, who had read de Gaulle's memoirs and admired the decisiveness of the man, could have failed to foresee a military response.

Europeans and Americans were treated coolly in Tunis, and reprisals were carried out against the French. As many French left Tunisia, people talked about complete cultural and educational Tunisification. The French language would be deemphasized in the schools, and a program was begun to replace French teachers with Tunisians.[16] As a result an impossible situation confronted the young nation that depended on the agreement signed with France in 1959 for technical and cultural cooperation.

In the United Nations the Afro-Asian bloc called for an emergency session of the General Assembly on Bizerte. The fifty votes necessary for the session were finally obtained, and the meeting was scheduled for August 21, with a French boycott assured. On August 26 the U.N. backed Tunisia on Bizerte 66 to 0, with 30 abstentions, among which were the United States and the United Kingdom. Although the United

States had abstained in the vote, they did put unilateral pressure on France which led to Tunisian-French negotiations in September and French agreement to withdraw all troops from Tunisian soil.[17] On October 15, 1964, the Tunisians completely took over Bizerte amid a gala ceremony attended by President Nasser of Egypt and President Ben Bella of Algeria. Plans were developed to make an industrial complex of the Bizerte area with the help of Western European and American capital.[18]

After the Bizerte crisis Tunisian-French relations slowly improved. Normalization of cultural and technical cooperation was announced on October 19, 1961. French culture is deeply embedded in Tunisian society partly because most of the Tunisian government officials received their university training in France. In April, 1963, extensive Tunisian-French talks designed to extend cooperation between the two antagonists opened in Paris. The talks resulted in new cultural and economic agreements between the two nations.

Economic Plan

The overwhelming problem for independent Tunisia is economic. How can a country with limited resources and a growing population meet its economic demands? Agriculture, which contributes about 40 per cent of the gross national product and about 55 per cent of the exports, is the bedrock of the Tunisian economy.[19] More than 70 per cent of the labor force is engaged in agriculture. In 1958 the slogan of an agricultural campaign was "Each year 70,000 more mouths to feed and 10,000 hectares of land destroyed by erosion."[20] Uncertain rainfall has always played havoc with Tunisian agriculture. One writer suggests a massive program for olive planting since there is a good world market for olive oil.[21] However, like everything else, olive production fluctuates between good and bad growing seasons. In the poor season of 1952 only 35,000 metric tons of oil were produced, whereas the unusual bumper-crop year of 1958 produced 120,000 metric tons. Revenue from the export of olive oil amounted to 23 million dollars in 1961. These exports are so fundamental to the economy that recently when domestic production was low Tunisia met her foreign trade commitments and then imported vegetable oils to mix with olive oil for domestic use. Grain production is also important for Tunisia, and although the average yield of hard and soft wheat and barley has increased, it still has not met the need, and wheat is imported to help support the work-relief program.

Water is a vital key to the Tunisian economy. In the Medjerda River Valley, where an extensive irrigation network is in operation, a thriving agricultural economy is feasible. However, in the central and southern regions, where the rainfall is scarce, drought is an ominous specter. Here the rain comes suddenly and hard, causing floods and erosion. A project planned in 1963 to capture water in Roman-type cisterns and water collection basins on the highlands of the Base Valley of the Medjerda would conserve water in the hills, preventing silting of the irrigation ditches in the valley when rainfall rushes from the denuded mountains.[22] By use of siphon tubes the stored water could be available for irrigation in the valley without need of machinery. In Libya 8,381 Roman-type water cisterns are in use, and the extension of such a system throughout Tunisia is a possibility.[23]

Citrus fruits are an important export item in years of good production, and experiments are being conducted in rice and cotton growing as well as in table grape production. Wine grapes, with an export value of 19 million dollars in 1961, are a coveted trade commodity because the high alcoholic potential of Tunisian grapes makes their wine a perfect blend when mixed with the weaker French wines.

The processing of agricultural products is one of the chief small industries in Tunisia. Vegetable canning and packing as well as the processing of fruit juices and fish products are important small-scale industries. As a recent economic report indicates, there are some real obstacles to heavy industrialization:

> Consumer industries have been hampered in the past by the ease with which goods could be processed in France, the relatively small population and its low purchasing power, a shortage of skilled industrial labor, and again the high cost of fuel.[24]

An estimated $5,400,000 per year may be added to the export figure since the construction of a pulp plant for processing esparto grass (alfa) at Kasserine. Part of the paper-making process will be done in Tunisia, after which the processed pulp will be shipped to England. The large plant, however, has caused some problems. It will consume almost three-fourths of the precious water supply of Kasserine and will discharge waste material, some of which is harmful to agriculture because it renders the water useless for irrigation.

Mining contributes about 8 per cent of the gross national product, and minerals make up approximately 30 per cent of Tunisian exports. The chief minerals are phosphate rock, iron ore, lead, and zinc. Several feasibility studies are being conducted to see if greater advantage can be taken of mineral wealth.

Tunisia suffers from an excess of imports over exports. Without a large source of domestic fuel the imbalance cannot be overcome by industrialization. Although some natural gas is available, there is not enough for heavy industrialization, but Tunisia expects to get more natural gas in the future from Algeria.

Unemployment and population growth are significant variables in the Tunisian economy. Unemployment figures have averaged around 10 per cent of the population, or close to 400,000 persons. However, making good use of the United States Food for Peace programs, Tunisia has begun extensive work-mobilization projects, more dramatically labeled, "Struggle Against Underdevelopment." Nearly 300,000 laborers are employed part-time through this plan, under which the government pays them in money and American surplus food. These laborers work on land clearance, reforestation, housing development, and other useful projects. Still underemployed, they are, nevertheless, better off than before the program was started. Estimates suggest that about 100,000 workers are still unaccounted for in the laboring force and are presumably unemployed at least most of the year.

The population has been growing faster than national productivity. Each year almost 23,000 people are added to the labor force, and since 50.9 per cent of the population is under twenty years of age, the birth rate will not diminish.[25] While the total population went up 68 per cent from 1921 to 1951, the urban increase was 165 per cent, compared to a rural increase of 45 per cent. Tunis itself represents nearly one-sixth of the population of Tunisia.[26]

Attending the shift to urban areas in search of employment are the psychological and sociological problems that result when the nomad or seminomad is cut off from family and tribal customs.[27] Both the Neo-Destour Party and the labor syndicate have tried to substitute for the lack of family ties by involving the newcomers in the political and economic life of the state. However, not all sociological factors militate against progress. Because Tunisia is a country of young people, it is easier for the government to attack tradition. Realizing that the young are impressed by action and often respond eagerly to change, the government planned to attack the demographic problem. Although birth control devices can be sold freely, cultural and economic factors hinder such a program. Arabs have great pride in family, and even if they decided to limit its size, the cost of contraceptives would strain most meager budgets. With children needing food, one would not be likely to use the money for contraceptives. The Bourguiba government requested Ford Foundation aid in 1963 for an experiment in family planning. With the aid of this grant twelve maternal and child health centers are being established to help teach family limitation and child care.[28]

All factors considered, obviously a bold and extensive economic plan was essential for Tunisia. In response a Secretariat of State for Planning and Finance was created in 1961, with Ahmed Ben Salah in charge. Back in favor, he finally acquired the position he had wanted in 1957. The plan that resulted was divided into two parts, first, a three-year period of preparation, a triennial plan (1961-1964), followed by a seven-year period that would make the nation nearly self-sufficient by 1971. It was apparent that serious disequilibriums in the economy had to be corrected. New jobs would have to be created. In addition the international trade balance remained discouraging: the total exports in 1960 equaled only 60 per cent of the imports. To overcome these serious problems a socialized economy was decided upon, with some private enterprise existing within the framework of the plan. Above all, the 1962 plan was designed to end the unequal distribution of wealth left over from the colonial period and to raise the standard of living of all Tunisians. It is hoped that by the end of the ten-year plan the economy will be in a position to "take off" and that it will become completely self-sufficient by 1973. To do this Tunisia must maintain an annual increase of the gross domestic product equal to 6 per cent.

The plan provides for reform and new direction in the following areas: agriculture, industry, foreign trade, credit structure, and government administration.[29]

In agriculture small holdings are to be regrouped into farms of optimum size so that modern machinery and scientific methods can increase the yield. Agricultural cooperatives for production, irrigation, and all aspects of farm operation will be created. Cooperatives were legalized in a 1934 statute, which was amended in 1958 to allow their more rapid spread.[30] The most successful area containing irrigated cooperatives is in the Medjerda River Valley northwest of Tunis. For example, the government operates the model agricultural cooperative of El-Habibia. Here families live in government-constructed houses on irrigated land. At the center of the village is a mosque, an assembly hall, administrative offices, a packing and shipping warehouse, and a factory for processing rice. The plan would consolidate farms under 25 acres, allowing the use of mechanized equipment.[31] On larger farms under the cooperative program, replacement of animal power with small tractors would reduce the amount of fodder needed for domestic purposes; feed could then be exported.

Recently Tunisia took a big step in land consolidation by the absorption of European-owned farms. In March of 1963 Tunisia and France signed an agreement providing for a gradual take-over of these lands with France assuming 90 per cent of the cost of compensating the landowners. However, in May, 1964, the Tunisian National Assembly passed a law which provided for the immediate absorption of about one million acres.[32] This move brought an emergency French cabinet meeting, presided over by President de Gaulle, and the announcement that France had suspended economic aid to Tunisia. Undaunted, several days later Tunisia took over 296,000 acres of French land and required that each citizen subscribe to national loans according to his income to make up for the loss of French aid.[33] All communally-owned tribal lands of central and southern Tunisia were also brought under state control.

Simultaneously with French land confiscation Tunisia acquired ninety-eight Catholic Church properties through an agreement with the Vatican. Only five Catholic churches remain open in the country. Many of the confiscated churches had been idle since the large-scale exit of Europeans. However, one of the greatest blows to Christian prestige was the announcement that the Cathedral of Saint Louis at Carthage, so famous in Catholic history, will become a national archaeological museum.

In the past too many Tunisian raw materials were extracted and sent abroad for processing. The new plan calls for the construction of processing industries. Besides the cellulose plant to make paper pulp from alfa grass in Kasserine, a phosphate processing plant is operating in Sfax, and canning of fruit juices will be done in a new plant at Grombalia. Oil refineries, sugar-beet refineries, textile mills, iron and steel mills, mineral processing, increased tourism, and the expansion of cement production are planned. These domestic enterprises will not only create jobs, but will supply consumer goods, thereby reducing the large excess of imports. The government will encourage primary industries such as chemicals and steel. Where key industries are concerned, the state will be involved in management. Private enterprise may exist if it does not interfere with economic planning.

A national banking system has been created, with the government *Banque Centrale* in control of all important transactions of the private banks. Because of the government's concern over adverse foreign exchange, the *Banque Centrale* stringently prevents the flow of private capital out of Tunisia. Since many employees are inexperienced in finance, the system is cumbersome, and the business of international banking in Tunisia is often held up pending permission for the *Banque Centrale*.[34] It has been known to take the *Banque Centrale* three months, under frequent prodding, to act on a simple request to open an account in a Tunis bank. Such an inefficient system has rendered the flow of foreign capital to Tunisia almost impossible. Reorganization of the banking system is imperative if Tunisia is to attract foreign capital and investment. Fortunately, the plan provides for national banks specializing in industrial credit and agricultural credit, and a bank dealing with cooperatives.

Reform of the government administration is projected in order to strengthen the power of the state, especially in economic matters. To be fully implemented, central authority must penetrate every region and governorate. A National School of Administration was established for training government officials, with an examination system to determine promotion. Replacement of European officials by Arabs will follow as soon as enough are trained.[35]

In the areas of education, housing, and human dignity the plan intends to improve the life of every Tunisian. President Bourguiba has described the fight against underdevelopment as more difficult than the struggle for independence. But it is hard for people to remain enthusiastic about a long-range plan unless perceptible progress is made to offset their depression from the poverty around them. Battling against the French for the specific purpose of independence was unquestionably more exciting than the tedious process of economic development with its attendant sacrifices.

On May 28, 1963, the National Assembly heard a lengthy report on the first year of the triennial plan, presented by Ahmed Ben Salah, Secretary of State for Planning and Finance. His report in general was optimistic: he announced an eight per cent increase in production over 1960, which was a prosperous year, and a twelve per cent increase over 1961, which was a mediocre year.[36] The secretary then reviewed every major accomplishment of the year in the economic, social, and cultural realms. Nowhere did he mention the dependence of the plan upon foreign aid. Ben Salah was later questioned about the possibilities of allowing farmers of southern Tunisia to trade more freely in Libyan markets, an acceleration of trade and commerce in all ports, and a freer tourist exchange. His reply was a dismissal of all the questions on the basis that underdevelopment dictated the present austerity program.[37]

American economic aid has been indispensable to Tunisia. An economic, technical, and related assistance agreement was signed with the United States in March, 1957. Under this accord the Tunisian government submits project proposals, and upon U.S. approval of a project, Tunisia contributes manpower and resources as the economy permits. Financial and technical help is furnished by the United States, but the initiative for developing a project rests with Tunisia. The United States agreed to give "to the people of Tunisia full publicity concerning programs hereunder."[38] Assistance under this agreement amounted to approximately 170 million dollars to the end of fiscal year 1962. Since 1959 another hundred million dollars of surplus agricultural commodities have been sent to Tunisia; they have helped support child-feeding programs, Algerian refugees in Tunisia, and a work-relief program. By 1963 American surplus wheat was being sent in sufficient quantities to support a work-relief program of 200,000 persons working full time.[39] In 1963 the United States announced that 180 million dollars would be loaned to Tunisia to support the first three years of the economic plan.

Tunisia is a long way from being financially independent. From 1957 to 1963 total United States aid (grants, loans, food) amounted to over 350 million dollars, or around $12 per year for every Tunisian during this six-year period. In 1962 foreign aid in grants and loans from all countries accounted for about 50 per cent of the Tunisian capital budget.[40]

President Bourguiba proudly announced to the National Assembly in April, 1966, that over the past ten years Tunisia had increased its net production by 62 per cent, with industrial production rising by 112 per cent, and agricultural production by 33 per cent.[41] This increase is close to what the ten-year plan hopes to maintain through 1972.

Search for Identity

An intangible problem that new nations have might be called a search for identity. How can they disassociate themselves from the power that dominated them for so long and give expression to their own culture and history? The search involves all aspects of life: actual take-over of political reins, development of the fine arts, education, and literary and historical expression.

When a native government assumes the functions of highly trained colonizers, a completely smooth transition is impossible. The French had jealously prevented the Tunisians from holding the top positions in the government; therefore, Tunisia urged especially the skilled Frenchmen and Europeans to remain for a period. Some did choose to remain, like the French Director of Public Works, who with tears in his eyes finally handed over the department to Tunisians. Others began to leave soon after independence, their numbers growing until their exit took on the proportions of a mass exodus of European technicians and entrepreneurs. For example, of about 180,000 French and 50,000 Italians in Tunisia in 1956, only 50,000 French and 20,000 Italians remained by 1964.[42] From 1956 to 1960 there was a 23 per cent reduction in the number of doctors practicing in the country, and another exodus of doctors followed the Bizerte incident. The doctor-per-inhabitant ratio remains appallingly low in the face of a great population growth. Not only did Tunisia suffer from the loss of skilled personnel, but money was being drained from the country. Strong measures were taken to counter the outpouring of capital: curtailment of luxury imports, price controls, and a generally fixed line on wages. The government has used foreign aid for technical education, but only time can bring results.

A country beset with problems of underdevelopment has little time to dwell on the past. History is a luxury of developed societies. In Tunisia the intellectuals have been preoccupied with the battle to improve the new nation. Yet Tunisia has reached a stage of development where a sense of history would be valuable. Wisely, Bourguiba recognizes the role that history can play in creating a national identity. In 1964 he called the party leaders together and explained, "In order to set national sentiment on firm foundations, we must also give the people a full picture of their past, that is to say, the history of the generations that preceded them."[43] He urged historical studies on three levels: first, interpretive scientific studies on the scholarly level in Arabic and French; second, textbooks for secondary schools showing the broad lines of Tunisian history; and last, popular publications for the general reader.[44] President Bourguiba established a *Centre Culturel International* with a building in Hammamet on the sea. Here foreign scholars can write and study surrounded by beauty. An impressive center to display Tunisian art and handicrafts has been opened in Tunis. Such projects help Tunisia communicate its artistic and cultural heritage to others.

Party Control

To the traveler and observer Tunisia seems to be psychologically ready to handle its problems. One is impressed by the friendliness of the people and the seriousness with which they approach their tasks. Many argue that dedication to future development justifies and, indeed, necessitates a one-party structure and a government based on a presidential constitution. To waste energy in political bickering would be tragic in a time of crisis, they argue. Neo-Destourians feel that they must lead the people, many of whom are ignorant of politics and incapable of political freedom and expression. President Bourguiba has thus analyzed the sociological situation:

> We must look reality in the face. Tunisia consists of separate social layers and does not yet enjoy that complete harmony which makes up the balance of a nation. Perhaps here again it is a manifestation of underdevelopment. A large part of our people still live in prehistoric conditions. We are still dealing with nomadic customs and the *gourbi* may be considered a stage in advance of the tent. We are trying by every means to settle people on the land.[45]

The psychology of revolution is interesting. During the struggle with France the nationalists constantly referred to the desires and ideas of the Tunisian people, but after independence the same leaders spoke of the absence of national feeling and unity. Actually, there was no definitive national will or aspiration—it had to be invented for the purposes of the fight and later nurtured for the survival of the new state. The revolution from beginning to end had been directed by an ambitious and powerful minority. A decision for either retaining or sharing power had to be made after the revolution was won. The Neo-Destour Party decided to retain complete power for the purpose of meeting the serious problems facing Tunisia. In November, 1959, and again in 1964, a resounding vote of confidence was given to Bourguiba and the party when the leader was overwhelmingly elected president for his first and second five-year terms.[45] The whole governmental edifice rests on the power and the personality of President Bourguiba.

A study of Bourguiba's life reveals a truly remarkable leader. Despite discouragments he never lost sight of his goal of Tunisian independence. After independence the new objective of rising above underdevelopment consumed his attention. When some speculators violated government regulations, they were given severe punishments, and President Bourguiba told the assembled party elite, "I can, when the time comes, inflict the harshest punishment, since to me, the nation's interests always come before any individual interest."[47] In a country with a seventy-two per cent illiteracy rate President Bourguiba has used his weekly radio talks to inform the nation and to act in a sense as the "nation's conscience," sometimes praising, sometimes scolding.[48] An authoritarianism has resulted that could become despotic, were it not for President Bourguiba's sincere paternalism and dislike of coercive measures and his preference for persuasion.[49]

Certain traditions remain unshakable even under the attack of such an overwhelming personality. Bourguiba's attempt to abolish the observance of Ramadan (Muslim month of fasting), because it slowed down economic development, has been a failure. Before Ramadan began in 1960 (February), President Bourguiba argued that the struggle against underdevelopment was so important that it was a modern form of holy war or *jihād* and therefore should take precedence over fasting, which made people sluggish and unable to work to capacity. The president's 1960 speech on Ramadan was addressed to the young. He reminded them that the "struggle for daily bread went beyond the armed conflict."[50] The economic crisis warranted Qur'anic exceptions on fasting, asserted the president. In addition, he admonished, "In order for Africa to attain the level of power, of culture and prosperity of Europe or America, it is necessary for you to work, to conquer apprehensions, superstitions and social constraint."[51] Nevertheless, Ramadan was observed, although Bourguiba succeeded in having the cafés closed at midnight to discourage all-night activities. The following year he spoke against fasting, but not so vehemently. On March 6, 1962, prior to Ramadan Bourguiba toasted modernization with fruit juice but was silent when the fast began, probably because the shock of Bizerte was still reverberating throughout the land. The issue was more than a dispute with the "old turbans," Bourguiba's name for the conservative religious leaders; it so stirred the nation that the president softened his attack. Persuasion had little effect on traditional religious belief, and force would have been folly.

Despite Bourguiba's undeniable popularity he has reported several plots on his life. Chaos and anarchy would surely have developed if the plots had succeeded. Factionalism would have run wild without any leader having the personality, power, or popularity to immediately restore order out of chaos. The 1962 assassination attempt[52] shocked the president profoundly, "I might easily have departed this life before this 18th of January. The question had even arisen as to whether I was to be killed in my bed or whether my residence was to be shelled."[53] In analyzing the plot President Bourguiba accused the following: diehard Youssefists, Communists, *fellaghas*, a few army officers, and some Algerians aiding the Youssefists. Approximately one hundred people have been brought to trial before the Permanent Military Tribunal of Tunis. Some were sentenced to prison, but only the leaders were put before the firing squad. The statements of the accused before the court give the impression of an ill-conceived and ill-directed plot, which seemed to have as its origin solely a desire for power. The dangerous result of such an affair is that the government will become overly cautious and defensive, considering all criticism as subversive. The president, narrowly escaping death, may become a martyr wielding great power. Freedom of expression or even the right to grumble sometimes serve as important safety valves in a society. Tunisians are a very expressive people and like to give vent to their opinions. A security system that is too strict creates pressure, and it has been tightened in Tunisia since the plot.

In his speech on the 1962 plot Bourguiba also said that Communists complained about his palaces, which number four with a fifth under construction. In commenting on these expensive residences a domestic servant in Tunis remarked, "Bourguiba makes a good Bey." The problem is that in a Muslim culture ostentation is suspected by people in general, not just Communists. An Arab's home is not pretentious from the outside, nor if he is wealthy does he flaunt his wealth in public. These customs lie deep in the culture. President Nasser of the United Arab Republic was once praised for being a person who "settles down to a way of life supremely wise, neither artificially modest, nor scandalously sumptuous."[54] When one of Nasser's brothers tried to use family influence for personal benefit, Nasser quickly rebuked him. It would be unfair to accuse Bourguiba of being "scandalously sumptuous," but an inclination to display of wealth must be avoided. Similarly, Moroccan King Hassan's recent purchase of luxury goods in the United States has been criticized at home. Bourguiba argues that all palaces belong to the state and that "the day I die, I shall be found to have been poorer than when I started my political career."[55] He also maintains that he spent so many years in French jails for his patriotism that he deserves some comforts. Nevertheless, considerable criticism and "café comments" have been voiced about his expenditures.

It is difficult for any revolutionary leader to sustain afterward the popularity he enjoyed during the revolution. Some attribute the partial loss of Bourguiba's popularity to his divorce and second marriage, and others mention the Bizerte catastrophe of 1961 as a presidential mistake. In any event, despite the tarnished spots, no other leader can rival the president's popularity. Bourguiba, while exhibiting the assurance of a leader, never claimed infallibility.

The record of Bourguiba's government, even before the 1962 plot, reveals that it would not tolerate opposition or, indeed, even much criticism. This fact is most evident in the relationship with the press. In November of 1956 the government passed a press regulation law requiring that all local, as well as foreign, papers or journals be approved by the Secretariat of State of Information. Failure to comply could mean seizure of the publication and removal from the newsstands.[56] In January, 1957, the newspaper *La Presse* was suspended by government order. All the facts behind the ban were not known, but the paper had accused the government of giving too little help to the Algerians, especially since the French seized the airplane in which Ben Bella and his colleagues were flying. The paper reappeared in February, declaring, "Our destiny lies with that of Tunisia and with its new destiny, which will be what God wills,"[57] and reaffirming determination to print the news objectively with commentary loyal to the government. Three daily newspapers appear with French language editions: *La Presse, Le Petit Matin,* and *L'Action.* Both *Le Petit Matin,* founded in 1922, and *L'Action,* started in 1955, represent the Neo-Destourian point of view, with *L'Action* an undisguised party spokesman.[58] None of the three papers publishes criticism of the government.

An interesting periodical that started out with the title *L'Action,*[59] later became *L'Action Afrique,* and is now entitled *Jeune Afrique* felt the power of Bourguiba's anger. Beginning in 1957 this journal published a series of articles criticizing Bourguiba for being too weak in dealing with the French. After the bombing of Sakiet Sidi Youssef, the articles became more critical. An enraged Bourguiba not only closed the magazine but verbally lashed Mohamed Masmoudi, who wrote for the journal. Masmoudi was dismissed from the government.

Eventually the successor of *L'Action,* entitled *Afrique Action,* began publication in October, 1960, and Mohamed Masmoudi was brought back into the cabinet as minister of information. After the Bizerte affair an article in *Afrique Action,* obviously with Masmoudi's approval, attacked the whole concept of personal power as practiced by Bourguiba. Bourguiba survived the attack by allowing a little freer debate within the party. However, Masmoudi was expelled from the Political Bureau and turned to a career in journalism with the magazine, which was allowed to continue under the title *Jeune Afrique.*[60] In an article entitled "Eleven Years Later," written after the plot on Bourguiba's life, Masmoudi evaluated the president's rule favorably:

> Bourguiba returned to us, not from Kef, but from beyond the tomb, almost resurrected. This return should constitute a new point of departure for the sacred union of all Tunisians. Union for work in dignity and discipline. Union in order that our young republic can go forward without risks of stumbling on meanness, pettiness and murderous slander.[61]

After selling automobiles for a while, Masmoudi returned to the government, serving as ambassador to France.

The problem of authoritarianism is a relative one in Tunisia. Few would deny the importance of President Bourguiba's leadership in the post-revolution period in Tunisian history. He is offering the stability and direction necessary for the success of the economic plan. At the same time the voices calling for political liberalism, though not loud, cannot be completely ignored. Some intellectuals fear that unrestrained Neo-Destourian control might lead to coercive dictatorship under Bourguiba's successor. Again the hub of criticism is the Paris section of the *Union Générale des Etudiants Tunisiens* (UGET). In February, 1963, the Paris bureau passed a motion condemning the interdiction of the Communist Party in Tunisia and asked for liberty of the press and freedom of expression. When elections were held for the Paris bureau, the coalition of leftists, comprising Communists, progressives, and Arab socialists, defeated the Neo-Destourian list. It remains now for this group to work within the national UGET for a series of reforms changing the student scholarship system to allow greater freedom from party control.[62] This schism in the syndicate reveals resentment against the party for using the student organization for political purposes. Even in Tunisia itself there is evidence that many members of the UGET feel they should not be integrated with the party. Although the National Council of the Neo-Destour Party asked for complete unity and integration, the 1963 elections within UGET have shown that nonintegrationist candidates won over their Destourian rivals.[63] Later the Paris section of the UGET fell under loyalist control, but other political pressures grew from economic conditions.

It is imperative that Tunisia improve the economy and eradicate unemployment. To do this with an annual population increase of 2.2 per cent is a difficult task. Harmonious relations between the party and the UGTT (labor syndicate) are based upon continuing economic success. The UGTT has no freedom to act on economic affairs independently of the government. Today minimum wages are set by two labor commissions, one in the North and the other in the South. Each commission has two representatives from management, two from labor, and a government inspector. All disputes are settled by the Secretary of State for Social Affairs.

In the summer of 1965 a dispute broke out between the Party and the UGTT. Habib Achour, general secretary of the labor federation, accused the government of planning to eliminate him because he wanted to cooperate more closely with international labor organizations. The labor leader was arrested, and both he and his successor, Ahmed Tlili, were "excommunicated" from the Destourian Socialist Party by the Political Bureau for "acts of insubordination designed to discredit our republican regime."[64] A new secretary-general of the UGTT, Bashir Ballagha, was elected and promptly made a pact of loyalty with the Destourian Socialist Party (PSD).

In 1963 municipal elections only candidates approved by the party were placed before the voters, while in the previous elections of 1957 and 1960 local independent lists were allowed. Some of the independents had been elected in 1957. President Bourguiba commented on the 1963 elections.

> The candidates endorsed by the party have been elected by more than 80 percent of the electorate; the remainder comprised, as M. Mehiri had indicated, Communist elements or impenitent adversaries who protested by not voting or by scratching names from the lists. These results will be studied, in place of other means permitting the disclosure of the currents of opinion.[65]

Abstention and scratching names from the list seemed to alarm the party, and it actually campaigned, strangely enough, against abstention, giving the impression that it feared a large defection. The secretary-general of the party, Bahi Ladgham, called abstention "a grave error which it is necessary to remedy."[66]

Another interesting aspect of the 1963 election was that Bourguiba did not run for mayor of Monastir, his native village, a position he had held for ten years. Instead, his son, Habib Bourguiba, Jr., was the unopposed party candidate for mayor of Monastir. The return of the president's son from his ambassadorial post in Washington and his appointment to the cabinet as secretary of state for cultural affairs and information touched off rumors that Bourguiba was picking his successor. This point of view was supported by later developments. After winning a second term by a huge vote, President Bourguiba reshuffled his cabinet, making his son foreign minister. Former Foreign Minister Mongi Slim became personal representative of the president.[67] Nevertheless, in the past President Bourguiba has carefully avoided any implied succession. For example, Bahi Ladgham, who had the title of Vice-President of the Council, which might have put him first in line, was given the less auspicious title Secretary of State to the Presidency charged with Coordination and National Defense. The constitution provides that upon the vacancy of the presidential office, "the members of the government shall appoint from among themselves a temporary head of state."[68] The National Assembly would then convene and elect the successor. Some observers feel that the very lack of a specific successor designated by the constitution will cause a serious intraparty fight in the Political Bureau of the Socialist Destour Party.

Education

After viewing many of its problems, the Tunisian government decided to expand the educational system. The present literacy rate is estimated at 28 per cent of the population. In response the party has included an ambitious educational program in its economic plan. Through French and American aid a program of construction and staffing of primary, secondary, agricultural, and vocational schools, plus the new University of Tunis, has been implemented. As the educational level rises, the country's economy must be able to offer employment to an eager group of young people graduating from the secondary schools and the university at home, as well as from graduate schools abroad. In an emotional speech which brought tears to his eyes President Bourguiba reported on education to the National Assembly, which was celebrating the tenth anniversary of the president's presentation of independent Tunisia's first government to the Constituent Assembly, predecessor of the National Assembly. He reported that there were 734,000 primary school pupils compared to 200,000 ten years earlier, 80,000 secondary students compared to 15,500, and 5,000 attending an institution of higher education compared to 1,350.[69]

American Peace Corps volunteers are making a significant contribution to Tunisian education. By 1964 there were seventy volunteers teaching in Tunisia, with the teaching program scheduled to be expanded by the Corps. In 1965 twenty-two Peace Corps nurses were helping train Tunisian nurses.[70] Since

Tunisia has been eager to receive members of the Peace Corps, she has been one of the countries in which the Corps has started a major program.

Maghreb Relations

Early in his political career Bourguiba was interested in some type of Maghreb organization binding Morocco, Algeria, and Tunisia. All three countries had a great similarity of economy and culture; it seemed to be a natural union. In speaking on the Algerian situation Bourguiba pledged, "We will struggle side by side to free the Arab Maghreb from servitude, and to make it a strong and united group, which will have its own influence and its own prestige."[71] The preamble of the Tunisian constitution dedicates the government to work toward the ideal of a Maghreb union. The government has adopted the policy of supporting African unions based on economic cooperation but not on political ideology. Its reasoning was candidly stated by Tunisia at the Addis Ababa Conference of Independent African States in May, 1963. Tunisia asserted that too much energy is wasted in ideological bickering to the neglect of areas where economic cooperation would be mutually beneficial. For example, why not combine the oil refining industry for the Maghreb rather than compete with one another? The Maghreb needs close economic ties with the European Common Market; geography has dictated that the Maghrebian market lies in Western Europe.

The greatest obstacle to Maghreb cooperation has been the political bickering that Tunisia warned against. President Bourguiba and Algerian president Ahmed Ben Bella had personality differences as well as differing points of view on the pace of Arab socialism. Bourguiba regarded Ben Bella as a young radical more prone to follow the dictates of Nasser than the necessities of the Maghreb.[72] Algeria, in the opinion of Bourguiba, had never given Tunisia enough credit for aid during the Algerian war, and President Bourguiba did not hesitate to tell Ben Bella this in a fatherly manner. President Ben Bella, head of a much larger state than Tunisia, was in no mood for any father-and-son talks. The disputed border between southern Tunisia and Algeria is another source of friction and may become a serious issue because oil reserves appear to lie in the area.

A tense situation further divided the two countries after the 1962 plot on Bourguiba's life. When a group of Youssefists involved in the plot took refuge in Algeria, Bourguiba recalled the Tunisian ambassador in Algeria and warned that "Tunisia, which was not afraid to stand against France, will not show itself weak before Mr. Ben Bella."[73]

Enabling the presidents of the three North African Arab republics to meet, the Addis Ababa Conference offered an opportunity for improved relations. Speaking of his conferences with President Nasser of the United Arab Republic and President Ben Bella of Algeria, Bourguiba exclaimed:

> I have the impression that these two meetings have been fruitful and that they have allowed all misunderstandings to dissipate. This was able to reinforce the ties of fraternity, friendship and loyal and sincere cooperation among our countries.[74]

Following these meetings, Tunisia and Algeria reestablished diplomatic relations on the ambassadorial level, and relations steadily improved. In July, 1964, economic officials of the two countries held talks and announced plans to

> coordinate production of glass, car assembly, iron and fertilizer processing and radio assembly plants. The statement stipulated that an Algerian trade center will be created in Tunis and that Algeria and Tunisia would jointly study the possibility of building a dam on the Medjerda, on the Tunisian-Algerian border.[75]

Relations between Tunisia and Morocco are normal, but a border dispute has strained Algerian-Moroccan relations. All three Maghrebian states have different political and economic philosophies. Morocco has a constitutional monarch who is cautious about economic change. Algeria has a republican government which pledges rapid socialization, while Tunisia's republic has moved more slowly in the path of Arab socialism. Only Morocco allows opposition political parties to exist. With all these differences political unity seems remote, but the surprise factor is the economic. Future economic demands may bring the Maghreb dream to fruition, but few dreams are accomplished rapidly.

On June 19, 1965, Colonel Hourai Boumedienne deposed Ben Bella as president of Algeria. Generally Tunisian-Algerian relations should improve, since there is no personal animosity between the two presidents. However, much depends upon the relationship between Tunisia and the Arab League. During a March, 1965, tour of the Eastern Mediterranean, President Bourguiba called on the Arab states to adopt a less antagonistic attitude toward Israel. His request angered the Arab League, and Tunisia has since declined to participate in League activities. Algeria, unlike Tunisia, has retained close ties with the Arab League. Tunisia would look with disfavor on a close alliance between Algeria and Egypt, which might endanger the more moderate foreign policy expressed by Bourguiba.

Conclusion

The perennial problems of Tunisia have remained despite the type of government, foreign or domestic. A paucity of natural resources in a parched land has brought poverty throughout history. Various governments have struggled with this dilemma, but none has been so dedicated or so determined to supply the answers as the present one, which, after all, is Tunisia's own. During the early protectorate France made a substantial contribution to Tunisia. Corruption within the Bey's government and the financial bungling of mameluke officials were eradicated. Men of ability like Paul Cambon superimposed an orderly government on a country splintered by tribal disputes. Unfortunately, in true nineteenth-century style, the political and economic reforms too often benefited Europeans in Tunisia and neglected the illiterate populace—a situation the twentieth century would not tolerate. Nationalist agitation and French stubbornness turned the constructive protectorate into a garrison state. The ensuing bitter struggle left a bruised land for the independent state to heal.

Throughout Africa and Asia similar stories are unfolding. Most new states have created monolithic one-party governments and socialized economies to solve their problems. Undoubtedly this provides the machinery for a direct and rapid attack on underdevelopment. However, a socialized economy need not be wedded to an authoritarian political system. When the people have been fed, the standard of living improved, and the educational level advanced, will the party itself be the victim of attack? When nations reach a degree of sophistication and maturity, will the people shout "freedom" as vehemently as they earlier shouted "independence"? Wise rulers will not overlook this possibility, and Tunisia shows many signs of prudence.

In Tunisia a new generation is beginning to move into positions of leadership. Its members were not active in the revolt against France, and many are graduates of the University of Tunis or of universities abroad other than French. Being less Francophile, they tend to look to the United States and, in a few cases, to Russia for help. The new government now has its chance, but it must have continued outside help. For the sake of a fine people one can only hope that history will be able to speak favorably of Tunisia's efforts.

APPENDIX
GLOSSARY
BIBLIOGRAPHY
NOTES
INDEX

APPENDIX

1881-1882 Théodore Roustan (resident-minister)

1882-1886 Paul Cambon (resident-minister, until the title was changed to resident-general)

1886-1892 Justin Massicault

1892-1894 Charles Rouvier

1894-1900 René Millet

1900-1901 Monsieur Benôit (acting resident-general)

1901-1906 Stéphen Pichon

1906-1918 Gabriel Alapetite

1918-1921 Etienne Flandin

1921-1929 Lucien Saint

1929-1933 François Manceron

1933-1936 Marcel Peyrouton

1936-1938 Armand Guillon

1938-1940 Eirik Labonne

1940 June 5 to July 25
Marcel Peyrouton

1940-1943 Admiral Esteva

1943, May 15 to June 25
General Alphonse Juin (acting resident-general)

1943-1947 General Charles Mast

1947-1950 Jean Mons

1950-1952 Louis Perillier

1952-1953 General Jean de Hautecloque

1953-1954 Pierre Voizard

1954 to internal autonomy, 1955
General Boyer de La Tour

GLOSSARY

achour: tax on wheat and barley land

alfa or esparto grass: reed-like plant used in mat-weaving or basket-making; the cellulose of alfa is used in paper manufacture

al-Fatat: society calling for full Arab freedom from Turkish control

al-Kahtaniva: society that called for Turko-Arab cooperation

cadis: Islamic judge

caid: tribal leader, local administrator

caidat: territory administered by a *caid*

chechia: red hat worn by Muslims in North Africa

colon: refers to European "settlers"

delga-en-nour: high quality date grown in southern Tunisia

destour: constitution

Djama'a Zitouna: theology school of the Mosque of the Olive Branch in Tunis

djema'a: a committee serving a religious function

enzel: land rental contract under malekite rite

fellagha: Tunisian underground fighter against the French

fellah (plural-*fellaheen*): peasant, tiller of the soil

gourbis: primitive huts, usually stone with mudplastered walls

habous: land held in religious trust

hadith: a tradition, some saying of the Prophet

hadith al khamis: President Bourguiba's "Thursday Talk" to the people

hanefite: an orthodox rite of Muslim law brought to North Africa by the Turks

imam: leader of the Muslim prayer service

jihād: Islamic holy war

kasbah: fortified section of the medina

khalifa: administrative assistant to the *caid* or a representative of Allah or of a Prophet

khammes: peasants working for a landowner

kouttabs: small Qu'ranic schools

Maghreb: Northwest Africa, means "western land" in Arabic

malekite: an orthodox rite of Muslim law

mameluke: Turkish slave in North Africa

medina: Muslim section of a city

medjba: tax levied on rural but not urban populations

melk land: land held under the Anglo-Saxon concept of individual ownership

meskins: a poor Tunisian

mgharca: contracts using European capital and Tunisian labor for agricultural production

mokhaddems: overseers who administered private *habous*

mrazla: a written judicial decision

mufti: religious jurisconsult

oudjak: Tunisian policeman

outika: document confirming a lost title to land

Ouzara: central Tunisian administration

ouzara court: secular court

piaster: a Tunisian unit of currency

rabta: a store of grain for the poor

Ramadan: Islamic month of fasting during the day

sahel: coast

sharaa: religious law

sheikh: elder of a tribe with administrative power

Sheikh-el-Islam: leading Muslim official

sirocco: hot wind off the Sahara

souk: bazaar, marketplace

sunna: Muslim traditions including sayings of Muhammad

wakf: Eastern Arab term for *habous*

zitoun: olive

zouave: an Algerian serving in the French army

BIBLIOGRAPHY

Government Publications

TUNISIAN PROTECTORATE

Direction de l'Agriculture et du Commerce, *Notice sur la Tunisie* (Tunis, 1903).
Direction Générale de l'Enseignement Public, *Conférences sur les administrations tunisiennes* (Sousse, 1899).
Direction des Forêts, *Notice sur les forêts de la Tunisie* (Tunis, 1889).
Journal Officiel Tunisien, 1890-1957.
Résidence Générale de la République Française, *Notice générale sur la Tunisie*, 1881-1921 (Toulouse, 1922).
Direction Générale des Travaux Publics, *Les travaux publics du protectorat français en Tunisie*, 3 vols. (Tunis, 1900).

TUNISIAN REPUBLIC

République Tunisienne, *Status, Coopérative Agricole; Société Civile particulière à personnes et capital variable* (Tunis, 1958).
Secretariat of State for Cultural Affairs and Information, *United States Aid Program to Tunisia*, March, 1963.
———, *Constitution of the Tunisian Republic* (Tunis, 1960).
———, *Speeches of President Habib Bourguiba* (seventeen of these were read; complete titles are given if they are footnoted).
———, *Tunisian-American Relations* (Tunis, 1959).
———, several books explaining modern Tunisia were published by the Secretariat: *Tunisia Works*, 1960; *Tunisian Development 62-71*, 1962.
Journal Officiel de la République Tunisienne, 1957 to date.

TUNISIAN SYNDICATES

Union Générale des Etudiants Tunisiens, *Travaux du premier congrès national*, Paris, July 10-13, 1953.
Néo-Destour and U.G.E.T., *Brochure du vᵉ anniversaire de l'assassinat de Ferhat Hached*, Tunis, December, 1957.

Néo-Destour, *Bulletin du Néo-Destour de la France,* February 1, 1955, # 6.

FRANCE

Ministère des Affaires Etrangères, *Documents diplomatiques; Affaires de Tunisie, 1870-1881* (Paris, 1881).
———, *Documents diplomatiques français,* 10 vols., 1871-1914 (Paris, 1929).
———, *Rapport au président de la République sur la Tunisie en 1881-1890* (Paris, 1890).
———, *Documents diplomatiques; Afrique, 1881-1898* (Paris, 1898).
Ambassade de France, *Tunisian Affairs,* New York, Bulletins Nos. 1-9.
Ministère du Commerce, *Bulletin consulaire français,* 22 vols. (Paris, 1877-1891).
Présidence du Conseil, *Facts and Figures about French North Africa* (Paris, 1952).
Sénat et Chambre de Députés: *Journal Officiel, 1881-1892; Débats parlementaires, 1881-1892; Documents parlementaires, 1881-1892.*

GREAT BRITAIN

Foreign Office, *British and Foreign State Papers* (London, 1881).
———, *Reports from Her Majesty's Consuls on the Manufactures, Commerce, etc. of their Consular Districts* (London, 1881-1883).
———, *Reports from Her Majesty's Diplomatic and Consular Officers Abroad* (London, 1886-1890).
Parliament: *Accounts and Papers* vol. XCIX, Papers by Command Nos. 1-8.
Parliament: Great Britain, *3 Hansard,* CCLXXXVI, (1881).

UNITED STATES

United States Agency for International Development, *Report on Water Conservation,* unclassified (Tunis, 1963).
Department of Commerce, *Tunis: Its Resources, Industries and Commerce with Reference to United States Trade* (Washington, 1923).
———, "Economic Developments in Tunisia 1958," *Economic Reports* (Washington, 1959).
———, "Basic Data on the Economy of Tunisia," *Economic Reports* (Washington, 1959).

Department of State, *Consular Letters*, Tunis, vols. XII, XIII, 1877-1906.
———, *Consular Letters*, Tunis, decimal series, 1906-1910.
———, *Consular Letters*, Tunis, microfilm 1910-1930.
———, *Treaties and Other International Acts Series 3794*, Economic, Technical and Related Assistance Agreement between the U.S. and Tunisia, March 26, 1957.

Collections of Laws, Treaties, and Diplomatic Documents

Bompard, Maurice (ed.), *Législation de la Tunisie; Recueil des lois, décrets et réglements en vigueur dans la Régence de Tunis au 1er janvier 1888* (Paris, 1888).
———, *Législation de la Tunisie; Supplément du 1er janvier 1896* (Paris, 1896).
Girault, Arthur, *Principles de colonisation et de législation coloniale*, 5 vols. (Paris, 1928).
Rouard de Card, E., *Traités de la France avec les pays de l'Afrique du Nord* (Paris, 1906).
Khalil, Muhammad (ed.), *The Arab States and the Arab League; A Documentary Record*, 2 vols. Khayat's (Beirut, 1962).
Knaplund, Paul (ed.), *Letters from the Berlin Embassy 1871-1874, 1880-1885*, American Historical Association (Washington, 1944).
Charter of the United Nations
Commission Internationale Contre le Régime Concentrationnaire, *Live Blanc sur la détention politique en Tunisie* (Brussels, 1952).

Memoirs and Correspondence

Cambon, Paul, *Correspondance 1870-1924*, 3 vols. (Paris, 1940).
Ferry, Jules, *Lettres de Jules Ferry 1846-1893* (Paris, 1914).
Freycinet, Charles de, *Souvenirs 1878-1893* (Paris, 1914).
Grüssenmeyer, A. C. (ed.), *Vingt-cinq années d'episcopat en France et en Afrique, Documents biographiques sur son éminence le Cardinal Lavigerie; Archevêque de Carthage et d'Alger, Primat d'Afrique*, 2 vols. (Algiers, 1888).
Juin, Maréchal Alphonse, *Mémoires; Alger, Tunis, Rome* (Paris, 1959).

Books

Anthony, John, *Tunisia; A Personal View of a Timeless Land,* Scribner (New York, 1961).

Ardant, Gabriel, *La Tunisie d'aujourd'hui et de demain* (Paris, 1961).

Aron, Robert, *The Vichy Regime 1940-44,* Macmillan (New York, 1958).

Barbour, Nevill, et al., *A Survey of North West Africa,* Oxford University Press (London, 1962).

Berque, Jacques, *Le Maghreb entre deux guerres* (Paris, 1962).

Bertrand, Louis, *Devant l'Islam, part II, Le centenaire du Cardinal Lavigerie* (Paris, 1926).

Bourguiba, Habib, *The Advancement of Africa,* Secretariat of State for Cultural Affairs and Information (Tunis, 1960).

———, *Towards Peace in Algeria,* Secretariat of State for Cultural Affairs and Information (Tunis, 1959).

———, *La Tunisie et la France; Vingt-cinq ans de lutte pour une cooperation libre* (Paris, 1954).

Brace, Richard M., *Morocco—Algeria—Tunisia,* Prentice-Hall (Englewood Cliffs, N. J., 1964).

Broadley, A. M., *The Last Punic War; Tunis, Past and Present; With a Narrative of the French Conquest of the Regency,* 2 vols., William Blackwood & Sons (London, 1881).

Brown, Leon C. (ed.), *State and Society in Independent North Africa,* The Middle East Institute (Washington, 1966).

Cambon, Henri, *Histoire de la Régence de Tunis* (Paris, 1948).

Carter, G. (ed.), *African One-Party States,* Cornell University Press (Ithaca, N.Y., 1962).

Constant, Paul Henri d'Estournelles de, *La Politique française en Tunisie; Le Protectorat et ses origines 1854-1891* (Paris, 1891).

Day, Georges, *Les Affaires de la Tunisie et du Maroc devant les Nations Unies* (Paris, 1953).

de Lanessan, Jean M.A., *La Tunisie* (Paris, 1887).

Despagnet, Frantz, *La Diplomatie de la troisième république et le droit des gens* (Paris, 1904).

———, *Essai sur les protectorats* (Paris, 1896).

de Villiers, G., *Derrière le rideau tunisien* (Paris, 1955).

Douglas, Norman, *Fountains in the Sand; Rambles among the Oases of Tunisia,* Martin Secker (London, 1912).

Exposition Coloniale de Marseille, *Editions,* 12 vols. (Marseille, 1905-07) :
  *Les Colonies françaises au début du XX*ᵉ *siècle,* vol. I. (1906).
  Les Ressources agricoles et forestières des colonies françaises, vol. IV (1907).
  Les Productions minérales et l'extension des exploitations minières, vol. V (1907) .
  L'Industrie des pêches sux colonies, vol. VI (1906) .
  Histoire de l'expansion coloniale de la France depuis 1870 jusqu'en 1905, vol. X (1905) .
Fanjans, Roman, *Alerte en Afrique du Nord* (Paris, 1953) .
Faucon, Narcisse, *La Tunisie avant et depuis l'occupation française; Histoire et colonisation,* 2 vols. (Paris, 1893) .
Fauvet, Jacques, *La IV*ᵉ *République* (Paris, 1959) .
Fitoussi, Elie et Benazet, Aristide, *L'Etat tunisien et le protectorat français; Histoire et organisation, 1521 à 1931,* 2 vols. (Paris, 1931) .
Ford Foundation, *Tapestry for Tomorrow* (New York, 1964) .
Gallagher, Charles F., *The United States and North Africa; Morocco, Algeria and Tunisia,* Harvard University Press (Cambridge, 1963) .
Ganiage, Jean, *Les Origines du protectorat français en Tunisie, 1861-1881* (Paris, 1959) .
Garas, Felix, *Bourguiba et la naissance d'une nation* (Paris, 1956) .
Gray, Ezio, Marcia, *Italy and the Question of Tunis* (Milan, 1939) .
Hahn, Lorna, *North Africa, Nationalism to Nationhood,* Public Affairs Press (Washington, D. C., 1960) .
Halpern, Manfred, *The Politics of Social Change in the Middle East and North Africa,* Princeton University Press (Princeton, N.J., 1963) .
Hammerton, Thomas, *Tunisia Unveiled,* Hale (London, 1959) .
Hanotaux, Gabriel et Martineau, Alfred, *Histoire des colonies françaises et de l'expansion de la France dans le monde,* 6 vols. (Paris, 1931).
Huc, Paul, *L'Oeuvre politique et économique du protectorat français en Tunisie* (Toulouse, 1924).
Julien, Ch.-André, *L'Afrique du Nord en marche; Nationalismes musulmans et souveraineté française* (Paris, 1953) .
Lacouture, Jean, *Cinq hommes et la France* (Paris, 1961) .

Laitmen, Leon, *Tunisia Today,* Citadel (New York, 1954) .

Lallemand, Charles, *La Tunisie, pays de protectorat française* (Paris, 1892) .

Leroy-Beaulieu, Paul, *L'Algérie et la Tunisie* (Paris, 1897) .

Le Tourneau, Roger, *Evolution politique de l'Afrique du Nord Musulmane 1920-1961* (Paris, 1962) .

Liebesney, Herbert, *The Government of French North Africa,* University of Pennsylvania Press (Philadelphia, 1943) .

McGuire, Edna, *The Peace Corps; Kindlers of the Spark,* Macmillan (New York, 1966).

Maroc et Tunisie; *Le Problème du protectorat* (Paris, 1953) .

Micaud, Charles A., Brown, Leon C., Moore, Clement H., *Tunisia; The Politics of Modernization,* Praeger (New York, 1964) .

Moore, Clement H., *Tunisia Since Independence,* University of California Press (Berkeley, 1965) .

Nickerson, Jane S., *A Short History of North Africa,* Devin-Adair (New York, 1961).

Olivier, Louis (ed.), *La Tunisie* (Paris, 1899) .

Paul Cambon, Ambassadeur de France, 1843-1924, par un diplomate, (written by Henri Paul Cambon, the son of Paul Cambon), (Paris, 1937).

Pellegrin, Arthur, *Histoire de la Tunisie depuis les origines jusqu'à nos jours* (Tunis, 1948) .

Pickles, Dorothy, *The Fifth French Republic; Institutions and Politics,* Praeger (New York, 1962) .

Pickthall, Mohammed M. (trans.), *The Meaning of the Glorious Koran* (New York, 1953) .

Piolet, J. B. (S.J.), *La France hors de France* (Paris, 1900) .

———, *Les Missions catholiques françaises au XIXᵉ siècle,* 5 vols. (Paris, 1903) .

Piquet, Victor, *La Colonisation française dans l'Afrique du Nord* (Paris, 1912).

Rambaud, Alfred, *Jules Ferry* (Paris, 1903) .

Roberts, Stephen H., *History of French Colonial Policy 1870-1925,* 2 vols., P.S. King & Sons (London, 1929) .

Rous, Jean, *Tunisie Attention* (Paris, 1952) .

Schacht, Joseph, *The Origins of Muhammadan Jurisprudence,* Oxford University Press (Oxford, 1950) .

Serres, Jean, *La Politique turque en Afrique du Nord sous la monarchie de juillet* (Paris, 1925).

Silvéra, Victor, *La Réforme des assemblées locales en Tunisie; Conseils municipaux et conseils de caidats* (Paris, 1953).

Taalbi, Abdelaziz, *La Tunisie martyre, Ses revendications* (Paris, 1920).

Tlatli, Salah-Eddine, *Tunisie nouvelle: Problèmes et perspectives* (Tunis, 1957).

Tournier, J., *Le Cardinal Lavigerie et son action politique 1863-1892* (Paris, 1913).

Vitry, Alexis, *L'Oeuvre française en Tunisie* (Paris, 1900).

von Grunebaum, G. E., *Modern Islam; The Search for Cultural Identity*, Vintage Book, Random House (New York, 1964).

Werth, Alexander, *Lost Statesman; The Strange Story of Pierre Mendès-France*, Abelard-Schuman (New York, 1958).

Zartman, I. W., *Government and Politics in Northern Africa*, Praeger (New York, 1963).

Zeine, Zeine N., *Arab-Turkish Relations and the Emergence of Arab Nationalism*, Khayat's (Beirut, 1958).

———, *The Struggle for Arab Independence*, Khayat's (Beirut, 1960).

Zéraffa, Michael, *Tunisie* (Paris, 1963).

Ziadeh, Nicola A., *Origins of Nationalism in Tunisia*, American University of Beirut (Beirut, 1962).

Periodicals

Arab Information Center, *Arab News and Views*, vol. X, No. 8, August 1, 1964.

Bourguiba, Habib, "Nationalism: Antidote to Communism," *Foreign Affairs*, XXXV, July, 1957, pp. 646-653.

Constant, Paul Henri d'Estournelles de, "Les Débuts d'un protectorat," *Revue des Deux Mondes*, vols. LXXIX, LXXX, February 15, 1887, March 15, 1887.

de la Far, André, "Nouveau départ en Tunisie," *Monde Nouveau Paru*, April, 1954, No. 78, pp. 5-10.

de Maupassant, Guy de, "Vers Kairouan," *Revue des Deux Mondes*, February 1, 1889, vol. 91, pp. 520-548.

de Montety, Henri, "Les Données du problème Tunisien," *Politique Etrangère*, March, 1952, pp. 447-466.

Gallagher, Charles F., American Universities Field Staff Reports Service, North African Series, 1961-1964.

Gorringe, H. H., "Tunis," *The Nation,* vol. XXVI, May 2, 1878, p. 289.

I.B.L.A., *Revue de l'Institut des Belles Lettres Arabes à Tunis,* "Tunisie, après cinq ans d'Indépendance," 24ᵉ année, Nos. 95-96, 1961.

Langer, W. L., "The European Powers and the French Occupation of Tunis," *American Historical Review,* XXXI, 1925-26, pp. 55-78; 251-265.

Lee, Dwight E., "The Origins of Pan-Islamism," *The American Historical Review,* vol. XLVII, January, 1942, pp. 278-287.

Leroy-Beaulieu, Paul, "La Colonisation française en Tunisie," *Revue des Deux Mondes,* November 15, 1886, vol. 78, pp. 373-406.

Lewis, Bernard, "The Quest for Freedom; A Sad Story of the Middle East," *Encounter,* March, 1964, pp. 29-40.

Lewis, William H., "The New Nomadism in North Africa," *The Middle East Journal,* Summer, 1957, pp. 269-281.

Ling, Dwight L., "The French Invasion of Tunisia," *The Historian,* August, 1960, pp. 396-412.

———, "Paul Cambon, Coordinator of Tunisia," *The Historian,* August, 1957, pp. 436-455.

Ling, Phyllis Cooper, "Washing Away Misconceptions in Tunisia," *World Outlook,* June, 1964, pp. 13-15.

McKay, Donald V., "The French in Tunisia," *The Geographical Review,* vol. XXXV, pp. 368-390.

Masmoudi, Mohamed, "Onze ans après," *Jeune Afrique,* January 21-27, 1963, p. 6.

Moore, Clement H., "Bourguibism in Tunisia," *Current History,* January, 1963, pp. 34-40.

———, "The Neo-Destour Party of Tunisia; A Structure for Democracy?," *World Politics,* April, 1962.

———, "Politics in a Tunisian Village," *The Middle East Journal,* Autumn, 1963, pp. 527-540.

Nouira, Hedi., "Le Néo-Destour," *Politique Etrangère,* July, 1954, 19ᵉ année, pp. 317-334.

Piel, Jean, "Le Cas tunisien," *Critique* No. 88, September, 1954, pp. 789-803.

Plauchut, Edmond, "La France en Tunisie; La Régence avant le protectorat," October, 1890, vol. 101, *Revue des Deux Mondes*, pp. 622-659.

Puaux, Gabriel, "La France en Tunisie," *La Revue de Paris*, February, 1953, pp. 41-50.

Ravussin, Che.-E., "Août 54 en Tunisie," *Esprit*, October, 1954, p. 517.

Réalités Tunisiennes (bi-mensuel).

Rigotard, Jean, "Les Réformes en Tunisie; Etude des dispositions législatives du 4 Mars," *La Nouvelle Revue Française d'Outre-Mer* No. 6, June, 1954, pp. 253-256.

Romeril, Paul E. A., "Tunisian Nationalism: A Bibliographical Outline," *The Middle East Journal*, Spring 1960, pp. 206-215.

Rondot, Pierre, "Accalmie ou apaisement en Tunisie?," *Etudes*, February, 1954, pp. 182-192.

Rosenfeld, Oreste, "Association dans l'égalite," *Preuves*, March, 1953, No. 25, pp. 54-56.

Roy, Jules, "L'Anxiété tunisienne," *La Revue de Paris*, August, 1953, pp. 22-28.

Sfeir, George N., "Fundamental Characteristics of the Tunisian Constitution," *The Middle East Journal*, Autumn 1959, pp. 446-448.

Silvéra, Victor, "De l'autonomie interne à l'indépendance de la Tunisie," *Revue Juridique et Politique de l'Union Française*, 10 année, No. 4, October-December, 1956, pp. 687-704.

———, "Réflexions sur la crise des rapports franco-tunisiens," *Politique Etrangère*, 23 année, No. 2, 1958, pp. 231-243.

———, "Du régime beylical à la République Tunisienne," *Politique Etrangère*, 22 année, No. 5, 1957, pp. 594-611.

———, "Le régime constitutionnel de la Tunisie," *Revue Française de Science Politique*, vol. X, No. 2, June, 1960, pp. 366-394.

Simiot, Bernard, "Tunisie pierre angulaire," *Hommes et Mondes*, February, 1954, pp. 329-342; March, 1954, pp. 555-562; April, 1954, pp. 98-105.

Tabone, Carmel, "L'Imbroglio juridique tunisien," *La Nouvelle Revue Française d'Outre-Mer*, April, 1954, pp. 145-149.

Taussig, H. G., "Tunis Emerges," *Africa Trade and Development*, July, 1962, pp. 11-13.

Valbert, G., "Le Régime du protectorat en Tunisie," *Revue des Deux Mondes*, November 1, 1886, vol. 78, pp. 193-204.

Variot, G., "Une Visite à l'hôpital arabe de Tunis," *La Revue Scientifique,* April 23, 1881, pp. 537, 538.

Vignon, Louis, "La France dans l'Afrique du Nord," *Revue Coloniale Internationale,* 1887, Tome I, pp. 142-146, 294-323.

Periodicals consulted in general: *L'Action, Afrique Action, Jeune Afrique,* all published in Tunis (specific references from these are footnoted).

Atlases and Encyclopedias

République Française, Gouvernement Général de l'Algérie, *Atlas d'Algérie et de Tunisie* (Algiers, 1924) .

Sorre, Max and Hardy, Georges (eds.) , *Atlas de l'Afrique du Nord* (Paris, 1939).

Universal Geography, 19 vols. J. S. Virtue & Co. (London, 1882-1897) .

Hughes, Thomas P. (ed) , *A Dictionary of Islam,* W. H. Allen (London, 1895) .

La Grande encyclopédie, 31 vols. (Paris, n.d.) .

The Encyclopaedia of Islam, 4 vols., Luzac (London, 1913-1934) .

Le Monde Economique, "World's Documents Series," Special Issue: Tunisia, June, 1956.

Encyclopédie Mensuelle d'Outre-Mer, "Tunisia 54" Special Number (Paris, 1954).

Newspapers

Tunis, *L'Action*

Tunis, *La Dépêche Tunisienne*

Tunis, *Independance*

Tunis, *Mission* (hebdomadaire politique paraissant le vendredi)

Tunis, *La Nation Tunisienne*

Tunis, *Le Petit Matin*

Tunis, *La Presse*

Tunis, *La Voix du Tunisien*

Paris, *Le Figaro*

Paris, *Journal des Débats*

Paris, *Le Monde*

London, *The Times*

Boston, *Christian Science Monitor*

New York, *New York Times*

NOTES

The following abbreviated forms for frequently cited sources have been used throughout the notes:

Accounts and Papers: Great Britain, *Accounts and Papers Issued at the Command of Parliament, 1881.*

Conférences: Direction Générale de l'Enseignement Public, *Conférences sur les administrations tunisiennes* (Sousse, 1899).

Con. Lett.: Consular Letters, Tunis.

Direction de l'Agriculture, *Notice:* Direction de l'Agriculture et du Commerce, *Notice sur la Tunisie* (Tunis, 1903).

Documents diplomatiques, françaises: France, Ministère des Affaires Etrangères, *Documents diplomatiques françaises, 1871-1914,* 1st series.

Documents diplomatiques . . . Tunisie: France, Ministère des Affaires Etrangères, *Documents diplomatiques, affairs de Tunisie, 1870-1881.* (This is the French Yellow Book on Tunisia.)

J.O.R.T.: Journel Officiel de la République Tunisienne.

J.O.T.: Journel Officiel Tunisien.

Notice générale 1881-1921: Résidence Générale de la République Française, *Notice generale sur la Tunisie 1881-1921,* (Toulouse, 1922).

I

1. Tunisia has an area of 48,300 square miles, which is about the size of the state of Louisiana. The land is measured in hectares under the metric system. A hectare is equivalent to 2.471 acres.

2. Norman Douglas, *Fountains in the Sand: Rambles among the Oases of Tunisia* (London, 1912), p. 224.

3. *Universal Geography* (London, 1882-97), XI, 124.

4. Paul Leroy-Beaulieu, *L'Algérie et la Tunisie* (Paris, 1897), pp. 346, 347. More recent figures from the Gouvernement Général de l'Algérie, *Atlas, d'Algérie et de Tunisie* (Algiers, 1924), Fascicule V,

give these annual averages: in the mountains of Kroumir as high as 55 to 62 inches; in the northeastern area around Tunis about 20 inches; in the southern oases only 4 inches.

5. *Encyclopaedia of Islam* (London, 1913-1934), I, 704.

6. H. H. Gorringe, "Tunis," *The Nation*, vol. XXVI, May 2, 1878, p. 290.

7. *Con. Lett.* XII, Nov. 12, 1877, dispatch 254.

8. Although the present Tunisian government is trying to replace the *gourbis* as rapidly as possible, many still exist in central and southern Tunisia.

9. E. Rouard de Card, *Traités de la France avec les pays de l'Afrique du Nord* (Paris, 1906), p. 128 (article X).

10. Ibid., pp. 106, 107.

11. Ibid., p. 204, article II.

12. A man by the same name, Hussein Bey, established the Hussein dynasty in 1705. He was a Greek adventurer with very little Arab or Turkish blood. After settling the dispute with Algeria, he founded the dynasty that ruled until 1957, when the monarchy was abolished.

13. Rouard de Card, *Traités*, pp. 213-15.

14. This patch of land, near the site of ancient Carthage, was said to be where Saint Louis died of the plague in August, 1270.

15. Jean Serres, *La Politique turque en Afrique du Nord sous la monarchie de juillet* (Paris, 1925), p. 143.

16. Ibid., pp. 371, 372.

17. Gabriel Hanotaux et Alfred Martineau, eds., *Histoire des colonies françaises* (Paris, 1931), III, 392. The section on Tunisia was written by Georges Hardy, the Director of the Colonial School.

18. Serres, *La Politique turque*, pp. 351, 352.

19. Jean Ganiage, *Les Origines du protectorate français en Tunisie, 1861-1881* (Paris, 1959), p. 71.

20. A. M. Broadley, *The Last Punic War* (London, 1882), I, 110, 111.

21. Ganiage, *Les Origines*, p. 73. Public intoxication is practically nonexistent in Tunisia today, which raises the question of either a prejudiced report from Consul Roches or the possibility of a much better disciplined society today.

22. Henri Cambon, *Histoire de la Régence de Tunis* (Paris, 1948), p. 113.

23. Arthur Pellegrin, *Histoire de la Tunisie* (Tunis, 1948), p. 164.

24. Hanotaux et Martineau, *Histoire,* III, 397.

25. Paul Henri d'Estournelles de Constant, *La Politique française en Tunisie* (Paris, 1891), p. 33.

26. Hanotaux et Martineau, *Histoire,* III, 396.

27. Victor Piquet, *La Colonisation française dans l'Afrique du Nord* (Paris, 1912), p. 346.

28. This position was held by a Frenchman throughout the existence of the Financial Commission. Victor Villet held the office from 1869 until 1874. He was also vice-president of the Financial Commission, and the president was the Bey's minister of finance, Mustapha Khaznadar.

29. France, *Journal Officiel,* August, 1882, p. 2103.

30. Paul Huc, *L'Oeuvre politique et économique du protectorat français en Tunisie* (Toulouse, 1924), p. 42.

31. *Documents diplomatiques . . . Tunisie,* p. 8.

32. Ganiage, *Les Origines,* p. 179.

33. Ibid., p. 426.

34. Ibid., p. 427.

35. Khéréddine was a mameluke of Circassian origin from the Caucasus. Born between 1825 and 1830, he was enslaved by the Turks and sold in Tunis about 1840. He was raised at court, where he held many official positions. In turn he had been president of the Financial Commission, president of the Grand Council and head of a mission to Turkey which brought about closer relations between the Porte and the Regency. He later became an official in the Turkish government and died in Constantinople in 1889.

36. d'Estournelles de Constant, *La Politique française,* pp. 74, 75.

37. *Conférences,* pp. 15, 16. This same idea is expressed in Elie Fitoussi et Aristide Benazet, *L'Etat tunisien et le protectorat français; Histoire et organisation, 1521 à 1931,* vol. I, 115. The American consul expressed a similar view of Khéréddine; see *Con. Lett.,* XII, dispatch 270.

38. d'Estournelles de Constant, *La Politique française,* pp. 76, 77.

39. *Con. Lett.,* XII, January 21, 1879, dispatch 24.

40. Ibid.

41. Franz Despagnet, *La Diplomatie de la Troisième République et le droit des gens* (Paris, 1904), p. 221.

42. *Con. Lett.*, XII, January 21, 1879, dispatch 24.

43. For an account of the attitude of the powers toward Tunisia, especially Bismarck's policy, see William A. Langer, "European Powers and the French Occupation of Tunis," *American Historical Review*, XXXI (Oct. 1925, Jan. 1926), pp. 55-78; 251-65.

44. *Accounts and Papers*, no. 2886, p. 2.

45. Ibid., p. 4.

46. Paul Knaplund, ed., *Letters from the Berlin Embassy* (Washington, 1944), p. 124.

47. *Documents diplomatiques, françaises*, II, 412.

48. Knaplund, *Letters from the Berlin Embassy*, p. 220.

49. *Documents diplomatiques, françaises*, II, 127.

50. Ezio M. Gray, *Italy and the Question of Tunis* (Milan, 1939), p. 13. See also Helen B. Metcalf, "French and Italian Rivalry in Tunisia" (unpublished doctoral dissertation, University of Maryland, 1942).

51. *Documents diplomatiques, françaises*, II, 394.

52. The English journalist and lawyer A. M. Broadley quotes from the convention to show that it was a mythical monopoly: see his *Tunis Past and Present* (London, 1882), I, 185. The text of the convention is in E. Rouard de Card, *Traités de la France avec les pays de l'Afrique du Nord* (Paris, 1906), pp. 228-32.

53. Hanotaux et Martineau, *Histoire*, III, 403.

54. d'Estournelles de Constant, *La Politique française*, p 95. See also Eugene Staley, *War and the Private Investor* (New York, 1935), 346. Important as the purchase was, there is danger of overemphasizing it; economically the Italian railroad was not a serious threat after France received the right to cut a shipping channel across the Lake of Tunis and to build a harbor for the city of Tunis.

55. *Con. Lett.*, XII (1878), dispatch 270.

56. Ibid., dispatch 271.

57. Ibid., (1879), dispatches 47, 57, enclosure A.

58. *Documents diplomatiques, françaises* II, 375.

59. Charles de Freycinet, *Souvenirs, 1878-1893* (Paris, 1914), p. 168.

60. Despagnet, *La Diplomatie de la Troisième République*, p. 223.

61. *Documents diplomatiques . . . Tunisie*, pp. 114-18.

62. Henri Cambon, *Histoire de la Régence*, p. 144.

63. *Accounts and Papers*, no. 2887, p. 8.

64. Great Britain, *3 Hansard,* CCLXII (1881), p. 1327.
65. *Accounts and Papers,* no. 2887, p. 19.
66. *Con. Lett.,* XII (1881), dispatch 79.
67. *Documents diplomatique . . . Tunisie,* supplement, pp. 26, 27.
68. Ibid., pp. xix, xxiv.
69. London *Times,* May 14, 1881; see *Documents diplomatiques, françaises,* IV; the entire first section is devoted to this dispute over Tunisia.
70. Full text published in Ministère des Affaires Etrangères, *Documents diplomatiques, Afrique, arrangements, actes et conventions, 1881-1898,* pp. 3-5.
71. Alfred Rambaud, *Jules Ferry* (Paris, 1903), p. 294.
72. France, *Journal Officiel,* May 23, 1881, p. 878.
73. London *Times,* May 16, 1881.
74. *Documents diplomatiques, françaises,* IV, 36 n. The dispute over Tunisia, which had calmed down in 1883, was revived under Fascist rule in Italy. Two examples of this revival were an anonymous pamphlet entitled *La Questione di Tunisi,* and the book *Italy and the Question of Tunis* by Ezio Maria Gray, who was vice-president of the Fascist Corporation of Professional Workers and Artists. Both of these appeared in 1939 and were strong pro-Fascist attacks on France.

II

1. The biographical material on Paul Cambon was taken from *Paul Cambon, ambassadeur de France, 1843-1924,* par un diplomate (Paris, 1937).
2. Paul Cambon, *Correspondance, 1870-1924* (Paris, 1940), I, 164.
3. Ibid.
4. Ibid., 161. Cambon's semi-invalid wife did not accompany him to Paris and spent only brief periods with him in Tunis; therefore, his correspondence with her is a valuable source of information.
5. Ibid., 170, 171.
6. Maurice Bompard, ed., *Législation de la Tunisie; Recueil des lois, décrets, et réglements en vigueur dans la Régence de Tunis au 1ᵉʳ janvier 1888* (Paris, 1888), p. xi.
7. d'Estournelles de Constant, "Les Débuts d'un protectorat," *Revue des Deux Mondes,* LXXIX (1887), p. 787.
8. Cambon, *Correspondance,* I, 174.

9. Henri Cambon, *Histoire de la Régence de Tunis* (Paris, 1948), p. 173.

10. Cambon, *Correspondance,* I, 180, 181.

11. The full text is published in France, Ministère des Affaires Etrangères, *Documents diplomatiques, Afrique, 1881-1898,* pp. 7-8.

12. France, *Journal Officiel,* April 2, 1884, p. 1001.

13. Ibid., p. 1003.

14. Ibid.

15. Ibid., p. 1002.

16. Ibid., p. 1003.

17. d'Estournelles de Constant, "Les Débuts d'un protectorat," *Revue des Deux Mondes,* LXXIX (1887), p. 804.

18. G. Valbert, "Le Régime du protectorat en Tunisie," *Revue des Deux Mondes,* LXXVIII (1886), p. 197.

19. France, Chambre des Députés, *Documents parliamentaires,* Aug. 1882, p. 2106.

20. *Documents diplomatiques, françaises,* IV, 493.

21. Ibid., 494 n.

22. d'Estournelles de Constant, *La Politique françiase en Tunisie* (Paris, 1891), p. 374.

23. *Accounts and Papers,* no. 3843, p. 15.

24. Arthur Girault, *Principles de colonisation et de législation coloniale* (Paris, 1928) V, 109

25. Cambon, *Correspondance,* I, 198-202.

26. Ibid., I, 211; Depienne was director of Tunisian finances.

27. The House of Representatives passed a joint resolution ending consular jurisdiction, which the Senate amended. The House took no action upon the amended resolution, so it failed to become law. *Command Papers,* 3843, Tunis (1884), pp. 7, 8. The American consulate in Tunis was discontinued by Congress on July 19, 1882, and reopened in 1890; therefore, the failure of the resolution to pass was of no consequence until 1890, and then only of minor consequence; United States, *Consular Letters,* XII, July 19, 1882, dispatch 107, National Archives.

28. Franz Despagnet, *Essai sur les protectorats* (Paris, 1896), p. 3.

29. d'Estournelles de Constant, "Les Débuts d'un protectorat," *Revue des Deux Mondes,* vol. LXXIX (1887), p. 786. Although

France did not immediately send a great number of officials to Tunisia, after the turn of the century the situation changed.

30. d'Estournelles de Constant, *La Politique française,* pp. 438, 439.

31. *Con. Lett.,* XIII, dispatch May 14, 1906.

32. Girault, *Législation coloniale,* V, 20. This *Ouzara,* meaning the Bey's general administration, should not be confused with the *ouzara* courts, see p. 58.

33. Bompard, *Législation,* p. 402.

34. Ibid., p. 431.

35. Cambon, *Correspondance,* I, 235.

36. Girault, *Législation coloniale,* V, 30.

37. Ministère des Affaires Etrangères, *Rapport au Président de la République sur la situation de la Tunisie en 1881-1890* (Paris, 1890), pp. 5, 6.

38. d'Estournelles de Constant, *La Politique française,* p. 443.

39. Girault, *Législation coloniale,* V, 32.

40. Bompard, *Législation,* p. 79.

41. Ibid., pp. 80-82.

42. *Conférences,* p. 69.

43. Louis Vignon, "La France dans l'Afrique du Nord," *Revue Coloniale Internationale* vol. I (1887), p. 319 n.

44. Victor Piquet, *La Colonisation française dans l'Afrique du Nord* (Paris, 1912), p. 341.

45. *Notice générale 1881-1921,* p. 44.

46. Girault, *Législation coloniale,* V, 57-65.

47. Joseph Schacht, *The Origins of Muhammadan Jurisprudence,* (Oxford, 1950), p. 1.

48. Ibid., p. 98.

49. Paul Huc, *L'Oeuvre politique et economique du protectorat français en Tunisie* (Toulouse, 1924), p. 111 n.

50. *A Dictionary of Islam* (London, 1895).

51. Louis Vignon, "La France dans l'Afrique du Nord," *Revue Coloniale Internationale,* vol. I (1887), p. 144.

52. d'Estournelles de Constant, *La Politique française,* p. 366.

53. Ibid., p. 368.

54. Ibid., and Girault, *Législation coloniale,* V, 138, 139.

55. Ibid.

56. d'Estournelles de Constant, "Les Débuts d'un protectorat," *Revue des Deux Mondes,* vol. LXXIX (1887), p. 809.

57. Ibid.

58. Girault, *Législation coloniale,* V, 110.

59. Ibid., 112, 113.

60. Ibid., 115.

61. *Rapport,* p. 46.

62. Great Britain, Foreign Office, *British and Foreign State Papers,* LXXI, 478.

63. Edmond Plauchut, "La France en Tunisie," Part I, *Revue des Deux Mondes,* vol. CI (1890), p. 636.

64. Ibid., p. 637.

65. d'Estournelles de Constant, *La Politique française,* p. 370.

66. *Rapport,* p. 52.

67. *Notice générale 1881-1921,* pp. 168-71.

68. *Encyclopaedia of Islam* (London, 1934), IV, 1907.

69. *Rapport,* p. 41.

70. Jean M. A. de Lanessan, *La Tunisie* (Paris, 1887), p. 248.

71. *Encyclopaedia of Islam,* IV, 1100.

72. de Lanessan, *La Tunisie,* p. 249.

73. Direction de l'Agriculture, *Notice,* p. 28.

74. Ibid., p. 29.

75. Ibid., p. 30.

76. Girault, *Législation coloniale,* V, 164.

77. Direction de l'Agriculture, *Notice,* p. 27.

78. Piquet, *La Colonisation française,* p. 374.

79. Direction de l'Agriculture, *Notice,* p. 35.

80. Gabriel Hanotaux et Alfred Martineau, eds., *Histoire des colonies françaises* (Paris, 1931), III, 428.

81. d'Estournelles de Constant, *La Politique française,* p. 422 n.

82. *Encyclopaedia of Islam,* IV, 855.

83. See the references to capitulation rights and the International Financial Commission in Chapter I.

84. Bompard, *Législation,* p. 422.

85. *Con. Lett.,* XIII, dispatch 39.

86. Dwight E. Lee, "The Origins of Pan-Islamism," *The American Historical Review,* vol. XLVII, Jan. 1942, passim. This article shows how vaguely and loosely the term is used.

87. Ibid., p. 279.

88. Ibid., p. 282.

89. Hanotaux et Martineau, *Histoire,* III, 459.

90. Huc, *L'Oeuvre,* p. 134.

91. For example, the trouble over private *habous* in 1920; see Hanotaux et Martineau, *Histoire,* III, 459-61.

92. Plauchut, "La France en Tunisie," Part III, *Revue des Deux Mondes,* vol. CII (1890), p. 317.

93. Guy de Maupassant, "Vers Kairouan," *Revue des Deux Mondes,* vol. XCI (1889), pp. 523, 524.

94. Girault, *Législation coloniale,* V, 183.

95. Leroy-Beaulieu, "La Colonisation française en Tunisie," *Revue des Deux Mondes,* vol. LXXVIII (1886), p. 391.

96. de Lanessan, *La Tunisie,* pp. 96, 97. This trend was also mentioned in Stephen H. Roberts, *History of French Colonial Policy,* (London, 1929), I, 272, 273.

97. Exposition Coloniale de Marseille, *Les Ressources agricoles et forestières des colonies françaises* (Marseille, 1907), IV, 63.

98. "Tunisia 54," Special Number, *Encyclopédie Mensuelle d'Outre-Mer* (Paris, 1954), p. 73.

99. Ibid., p. 74.

100. Charles Lallemand, *La Tunisie, pays de protectorat française* (Paris, 1892), pp. 22-5.

101. Arthur Pellegrin, *Histoire de la Tunisie* (Tunis, 1948), p. 156.

102. Piquet, *La Colonisation française,* p. 341.

103. Department of Commerce, *Tunis: Its Resources, Industries, and Commerce with Reference to United States Trade* (Washington, 1923), p. 23.

104. Ibid.

105. Exposition de Marseille, *Les Ressources agricoles,* IV, 40.

106. Plauchut, "La France en Tunisie," Part III, *Revue des Deux Mondes,* vol. CII (1890), p. 314.

107. de Lanessan, *La Tunisie,* pp. 27, 28.

108. Lallemand, *La Tunisie, pays de protectorat française,* p. 168.

109. Leroy-Beaulieu, "La Colonisation française en Tunisie," *Revue des Deux Mondes,* vol. LXXVIII (1886), p. 392.

110. Ibid., p. 383.

111. Exposition de Marseille, *Les Ressources agricoles,* IV, 71.

112. Ibid., 70 n.

113. Department of Commerce, *Tunis: Its Resources, Industries and Commerce,* pp. 48, 49.

114. *Conférences,* p. 374.

III

1. *Conférences,* p. 272.

2. Indeed, Tunisia became a lucrative trade area for Metropolitan France. The duty on items imported by Tunisia was usually 5 per cent less if they were brought from France or Algeria. *J.O.T.* March 6, 1953.

3. J. B. Piolet, *La France hors de France* (Paris, 1900), p. 576.

4. Ibid., p. 578. In his dissertation, entitled *The French Acquisition of Tunis* (Cornell University, 1939), Donald V. McKay devoted Chapter VI to an informative and interesting explanation of the effect that French geographical societies had in stimulating French colonial sentiment after 1870.

5. *Conférences,* p. 279.

6. Victor Piquet, *La Colonisation française dans l'Afrique du Nord* (Paris, 1912), pp. 355, 356.

7. Piolet, *La France,* p. 9 et seq.

8. Jean M. A. de Lanessan, *La Tunisie* (Paris, 1887), p. 98.

9. Piolet, *La France,* p. 577; the families of those listed and naturalized French were included in the remaining 7,000.

10. *Conférences,* pp. 276, 277.

11. Alexis Vltry, *L'Oeuvre française en Tunisie* (Paris, 1900), p. 73.

12. Direction de l'Agriculture, *Notice,* p. 10.

13. Ibid., appendix.

14. Stephen H. Roberts, *History of French Colonial Policy* (London, 1929), I, 274.

15. Maurice Bompard, ed., *Législation de la Tunisie; Resoueil des lois, décrets, et réglements en viguer dans la Régence de Tunis au 1er janvier 1888* (Paris, 1888), p. 383.

16. Narcisse Faucon, *La Tunisie avant et depuis l'occupation français; Histoire et colonisation* (Paris, 1893), I, 427 n.

17. Plauchut, "La France en Tunisie," Part I, *Revue des Deux Mondes,* vol. CI (1890), p. 624.

18. J. Tournier, *Le Cardinal Lavigerie et son action politique, 1863-1892* (Paris, 1913), pp. 3-6.

19. Ibid., p. 7.

20. Louis Bertrand, *Devant l'Islam;* Part II, *Le Centenaire du Cardinal Lavigerie* (Paris, 1926), p. 89.

21. Tournier, *Le Cardinal Lavigerie,* p. 8.

22. Bertrand, *Devant l'Islam,* p. 95.

23. J. B. Piolet, ed., *Les Missions catholique françaises au XIXe siècle* (Paris, 1903), V, 63.

24. Ibid., 66.

25. Ibid., 80.

26. A. C. Grüssenmeyer, ed., *Vingt-cinq années d'épiscopat en France et en Afrique, Documents biographiques sur son éminence le Cardinal Lavigerie; Archevêque de Carthage et d'Alger Primat d'Afrique* (Algiers, 1888), II, 11.

27. Ibid., 12.

28. Ibid., 14, 15.

29. Ibid., 20.

30. Bertrand, *Devant l'Islam,* p. 106.

31. Grüssenmeyer, *Vingt-cinq années,* II, 111, 112.

32. Ibid., 174.

33. *Paul Cambon, ambassadeur de France, 1843-1924,* par un diplomate (Paris, 1937), p. 54.

34. Grüssenmeyer, *Vingt-cinq années,* II, 32, 33.

35. Ibid., 176.

36. Ibid., 45.

37. Ibid., 182.

38. Elie Fitoussi et Aristide Benazet, *L'Etat tunisien et le protectorat français; Histoire et organisation, 1521 à 1931* (Paris, 1931), II, 811.

39. Phyllis Cooper Ling, "Washing Away Misconceptions in Tunisia," *World Outlook,* June, 1964, p. 15.

40. Mohammed M. Pickthall, trans., *The Meaning of the Glorious Koran* (New York, 1953), Surah II, verse 120.

41. Ibid., Surah V, verse 51.

42. Bertrand, *Devant l'Islam,* p. 104.

43. Grüssenmeyer, *Vingt-cinq années,* II, 320.

44. C. A. Micaud, L. C. Brown, and C. H. Moore, *Tunisia, the Politics of Modernization,* Praeger (New York, 1964), pp. 58, 75.

45. Plauchut, "La France en Tunisie," Part I, *Revue des Deux Mondes,* vol. CI (1890), p. 653.

46. *Con. Lett.,* XII, Nov. 26, 1877, dispatch 255; and Plauchut, "La France en Tunisie," Part III, *Revue des Deux Mondes,* vol. CII (1890), p. 333.

47. d'Estournelles de Constant, *La Politique française en Tunisie* (Paris, 1891) p. 450.

48. *Diplomatic and Consular Reports* (1886) , Part I, p. 28.

49. Piquet, *La Colonisation française,* p. 384.

50. *Notice générale, 1881-1921,* p. 411.

51. Cambon, *Correspondance 1870-1924* (Paris, 1940) , I, 218.

52. *Cambon,* par un diplomate, p. 60.

53. d'Estournelles de Constant, *La Politique française,* p. 454 n.

54. Piquet, *La Colonisation française,* p. 388.

55. Ibid., pp. 387, 388.

56. France, Présidence du Conseil, *Facts and Figures about French North Africa* (Paris, 1952) , p. 15.

57. d'Estournelles de Constant, *La Politique française,* p. 442.

58. Vitry, *L'Oeuvre,* p. 160.

59. Piquet, *La Colonisation française,* p. 392.

60. d'Estournelles de Constant, *La Politique française,* pp. 440, 441.

61. *Diplomatic and Consular Reports,* vol. I (1886) , p. 721. Robert Koch did not isolate cholera bacteria until 1883.

62. Ibid., pp. 133-35.

63. G. Variot, "Une Visite à l'hôpital arabe de Tunis," *La Revue Scientifique,* April 23, 1881, pp. 537, 538.

64. "Tunisia 54," Special Number, *Encyclopédie Mensuelle d'Outre-Mer* (Paris, 1954) , p. 43.

65. Ibid., pp. 35, 36.

66. Plauchut, "La France en Tunisie," Part I, *Revue des Deux Mondes,* vol. CI (1890) , p. 657.

67. Piquet, *La Colonisation française,* p. 389.

68. Fitoussi et Benazet, *L'Etat tunisien,* II, 485.

69. Piquet, *La Colonisation française,* pp. 393, 394.

IV

1. Nicola A. Ziadeh, *Origins of Nationalism in Tunisia,* American University of Beirut (Beirut, 1962) , p. 43.

2. The figures are found in Ziadeh, *Origins,* p. 33 and in Arthur Pellegrin, *Histoire de la Tunisie* (Tunis, 1948) , p. 207.

3. Henri Cambon, *Histoire de la Régence de Tunis* (Paris 1948) , p. 206.

4. Ibid., p. 196.

5. See pp. 112-14 for more details on the 1922 reform. While a reform in 1936 granted Tunisian representation in the Grand Council, this came no closer to satisfying the nationalist wishes than before.

6. For a list of the key Tunisian families see Pellegrin, *Histoire de la Tunisie,* p. 188.

7. Pellegrin, *Histoire de la Tunisie,* p. 203.

8. See pp. 121 and 122.

9. Henri Cambon, *Histoire de la Régence,* p. 205.

10. The American vice-consul, Alfred Chapelié, sent a dispatch which predicted a great economic future for the Bizerte area. *Con. Lett.,* vol., XIII, dispatch, August 18, 1896. Alfred Chapelié was born in Tunis and managed the famous Chapelié importation house until he went into banking in 1870. He married an American and later became vice-consul of the United States.

11. *Con. Lett.,* XIII, dispatch, September 9, 1900.

12. *Con. Lett.,* microfilm, dispatch, August 27, 1925.

13. Ibid., dispatch, November 8, 1918, quoting from *La Dépêche Tunisienne.*

14. Ibid., microfilm, dispatch, December 6, 1926.

15. Ibid., dispatch, May 17, 1927.

16. Ibid., dispatch, October 30, 1925. Three of the so-called Communists were banished for ten years and the others for five years.

17. Ibid., dispatch, June 20, 1925.

18. Curiously enough, the United States never renounced consular jurisdiction, and this resulted in a running debate between the two countries, with the French resident-generals largely ignoring politically and socially the American vice-consuls. In the heat of the dispute the American vice-consul Chapelié referred to Resident-General Millet's "violent and unsteady mind." *Con. Lett.,* XIII, dispatch, June 14, 1895.

19. See pages 80, 81.

20. Robert Aron, *The Vichy Regime, 1940-44,* Macmillan (New York, 1958), p. 339.

21. *Con. Lett.,* microfilm, dispatch, September 13, 1928.

22. By 1955 the state appointed the director of Collège Sadiki, assuring the public nature of the institution. *J.O.T.,* October 27, 1955.

23. Gabriel Hanotaux et Alfred Martineau, eds., *Histoire des colonies françaises* (Paris, 1931), III, 455, 456.

24. Ziadeh, *Origins,* p. 73.

25. Ibid., p. 80.

26. Henri de Montety, "Les Données du problème tunisien," *Politique Etrangère,* March, 1952, pp. 451, 452.

27. Habib Bourguiba, "Continuity of the National Struggle" (speech), April 9, 1962, Tunis, Secretariat of State for Cultural Affairs and Information, pp. 11-14.

28. Ziadeh, *Origins,* pp. 84, 85. Ali Bach Hamba went to France, where he died six years later.

29. Pellegrin, *Histoire,* p. 192 n.

30. Ibid., p. 191.

31. Ziadeh, *Origins,* p. 90.

32. Zeine N. Zeine, *The Struggle for Arab Independence,* Khayat's (Beirut, 1960), pp. 107-27.

33. Ibid., p. 224.

34. *Con. Lett.,* microfilm, dispatch, June 24, 1920.

35. Roger le Tourneau, *Evolution politique de l'Afrique du Nord musulmane, 1920-1961* (Paris, 1962), p. 66 n.

36. *Le Figaro,* April 28, 1922. A French lawyer in Tunis wrote a book entitled *Ce que la Tunisie demande à la France,* in which he showed Wilsonian influence on the Young Tunisians. Paul Huc, *L'Oeuvre, politique et économique du protectorat français en Tunisie* (Toulouse, 1924), p. 132.

37. Ibid., April 29, 1922.

38. Ibid., April 28, 1922.

39. Ziadeh, *Origins.,* p. 118.

40. The French section contained 56 members, 22 of whom directly represented large French economic interests in Tunisia, and the remainder were elected by individual French colons. The Tunisian section had 41 members selected by the Regional Councils and the Tunisian Chambers of Commerce and Agriculture.

41. Henri Cambon, *Histoire de la Régence,* pp. 307, 308.

42. Habib Bourguiba, a man of intelligence and intense energy, was born in Monastir on August 3, 1903, the son of an army officer who had seven older children. He took his elementary and secondary education in Tunis, where he attended Collège Sadiki and Lycée Carnot. In 1924 Bourguiba studied law in Paris. As a young lawyer with a French wife and a small son, he returned to Tunisia in 1927. Politics interested him more than law, and three years later he joined

254 / Notes for Pages 115 to 123

the editorial staff of *La Voix du Tunisien,* the newspaper of the Destour Party.

43. Jean Lacouture, *Cinq hommes et la France* (Paris, 1961) , p. 111.

44. Abdelaziz Taalbi, *La Tunisie martyre: Ses revendications* (Paris, 1920), p. 9.

45. Ibid., pp. 17-19.

46. Ibid., pp. 208-12.

47. According to Habib Bourguiba, Taalbi was disappointed by factionalism and strife within the nationalist movement. Taalbi was the victim of defamatory press comment. Bourguiba concluded, "Disheartened and discouraged, he left for the East, which he knew well and where he knew he could make an impression through his gift of oratory." Habib Bourguiba, *Lessons of Thirty Years of Struggle,* (speeches), Ksar Hellal, March 1, 1964, and Tunis, March 2, 1964, Secretariat of State for Cultural Affairs and Orientation, p. 29.

48. *Con. Lett.,* microfilm, dispatch, August 27, 1925.

49. Ibid., August 25, 1923.

50. Ibid., August 27, 1925.

51. Ibid., December 15, 1925.

52. Ibid., December 10, 1925, quoting the newspaper *L'Avenir Social.*

53. Henri Cambon, *Histoire de la Régence,* p. 231. See page 131.

54. *Con. Lett.,* microfilm, dispatch, September 16, 1926.

55. Ibid., March 3, 1928.

56. *Le Figaro,* April 12, 1931.

57. Habib Bourguiba, *La Tunisie et la France; Vingt-cinq ans de lutte pour une coopération libre* (Paris, 1954) , p. 27.

58. Ibid., p. 43.

59. Ibid., p. 52.

60. Habib Bourguiba, *Lessons of Thirty Years of Struggle* (speeches), Ksar Hellal, March 1, 1964, and Tunis, March 2, 1964, Secretariat of State for Cultural Affairs and Orientation.

61. Roger le Tourneau, *Evolution politique de l'Afrique du Nord Musulmane, 1920-1961* (Paris, 1962) , p. 76.

62. Henri Cambon, *Histoire de la Régence,* p. 239.

63. Bourguiba, *La Tunisie et la France,* p. 162.

64. Henri Cambon, *Histoire de la Régence,* p. 240.

65. Le Tourneau, *Evolution politique,* pp. 85, 86.

66. *Le Figaro,* April 16, 1938.

67. Ibid., April 13, 1938.

68. Habib Bourguiba, "Continuity of the National Struggle" (speech), Tunis, April 9, 1962, Secretariat of State for Cultural Affairs and Information.

69. Henri Cambon, *Histoire de la Régence*, p. 242.

70. Ibid., p. 243.

71. For an account of the battles see Maréchal Juin, *Mémoires; Alger, Tunis, Rome* (Paris, 1959) , pp. 117-74.

72. Le Tourneau, *Evolution politique*, p. 96.

73. Ibid., pp. 97, 98.

74. The *Nicham Iftikhar* was the highest decoration bestowed by the Bey.

75. Maréchal Juin, *Mémoires*, p. 188.

76. Ibid., p. 194.

77. Ibid., p. 193.

78. Secretariat of State for Information, *Tunisian-American Relations* (Tunis, 1959) , p. 60.

79. On April 8, 1964, Rachid Driss presented his credentials to the Department of State as the new ambassador to Washington, replacing Habib Bourguiba, Jr.

80. Felix Garas, *Bourguiba et la naissance d'une nation* (Paris, 1956) , p. 159.

81. Bourguiba, *La Tunisie et la France*, p. 189.

82. Garas, *Bourguiba*, pp. 160, 161.

83. Le Tourneau, *Evolution politique*, p. 111.

V

1. At the ninth congress of the UGTT in April, 1963, Habib Achour was elected secretary-general. *La Presse*, April 7, 1963.

2. *Le Monde Economique*, "World's Documents Series," Tunisia, June, 1956, pp. 44, 45.

3. Habib Bourguiba, *La Tunisie et la France; Vingt-cinq ans de lutte pour une coopération libre* (Paris, 1954) , p. 237.

4. *Mission* (hebdomadaire politique paraissant le vendredi) , August 31, 1951.

5. Gabriel Puaux, "La France en Tunisie," *La Revue de Paris*, February, 1953, p. 43.

6. The major Paris newspapers did not even report the speech.

7. Jean Rous, *Tunisie attention* (Paris, 1952), p. 107. (Italics are mine.)

8. *La Dépêche Tunisienne,* June 13, 1950.

9. *Le Figaro,* June 14, 1950.

10. The office of secretary-general, which was abolished by the 1922 reforms, was reestablished in 1935 but did not have as much power as it did before 1922.

11. *La Dépêche Tunisienne,* June 15, 1951.

12. Roman Fanjans, *Alerte en Afrique du Nord* (Paris, 1953), p. 32.

13. *Mission,* February 16, 1951.

14. Ibid., November 16, 1951.

15. Ibid., December 14, 1951.

16. *La Presse,* November 21, 1951.

17. *La Dépêche Tunisienne,* December 1, 1951.

18. Muhammad Khalil, ed., *The Arab States and the Arab League,* (Beirut, 1962), II, 88.

19. *Le Figaro,* December 15, 1951.

20. *La Dépêche Tunisienne,* December 15, 1951.

21. *Le Figaro,* December 17, 1951.

22. Pierre Rondot, "Accalmie ou apaisement en Tunisie?," *Etudes,* February, 1954, p. 185 n.

23. *As-Zohira,* December 19, 1951, reprinted in *Mission.*

24. *La Presse,* December 18, 1951.

25. *La Dépêche Tunisienne,* December 20, 1951.

26. *Mission,* December 21, 1951.

27. Ibid.

28. Oreste Rosenfeld, "Association dans l'égalite," *Preuves,* March, 1953, no. 25, pp. 54-6.

29. *Le Petit Matin,* December 21, 1951.

30. *La Nation Tunisienne,* January 23, 1949.

31. *Indépendence,* February 1, 1951.

32. *Le Figaro,* December 20, 1951.

33. *Indépendence,* February 22, 1951.

34. Victor Silvera, "Le Régime constitutional de la Tunisie," *Revue Française de Science Politique,* vol. X, no. 2, June, 1960, p. 392.

35. *Indépendence,* May 17, 1951.

36. Ibid.

37. *Maroc et Tunisie; Le Problème du protectorat* (Paris, 1953), p. 190.

38. Fanjans, *Alerte en Afrique du Nord,* p. 34.

39. Ibid., p. 35.

40. Felix Garas, *Bourguiba et la naissance d'un nation* (Paris, 1956), p. 192.

41. Fanjans, *Alerte en Afrique du Nord,* p. 63.

42. *Le Petit Matin,* November 22, 1951.

43. Bourguiba, *La Tunisie et la France,* p. 298.

44. Habib Bourguiba, "Nationalism: Antidote to Communism," *Foreign Affairs,* XXXV, July, 1957, p. 648.

45. *Le Petit Matin,* January 2, 1952.

46. Habib Bourguiba, "Loyalty and Civic Sense" (speech), March 12, 1962, Tunis, Secretariat of State for Cultural Affairs and Orientation, p. 12.

47. *Afrique Action,* October 14-20, 1961.

48. *Mission,* January 25, 1952.

49. Habib Bourguiba, "Decolonization and Cooperation" (speech), June 30, 1964, Tunis, Secretariat of State for Cultural Affairs and Orientation, p. 10.

50. Bourguiba, *La Tunisie et la France,* p. 442.

51. "Jean le Terrible" is French for Ivan the Terrible. Alexander Werth, *Lost Statesman, The Strange Story of Pierre Mendès-France,* Abelard Schuman (New York, 1958), p. 318.

52. *Le Petit Matin,* January 15, 18, 22, and 23, 1952.

53. Ibid., April 18, 1952.

54. *Le Figaro,* February 9 and 10, 1952.

55. *Mission,* February 8, 1952.

56. Rous, *Tunisie attention,* p. 127.

57. Garas, *Bourguiba,* pp. 204, 205.

58. *Mission,* February 8, 1952.

59. Fanjans, *Alerte en Afrique du Nord,* p. 19.

60. Ibid.

61. Rous, *Tunisie attention,* p. 77.

62. Jacques Fauvet, *La IVe République* (Paris, 1959), p. 208.

63. Ibid., p. 214 n.

64. Fanjans, *Alerte en Afrique du Nord,* p. 23.

65. Garas, *Bourguiba,* p. 197.

66. *New York Times,* December 7, 1952.

67. Commission Internationale contre le Régime Concentrationnaire, Livre Blanc sur la détention politique en Tunisie (Brussels, 1952), p. 10.

68. Ibid., p. 13.

69. Ibid., p. 79.

70. Ibid., p. 27.

71. Here is a copy of an arrest order:

Resolution

The General Commandant Superieur of the Troops of Tunisia,
In regard to the Beylical Decree of 1 Sept. 1939.

In regard to the Beylical Decree of 7 Oct. 1943, particularly paragraph 2 of article 2.

In regard to the residential order of 17 Jan. 1952 charging the military authority with the exercise of the powers of imprisonment determined by article 4 of the Beylical law of 1 Sept. 1939, paragraphs 1 and 2.

Order the arrest of

_____ for a period of

_____

(Signed) General Garbay

72. *Le Petit Matin,* August 9, 1953.

73. *Union Générale des Etudiants Tunisiens, Travaux du premier congrés national de l'union générale des étudiants tunisiens,* Paris, July 10-13, 1953, p. 83.

74. Bourguiba, *La Tunisie et la France,* p. 394.

75. *New York Times,* May 16, 1953.

76. *Maroc et Tunisie,* p. 199.

77. Fauvet, *La IVᵉ République,* p. 237.

78. Ibid., p. 231.

79. Ibid., p. 266.

80. Fanjans, *Alerte en Afrique du Nord,* p. 65.

81. *Le Petit Matin,* May 16, 1952.

82. Ibid., June 1, 1952.

83. Ibid., October 11, 1952.

84. *Mission,* January 18, 1952.

85. Khalil, *The Arab States,* I, 365.

86. Ibid.

87. Charter of the United Nations, Chapter I, Article I, paragraph 2.

88. Georges Day, *Les Affaires de la Tunisie et du Maroc devant les Nations Unies* (Paris, 1953), p. 18.

89. Ibid., p. 51.

90. *Maroc et Tunisie,* p. 217. François Mitterrand was in the cabinet of Joseph Laniel, from which he resigned twice in protest, once when France deposed the Sultan of Morocco, and again in 1953, when Pierre Voizard was appointed resident-general in Tunisia without a reform program. Mitterrand became minister of interior under Pierre Mendès-France and later minister of justice under Guy Mollet.

91. Khalil, *The Arab States,* I, 370.

92. Charter of the United Nations, Chapter I, Article II, paragraph 7.

93. Khalil, *The Arab States,* I, 370, 371.

94. Day, *Les Affaires de la Tunisie et du Maroc,* p. 46.

95. Ibid., p. 119.

96. *Le Petit Matin,* November 12, 1953.

97. Khalil, *The Arab States,* I, 371.

VI

1. For example, the order requiring press identification cards was abrogated. *J.O.T.,* March 12, 1954.

2. *Le Petit Matin,* October 28, 1953. His suspension of censorship was extremely brief; just two months later he stopped the distribution of the Moroccan newspaper *Paris* when it criticized him and the Bey. *New York Times,* December 17, 1953.

3. Ambassade de France, *Tunisian Affairs* no. 6, p. 6.

4. *Le Petit Matin,* February 24, 1954, italics mine.

5. Jean Rigotard, "Les Réformes en Tunisie; Etude des dispositions législatives du 4 Mars," *La Nouvelle Revue Française d'Outre-Mer,* no. 6, June, 1954, pp. 253-56.

6. Ambassade de France, *Tunisian Affairs,* no. 6, p. 8.

7. André de la Far, "Nouveau départ en Tunisie," *Monde Nouveau Paru,* April, 1954, p. 10.

8. Jacques Fauvet, *La IVᵉ République* (Paris, 1959), p. 268.

9. *Le Petit Matin,* May 28, 1954.

10. Habib Bourguiba, *La Tunisie et la France; Vingt-cinq ans de lutte pour une coopération libre* (Paris, 1954), p. 424.

11. Carmel Tabone, "L'Imbroglio juridique tunisien," *La Nouvelle Revue Française d'Outre-Mer,* April, 1954, pp. 148, 149.

12. Ambassade de France, *Tunisian Affairs,* no. 8, p. 3.

13. Bourguiba, *La Tunisie et la France,* p. 432.

14. *Le Monde Economique,* "World's Documents Series," Special Issue: Tunisia, June, 1956, p. 56.

15. Ibid., p. 57.

16. Ch.-E. Ravussin, "Août 54 en Tunisie," *Esprit,* October 1954, p. 517.

17. Ibid.

18. Tahar Ben Ammar was born in Tunis in 1885 in a middle-class family but by 1954 was a large landowner. He served as president of the Tunisian section of the Grand Council. Known as a moderate nationalist, he worked hard for Tunisian internal autonomy.

19. Ambassade de France, *Tunisian Affairs,* no. 7, p. 21.

20. *J.O.T.,* September 17, 1954.

21. *Le Monde,* August 6, 1954.

22. Dr. Etienne Burnet was head of the Pasteur Institute in Tunis from 1936 until 1943.

23. *Le Monde,* August 7, 1954.

24. Ibid., August 7 and 8, 1954.

25. Ambassade de France, *Tunisian Affairs,* no. 7, p. 4.

26. *Le Petit Matin,* August 14, 1954.

27. Fauvet, *La IVe République,* p. 286.

28. Felix Garas, *Bourguiba et la naissance d'une nation* (Paris, 1956) , p. 259.

29. Ibid., p. 262. It is interesting to note that this same leader was implicated in the plot to assassinate Bourguiba in 1963. In analyzing this plot Bourguiba said: "It is all the same for Lazhar Chraiti to go around in European-style clothes and wear a tarbush: he has remained what he was. You heard him talk before the court, like a hunted animal. After what he planned to do, he has the nerve to ask me to pardon him. Such agitators are a public menace. They are motivated by a spirit of rapine. It will take several generations to change this nomad mentality." *La Presse,* January 19, 1963.

30. *Le Monde,* August 20, 1954, reported that Ben Ammar and Masmoudi met with Bourguiba in his residence and received his approval for texts in the current negotiations with the French government.

31. Garas, *Bourguiba,* pp. 268, 269.

32. Ibid., p. 269.

33. *Le Petit Matin,* June 2, 1955.

34. Muhammad Khalil, ed., *The Arab States and the Arab League* (Beirut, 1962) , I, 373.

35. Ibid., 399-424.

36. Ibid., 424.

37. *Le Petit Matin,* July 13, 1955.

38. *New York Times,* June 29, 1955.

39. Ibid., July 9, 1955.

40. *Le Petit Matin,* August 28, 1955. For France the following personalities were pictured: President René Coty, Edgar Faure, Pierre Mendès-France, General Boyer de La Tour, Christian Fouchet, Pierre July; for Tunisia: the Bey, Habib Bourguiba, Tahar Ben Ammar, Mongi Slim, Mohamed Masmoudi, and Aziz Djellouli, who joined the other Tunisian negotiators during the latter phase of the Paris talks.

41. Ibid., August 24, 1955.

42. *L'Action,* October 31, 1955.

43. *Le Petit Matin,* October 8, 1955.

44. Ibid., October 18, 1955.

45. Ibid., November 1, 1955.

46. *L'Action,* November 7, 1955.

47. Ibid.

48. *Le Monde Economique,* "World's Documents Series," Tunisia, Special Issue: June, 1956, p. 43.

49. *Le Petit Matin,* January 12, 1956.

50. Ibid., January 29, 1956.

51. *Réalités Tunisiennes* (bi-mensuel), October 1, 1956.

52. *La Presse,* October 29 and 30, 1956

53. *New York Times,* August 15, 1961.

54. *La Presse,* January 19, 1963.

55. Victor Silvera, "Réflexions su la crise des rapports franco-tunisiens," *Politique Etrangère,* no. 2, 1958, p. 234.

56. Ibid.

57. *Le Monde,* August 1, 1954.

58. Victor Silvera, "Du Régime beylical à la République Tunisienne," *Politique Etrangère,* no. 5, 1957, p. 605.

59. Fauvet, *La IVe République,* p. 300.

60. Khalil, *The Arab States,* I, 445.

61. Werth, *Lost Statesman, The Strange Story of Pierre Mendès-France,* Abelard Schuman (New York, 1958), p. 354.

62. *L'Action,* May 2, 1955.

63. Ibid.

64. Werth, *Lost Statesman,* p. 370.

65. Ibid., p. 372.

66. *La Presse,* October 19, 1956.

67. *Réalités Tunisiennes* (bi-mensuel), October 15, 1956.

68. Silvera, "Du Régime," p. 605.

69. *Le Petit Matin,* January 29, 1952.

70. *L'Action,* January 2, 1956.

71. *New York Times,* March 16, 1956, and March 27, 1956.

72. Silvera, "Du Régime," p. 607.

73. *J.O.R.T.,* July 29, 1957.

74. Ibid., August 2, 1957.

75. Ch.-Andre Julien, *L'Afrique du Nord en Marche; Nationalismes musulmans et souverainete française* (Paris, 1953), pp. 80, 81. There were several hundred thousand party members led by about 26,000 militants. The militants were the highly trained political cadre that held tenaciously to Neo-Destourian principles.

76. Hedi Nouira, "Le Néo-Destour," *Politique Etrangère,* July 1954, p. 322.

77. Neo-Destour, *Bulletin du Néo-Destour de la France,* February 1, 1955, no. 6, p. 17.

78. Ibid., p. 20.

79. Victor Silvera, "Le Régime constitutionnel de la Tunisie," *Revue Française de Science Politique,* vol. X, no. 2, June, 1960, p. 392.

80. George N. Sfeir, "Fundamental Characteristics of the Tunisian Constitution," *The Middle East Journal,* Autumn 1959, p. 446.

81. *La Presse,* January 19, 1963.

82. *New York Times,* March 7, 1959. He was later released and his lands were not confiscated by the government. The charges against him were ill founded.

83. Ibid., November 25, 1958, and October 4, 1959.

84. See page 197.

85. *New York Times,* December 17, 1956.

VII

1. *Le Petit Matin,* March 10, 1956. France apologized to the U.S. for these attacks, which took place under the eyes of the French police. *New York Times,* March 11, 1956.

2. *Réalités Tunisiennes* (bi-mensuel), May 15, 1956.

3. *La Presse,* October 29, 1956.

4. *Réalités Tunisiennes* (bi-mensuel), June 1, 1957.

5. *Le Petit Matin,* March 20, 1957.

6. Jacques Fauvet, *La IVe République* (Paris, 1959), pp. 339, 340.

7. Ibid., p. 340.

8. *L'Action,* February 10, 1958. This is not to be confused with the daily paper of the same name, which was an official Neo-Destourian organ.

9. Fauvet, *La IVe République,* p. 341.

10. Jean Lacouture, *Cinq-hommes et la France* (Paris, 1961), p. 179.

11. *Réalités Tunisiennes,* 1st quarter, 1958.

12. *New York Times,* August 25, 1961. The last published account of the Tunisian dead was 1,800, but in private interviews with knowledgeable Tunisians the author has been led to believe that the actual figure was higher.

13. Ibid., July 23, 1961.

14. Ibid., July 25, 1961.

15. Ibid., July 29, 1961.

16. *Afrique Action,* October 14-20, 1961, p. 11.

17. *New York Times,* August 19, 1961. Bourguiba sent Cecil Hourani to the United States as his personal envoy to talk with President Kennedy and Dean Rusk about Bizerte.

18. *New York Times,* August 10, 1964.

19. Secretariat of State for Cultural Affairs and Information, *United States Aid Program to Tunisia* (Tunis, 1963), table I.

20. Ibid., table I. This means a present annual population increase of about 84,000 people.

21. Salah-Eddine Tlatli, *Tunisie nouvelle; Problèmes et perspectives* (Tunis, 1957), p. 282.

22. United States Agency for International Development, *Report on Water Conservation,* December, 1963, written by William J. Davis, Soils Adviser USAID, Tunisia. This project would transform the mountain Djebel Amar, northwest of Tunis, from a worthless piece of real estate into a water reservoir.

23. Ibid., p. 2.

24. U.S. Department of Commerce, "Basic Data on the Economy of Tunisia," *Economic Reports* (Tunis, 1959), p. 6.

25. Ibid., p. 1.

26. Jean Piel, "Le Cas tunisien," *Critique* no. 88, September, 1954, pp. 790, 791.

27. William H. Lewis, "The New Nomadism in North Africa," *The Middle East Journal,* Summer 1957, pp. 269-81. See also André Demeerseman, "Un Contraste saisissant: Personnalité actuelle et personnalité ancienne de la Tunisie," *IBLA, Revue de l'Institut des Belles Lettres Arabes à Tunis,* 1961, III-IV, pp. 223-49.

28. Ford Foundation, *Tapestry for Tomorrow* (New York, 1964), p. 43.

29. Secretary of State for Cultural Affairs and Information, *Tunisian Development 62-71* (Tunis, 1962), passim. This work explains the Tunisian ten-year economic plan.

30. République Tunisienne, *Statuts, Coopérative Agricole; Société Civile particulière à personnes et capital variables,* Tunis, 1958, passim.

31. Shortly after the establishment of the republic, steps were taken to put more *habous* land into production. See *J.O.R.T.,* November 2, 1957.

32. *New York Times,* May 13, 1964. Broken down as follows: 675,000 acres held by French, 110,000 acres held by Italians, and 37,000 acres held by Maltese. There were about 800 French farmers in Tunisia and 100 different French companies owning land.

33. Ibid., May 16, 1964. Tunisia has also received a 28-million-dollar loan from the Kuwait Fund for Arab Economic Development to help overcome the effects of the cancellation of French aid.

34. In Tunis Europeans and Americans tell incredible stories about the *Banque Centrale,* but the stories became much more credible after the author had some adverse experiences of his own. A high official of a French bank showed the writer a stack of requests that were waiting for the decision of the *Banque Centrale.*

35. Just as French officials took over the local government from the *caids,* the newly trained Tunisian officials are moving into control within each of the thirteen gouvernates (administrative provinces) of Tunisia.

36. *La Presse,* May 29, 1963.

37. Ibid., May 29, 1963.

38. *Treaties and Other International Acts Series 3794,* Economic, Technical and Related Assistance Agreement between the U.S.A. and Tunisia, March 26, 1957.

39. *La Presse,* April 4, 1963.

40. Secretariat of State for Cultural Affairs and Information, *United States Aid Program to Tunisia,* table 4.

41. *New York Times,* April 18, 1966.

42. *New York Times,* May 30, 1964.

43. Habib Bourguiba, "Value of Historical Studies" (speech), March 12, 1964, Le Kef, Secretariat of State for Cultural Affairs and Orientation, p. 15.

44. Ibid., p. 16.

45. Habib Bourguiba, "Lessons of An Ordeal" (speech), December 1, 1962, Tunis, Secretariat of State for Cultural Affairs and Information, p. 12.

46. President Bourguiba was elected to his second five-year term by 96.43 per cent of the registered voters, surpassing his 1959 election, when 91.7 per cent of the voters cast their ballots for him. *New York Times,* November 11, 1964.

47. Habib Bourguiba, "Loyalty and Civic Sense" (speech), March 12, 1962, Tunis, Secretariat of State for Cultural Affairs and Information, p. 9.

48. For an interesting analysis of the *hadith al khamis,* or "Thursday Talk," see Charles F. Gallagher, "Building a New Tunisia," American Universities Field Staff *Reports Service, North Africa Series,* January 30, 1961, vol. VII, no. 1, pp. 1-6.

49. For a discussion of Tunisian authoritarianism and an analysis of the Neo-Destour, see Charles F. Gallagher, *The United States and North Africa,* Harvard University Press (Cambridge, 1963), pp. 120-23. Also the chapter on Tunisia written by Charles F. Gallagher in G. Carter (ed.), *African One-Party States,* Cornell University Press (Ithaca, 1962). An important article on the party is Clement H. Moore, "The Neo-Destour Party of Tunisia; A Structure for Democracy?," *World Politics,* April, 1962, pp. 461-82. An informative study of political freedom in the Middle East is found in Bernard Lewis, "The Quest for Freedom; A Sad Story of the Middle East," *Encounter,* March 1964, pp. 29-40.

50. Gabriel Ardant, *La Tunisie d'aujourd'hui et de demain* (Paris, 1961), p. 68.

51. Ibid., p. 71.

52. See page 180.

53. *La Presse,* January 19, 1963.

54. *Jeune Afrique,* May 6-12, 1963, p. 6.

55. *La Presse,* January 19, 1963.

56. *Réalités Tunisiennes* (bi-mensuel), December 1, 1956, p. 8.

57. *La Presse,* February 5, 1957.

58. *Réalités Tunisiennes* (bi-mensuel), November 15, 1956, p. 31.

59. See page 263, note 8.

60. In Tunis some claim that Bourguiba physically attacked Masmoudi, hitting him so hard that his glasses flew off.

61. Mohamed Masmoudi, "Onze ans apres," *Jeune Afrique,* January 21-27, 1963, p. 6.

62. *Jeune Afrique,* May 13-19, 1963, p. 8.

63. Ibid.

64. *The Middle East Journal,* Autumn 1965, p. 511. At the Party National Congress in October, 1964, the name of the party was officially changed to the Socialist Destour Party, dropping the "Neo," which was originally used to distinguish the group from the Old Destourians.

65. *La Presse,* May 14, 1963.

66. *Jeune Afrique,* May 13-19, 1963, p. 8.

67. *New York Times,* November 12, 1964.

68. Constitution of the Tunisian Republic, Chapter III, Article 51.

69. *New York Times,* April 18, 1966.

70. Edna McGuire, *The Peace Corps; Kindlers of the Spark,* Macmillan (New York, 1966) pp. 131, 132.

71. Habib Bourguiba, *Towards Peace in Algeria,* Secretary of State for Information (Tunis, 1959), pp. 59, 60.

72. Clement H. Moore, "Bourguibism in Tunisia," *Current History,* January, 1963, p. 40.

73. *La Presse,* January 19, 1963.

74. Ibid., May 27 and 28, 1963.

75. *Arab News and Views,* vol. X, no. 8, August 1, 1964. Arab Information Center.

INDEX

Abadie, General: proclamation of, 123

Abbas, Ferhat, Algerian nationalist, 129

Acheson, Dean: on Tunisia, 157

Achour, Habib: labor leader, 131; leader of UTT, 186; arrested, 217

Addis Ababa Conference 1963, 220, 221

Ahmed Bey: visit to France 1846, 13, 14

Al-Afghani, Jamal-al-Din, 106

Alapetite, Gabriel: becomes resident general, 100

Al-Fassi, Allzl: Moroccan nationalist, 129

Al-Fatat: Arab secret society, 106

Alfa grass: uses of, 74

Algeria: French conquest, 12

Al-Habib, Muhammad Bey: and reforms of 1922, 114

Ali, Muhammad: and Arab nationalism, 105

Al-Kahtaniva: Arab secret society, 106

Arab nationalism: early beginnings, 105, 106; after World War I, 106, 107

Asker, Khalifa Ben: invades Tunisia, 110

As-Safi, Ahmed: secretary-general of Destour, 112

Authoritarianism, 212n

Azzedine Bey, Prince: slain, 154

Baccouche, Salaheddine: Tunisian prime minister, 148; on Schuman reforms, 150, 151; disgraced, 192

Badra, Mohammed: minister of social affairs, 132; and UN, 156

Balbo, Italo (Undersecretary of State): visit to Tunisia, 104

Ballagha, Bashir: secretary-general of UGTT, 217

Banque Centrale, 207 and n

Beauval, Charles de: French consul, 16

Belagaroui, Ahmed: attack on, 153

Ben Ammar, Tahar: Tunisian nationalist, 150; asked to form government, 169, biographical sketch of, 169n; French confidence in, 181, 182; resigned as premier, 183, 184; disgraced, 192

Ben Bella, Ahmed: Bizerte ceremony, 201; on Bourguiba, 220, 221; mentioned, vii

Ben Milad, A.: calls Neo-Destour Fascist, 142

Ben Salah, Ahmed: questions French sincerity, 179; sees economic crisis, 184, 185; dropped from the government, 186; in charge of the plan, 205; reports on the plan, 208

Ben Salem, Dr.: report on Cape Bon, 149

Ben Youssef, Salah: and Neo-Destour, 129, 130; wants full independence, 126; and UN, 156; attacks conventions, 173; returns to Tunis, 177; calls for free Maghreb, 177, 178; condemned to death in absentia, 179; assassinated, 180

Berbers, 6

Bey's power: reduced, 188

Bidault, Georges: on Tunisia and UN, 158

Bizerte Crisis: bloodshed, 199 and n, 200; UN debate, 200, 201